Faith-Based Inefficiency

Faith-Based Inefficiency

The Follies of Bush's Initiatives

BOB WINEBURG

 PRAEGER

Westport, Connecticut
London

Library of Congress Cataloging-in-Publication Data

Wineburg, Robert J.
  Faith-based inefficiency : the follies of Bush's initiatives / Bob Wineburg.
    p. cm.
  Includes bibliographical references and index.
  ISBN 0-275-99312-4 (alk. paper)
    1. White House Office of Faith-Based and Community Initiatives (U.S.)
2. Faith-based human services—United States. 3. Human services—
Government policy—United States. 4. Church and state—United States.
5. Conservatism—United States. 6. United States—Social policy—1993- I. Title.
  HV530.W543 2007
    361.7'50973—dc22   2006038664

British Library Cataloguing in Publication Data is available.

Library of Congress Catalog Card Number: 2006038664
ISBN-10: 0-275-99312-4
ISBN-13: 978-0-275-99312-2

First published in 2007

Praeger Publishers, 88 Post Road West, Westport, CT 06881
An imprint of Greenwood Publishing Group, Inc.
www.praeger.com

Printed in the United States of America

The paper used in this book complies with the
Permanent Paper Standard issued by the National
Information Standards Organization (Z39.48-1984).

10 9 8 7 6 5 4 3 2 1

Contents

Preface

STUCK

It doesn't make much difference now why I was absolutely immobilized upon starting this book, but a little journey will allow me to introduce myself and to state clearly what would have lingered beneath the surface of my writing had I pretended to be somebody I am not. I was somewhat hesitant to write this book because I wanted my academic colleagues to view this work as the definitive book about President George W. Bush's faith-based initiative, yet in my heart, I knew my pitch would certainly impede such approval. I planned to feign objectivity as I addressed his faith-based initiative, but after serious consideration, I knew I just could not do so. Still, I was going to don my white social science lab coat, retrieve my twenty years of notes and piles of data, and craft this book with the impartiality of a stereotypical scientist who allows facts seemingly to speak for themselves. Such works, especially ones secured with statistics, earn more tributes in the social sciences than a policy analysis in a seminarrative style like my latest creation.

I have carefully conducted four local research projects that were supported with external funds and faced peer review. I have run several focus groups and have completed studies exploring religious people and their reasons for engaging in service. In addition, I have spent numerous hours with practitioners to determine the different levels of religious involvement with human services in Greensboro, North Carolina, from the 1980s to the present. Since local human service systems around the country are more similar than not, the practical side of my work has been on just one community as I examined how social policy affects the design and delivery of church-based social services. Case studies from one place simply are not deemed legitimate, as demographic studies are, because they do not encompass concerns from a large enough territory. I do not question that judgment; it was drilled into me from my first doctoral research class.

Even so, I found myself in a quandary for days, unable to determine why I was at a standstill.

As I sat powerless, different excuses raced through my mind. For more than twenty years I have been fortunate enough to witness, with what I believe to be a unique perspective, the way religious congregations help others. Practitioners from far and wide, many of whom are my former students, frequently seek my advice, usually about how to write grants or how to arrive at consensus when debating contentious issues. My advice must have been sensible as they have continued to contact me. Most academics, for good reason, follow only the dominant features involved in issues of national social policy; they pay little attention to the significant details regarding a policy's impact on the community. Was I impressing the practitioner or simply deluding myself?

The gripping paranoia common to some academics had me frozen. "But I have a place with the powerhouses," I thought to myself. I have examined the more advanced questions relating to major social policies of the Reagan budget cuts; George H. W. Bush's "Thousand Points of Light" in his era of a "kinder, gentler nation"; Bill Clinton's efforts to change "welfare as we know it"; and George W. Bush's faith-based initiative. While doing so, I envisioned painting a detailed illustration of how those spiraling yet interconnecting changes impacted Greensboro's human service system. I convinced myself that I always saw the "curveball breaking" as it left the world of policy and spun toward the local communities, proving me to be a good singles hitter in the world of academic sluggers. Twenty years ago when the idea of church-based social services was a blip, I was writing frantically. Now with the world constantly focused on some dimension of religion, I was stuck in the batter's box; first base seemed miles away.

After twenty years, I am certain that large-scale social policies bring about great changes in local service delivery systems. After all, at the end of the day, programs are the expressions of policies. In my twenty-five-plus years as an academic, I finally determined that it is far more prestigious to explore the conflicts in values or legal issues surrounding a controversial policy than it is to argue the pros and cons of the programs they might create. Minor details are the dwarfs of major policy discussions. If one wants to make a major impact, he will not write about "trivial" matters like how policies play out on the ground. I was wedged between wanting my academic colleagues' approval for exploring the flaws in a huge policy and knowing that I will not win their approval until my findings are verified by those who conduct broader-reaching studies. I desired recognition for my theories and thought to myself, "If someone doesn't describe the details, how will others know what to look for when they do their large studies?" I was restless but stunned. Nothing seems worse to an academic than feeling irrelevant.

Far more details exist in local work, but they do not grab a reader's attention like critiquing the flaws in "ending welfare as we know it" or disproving the simple idea of mobilizing a "thousand points of light" to solve our vast social problems. What happens when a furniture factory that is the center of a community's economic life moves to China, and welfare, as we knew it, is gone? How do organizational leaders train a thousand points of volunteer light, integrate them into services, keep them occupied, and evaluate their effectiveness when budgets are cut and organizations are frenzied trying to meet the increased demands for more services and increased pressure for accountability? Such details dangle beneath the surface of catch phrases, and I was compelled to write about them no matter how it altered my ego. Therefore, I sadly abandoned the idea of writing the defining work on President Bush's faith-based initiative because I prefer writing about the details of what this policy has meant to the local human service system. My realization did not unglue me, however—something else did. I still sat for days waiting for my fingers to light up my computer monitor.

HEARING VOICES AND GETTING UNSTUCK

Trying to convince myself that I had something to say, as I sat steadfastly in my desk chair for days, was no fun. As a result, I directed my attention to finding the reason for my writer's block. Recovering from a health setback that kept me from writing the previous year, I was convinced that I was simply out of practice. While sitting at the computer in a stupor yet another day, I slipped into the once familiar hypnotic state where I used to do my best writing. I missed that zone because some old friends remain there—two voices of my inner thoughts—but I am not certain what exactly is going on because it is a dreamlike state. Nevertheless, those voices make sense out of the timeless, wordless stream of jumbled impressions, feelings, and ideas about my life's work, policy, and its implementation. Oddly enough, once the thoughts actually travel through my fingers and transfer words to the screen, my two voices start a surreal free-for-all, arguing over the effectiveness of placing ideas one way or another. We started a wrestling match once we became reacquainted. (I say *we* because once my fingers take over, a "conscious me" joins the effort.)

I kept hearing the positive voice say, "You have a truly unique story to tell." The cynical voice fired back, "No one is going to buy a story about a large and controversial policy from someone south of the Washington Beltway." "Nonsense!" said the first. "Covering twenty years of the twists and turns of the religious community's involvement in one town without a break is a huge contribution, and no one else has done it." The cynic retaliated with two quick rounds: "People are tired of Greensboro, North Carolina's religious community. Don't you remember ten years ago when Jon Van Til asked if you were still writing that same paper about Greensboro?" "He was joking," the positive voice countered smugly. The cynical voice retorted, "But you *are* still writing that paper!"

The quarrel continued. My positive voice took the floor: "You covered religion and the Reagan budget cuts. You told an essential story and placed that shift to increasing local development in a context that no one else captured! You covered religious social service development when the thousand points of light flickered on and off during Bush I's administration. You covered religion when Clinton ended welfare, and you not only told a good story but also warned the cheerleaders for more religious social services not to expect too much from the religious community; they can only do so much. And you were right—so get on with it!"

The cynical voice was unconvinced, telling me, "You have biases that eventually will leak out, and the experts will bury your work by calling it journalistic."

"State your biases up front and write! If people don't like the biases, they won't read the book. Criticism is part of this game!"

"Your point of view differs from most. They will criticize you."

"So what? This is not a popularity contest. It is about the truth, as you know it! Get on with the book!"

And so it went, back and forth.

OUT OF THE BLOCKS

Eventually I caved in and listened to the positive voice, so I will start in earnest by stating that this book is a continuing story of one community's religiously based social services and sectarian services and its reactions to continuing policy changes. I have witnessed, studied, and experienced these changes for almost three decades. What I have learned extends far beyond this community, as the following quick anecdote demonstrates.

In December 2004, I gave a presentation on how to effectively use the resources of the religious community to a conference sponsored by the State of Washington Family Policy Council. Not wanting to be labeled as an academic with a canned speech, I prepared by analyzing the city of Spokane's human service network and its relationship to its religious community so that I could weave a local frame of reference, or at least one from a community in the Washington State, into what I had to say in general. The paper copy of my PowerPoint presentation was inside the packet of materials provided to the attendees at registration. Before the presentation, one of the participants approached me and stated, "I see you are from Spokane." Thrilled, yet not quite sure of what he was referring to, I said, "No I am from Greensboro, North Carolina." Taken aback, he then asked me how was I able to get so much information about Spokane. I said it was all on the Web, and if one knew what to look for, it could be presented in a coherent way, as one community's system of services is very similar to another's, be it Greensboro or Spokane.

Before wrapping up this prologue, let me expose my two major biases. I am openly declaring them to avoid any misinterpretation of my point of view.

First, I have been a card-carrying member of a Reform Jewish religious congregation for most of my life. I am wary of people who want to convert me to Christianity. I am an observant Jew who had his temple desecrated with swastikas as a kid. I look to the government to protect our minority status. I favor faith-based social services if the rules of solid program development and legitimate separation of church and state are adhered to in the delivery of service. I also favor the kinds of mutual assistance that faith-based services provide informally, because that kind of assistance is the glue of civil society. I live in the South, so the fall 1999 Proclamation of the Southern Baptist Convention to Convert Jews, and its yearly reiteration, is, to me, at least a vestige of institutional anti-Semitism. Practically speaking, such proclamations instruct me to keep my antennae attuned when I am in a setting with fundamentalist-leaning Christians. I don't believe anyone is out to get me. I am merely sensitive to a reality that sometimes eludes the majority.

I don't want to be criticized for being nuanced, so what follows is in the clearest English I can muster: *The "faith" in the president's "faith-based initiative" may be defined as a marriage between the government and a group of Christians who believe effective social services can be delivered only if one accepts Jesus as his or her Personal Savior.* While I have not always believed that, I certainly do now. I will not devote this entire book to proving this point, but I will offer enough evidence for the reader to understand that my bias does, in fact, have some validity. Social service delivery is complex; success in generating change requires considerably more than merely believing change will occur.

My second bias is that *I filter ideas about social policies and their programs through a very particular set of lenses; they assess the interest level shown from the people who operate the local human service system—that interconnected hodgepodge of public, private nonprofit, self-help, and religious organizations. For an initiative to take root and show growth in local services, everyone in the varied agencies and organizations must collaborate to plan for change thoughtfully and effectively.* There are some pretty strong arguments out there against collaboration, but not from those who really know the culture of local systems. Individuals working within the entire social work system must develop a unified front in order to meet the needs of those they serve. How ironic that the people who usually determine the policies and funding allowances for such valuable human resources know very little about the issues and the range of services unique to each group. Rather than encouraging these organizations to support each other, the faith-based bureaucracy has promoted an unhealthy competition among them. President Bush's faith-based initiative has been a top-down, inside-the-Beltway effort that has promoted more competition for fewer dollars because the effort is not really geared to enhance effective service delivery but rather to promote right-wing evangelical Protestant social services while starving equivalent government programs.

This is neither the America I grew up to believe in, nor is it the way I was taught to design services to help those who don't have the means to help themselves: children, the elderly, the sick, and the disabled. So as I proceed, it is important to understand that the basis of my argument rests in those positions. I have been called a left-wing partisan, but the left-wing partisans I know have been against Bush's faith-based initiative from the get-go. I was not, and I wanted it to be done right because

I know the role congregations and religious organizations assume in local social services and have the deepest respect for social services coming from congregations and faith-based organizations. They are not going away. The Bush faith-based initiative could have done so much better to harness their spirits. This book argues against what George W. Bush has done and proposes a better way.

Acknowledgments

There are many people who helped influence this book. First, I'd like to thank the Reverend Odell Cleveland. He is my friend and colleague, without whom I never would have had the grounded vantage point from which to write with confidence. He read every word of this book even though he didn't always agree, except in the last three chapters. I must also include Bishop George Brooks of Mt. Zion Baptist Church in Greensboro, North Carolina, who not only had confidence in Odell but also let me in his church as if I were a member. I'd like to thank the staff and board of the Welfare Reform Liaison Project, too many to list here, who treat me as if I was one of them. Kurt Lauenstein, M.D., read chapter 4 and gave beautiful criticism from the layman's viewpoint. Richie Zwigenhaft, Ph.D., gave a beautiful but hard-hitting critique of chapter 6, as did Edward Queen, Ph.D. Bill Thornton of the Guilford County Department of Social Services helped here, too. My brother, Sam Wineburg, Ph.D., helped all along the way. Larry Weisman humbled me and made me a much more careful storyteller.

Lyn Rozelman was my editor and overseer throughout. She kept me using the English language and hit hard and often—which is what we academics need now and then. Suzanne Staszak-Silva, senior editor at Praeger, has been firm but gentle with me. My great friend Ram Cnaan brokered the interview with the elusive John Dilulio. John was gracious to give me as much time as I needed. Stanley Carlson Thies went out of his way to talk to me during a very busy time for him. Bob Jaeger and Diane Cone of Partners for Sacred Places opened their doors to hear me once again. Billy Terry taught me how the Washington grant game works from an insider's viewpoint. Tom Hamburger of the *Los Angeles Times* was a sounding board throughout, as was Michele Goldberg. Rebecca Sager, a Ph.D. student at the University of Arizona, and her mentor

Mark Chaves, Ph.D., were very helpful. I also want to thank John Rife, Ph.D., the former chair of my department, for supporting me all the way through. Brian Goldberg was a great supporter throughout. Diana Garland, Ph.D., was very helpful with chapter 2. Finally, my wife and kids, Cate, Zach, and Hannah, have always been there.

Regardless of who provided what help, I alone accept the responsibility for what is written here.

Introduction

Let me begin my policy analysis with the following assertion: From the beginning, President George W. Bush's Faith-Based Initiative had little chance of making a real impact, because his engineers did not seek input from any of the country's 19,000 cities and 3,000 counties. Much of their energy merely promoted the marriage between government and evangelicals on the right side of the political and religious spectrum, instead of thoughtfully integrating the amazing resources of the religious community into the web of services locally.

Part of my purpose for writing this book was to critique and to analyze more deeply the controversial reasons why the people charged to carry out the policy had no strategy for integrating this initiative into each community in the country. In the following pages, I try to unravel the complicated and controversial dimensions that stalled the initiative and, more importantly, held up any sober discussion about how to address some of the social problems facing communities. Hidden religious agendas from some of the president's architects, blurring the boundaries between church and state, politicians and "pals," and administrative rule changes that skirted the legislative process have hurt the cause for better faith-based social service delivery. These controversies caused enough damage to change a policy that could have harnessed the true spirit of religious community but instead steered us into different directions, yet another thorn in the continuing metareality underneath this initiative—the cultural war between liberals and conservatives.

I stand by these serious claims and support them throughout the book in different ways. Others have done extensive work on some of them,[1] so my policy analysis will pinpoint the initiative's real Achilles' heel: President Bush's corps of political engineers was simply naïve about the inner workings of local service systems. Even if the leaders in the armies of compassion won every political or religious battle, they still would have lost their war on poverty. You just don't start and end an urban poverty policy with catch phrases about how effective churches are in social service delivery, with no evidence to back up the claim and no strategy to get local "buy-in." From the beginning, little local acceptance surfaced, yet the media blitz that kicked off the initiative made it look like churches were the solution for our social service problems. Sadly, a policy that ignores the planning and groundwork to make implementation seamless is a poor policy. President Bush's rather ineffectual Faith-Based Initiative failed to yield the measurable results he had expected.

The tough-nosed analysis here will undoubtedly result in some critics labeling my work as simple partisan polemics. Considering myself an "old school" academic, I see shaping public discourse as being essential to academic life. It was primarily people outside the academy, mainly from conservative think tanks, that developed the Faith-Based Initiative, although several academics shaped and supported it as well. As a lifetime advocate for the poor, starting initially as a VISTA (Volunteers In Service To America) volunteer in 1973, I protest when programs designed to help society's most vulnerable are flawed. The Faith-Based Initiative was not designed to work in any measurable way because it was top-down, ideologically driven, and pathetically naïve about community social service systems.

I now know what works and what doesn't in program development and in creating sustained partnerships among churches, faith-based nonprofit organizations, and local government. Knowing how to work in those systems locally is crucial to making a success of any initiative that wants to use the resources of the religious community. Given my experience, much about what was supposedly new regarding President Bush's Faith-Based Initiative was not new to me at all, and there was no surprise in how a set of ideas about a social policy will play out when it is implemented with no plan to guide communities.

Over the years, there have been occasions when I have become impatient with my academic colleagues when they hedge and assert that not enough research exists to make a particular claim, even when the idea is as unworkable as this Faith-Based Initiative. I am deeply saddened that the architects and engineers of this initiative implied that the faith community could do more than it actually can. Professor Mark Chaves's book *Congregations in America* makes a strong case that not a large percentage of congregations nationally are involved in extensive social service activity. On average, those that are extensively involved, devote less than 3 percent of their total budget to social service delivery.[2] No major policy shift, as this one was supposed to be, could change the national pattern of service involvement by congregations without major planning, yet few academics dared to challenge the assumption that it could.

I have asked the promoters and academic supporters of this initiative for years now, sometimes forcefully, to explain how this effort would work locally; I have never received an answer. Now is the time to unzip what is shrouding this initiative, progressing slowly, carefully, and respectfully.

Acquaintances of mine know that I can occasionally be argumentative. If my position seems too emphatic or offensive, I apologize in advance.

Yet, those individuals who know me on a more familiar basis realize that I do not tread lightly; they are fully aware that I respect the dignity of every human being with whom I come in contact—friend or foe. In this book, I have avoided attacking people's character or criticizing people's ideas in an undignified way, but I have hit hard while balancing my point of view with fair-minded examples to support my claims. This was a difficult task, and I want the reader to understand my aims from the outset so the book does not appear unduly jagged. It is hard to go back and forth between the large policy and the local community, but I trust that I learned a few things from the similar effort in my last work, *A Limited Partnership*.[3]

TOP-DOWN POLICY ANALYSIS

The backbone of this book is the Bush administration's Faith-Based Initiative, so it is a policy analysis whose reach is far beyond one community. I was involved with an important strand in the genesis of this initiative during Bill Clinton's presidency, roughly during a span of seven years from 1993 to 2000. It was this involvement that led to my concern that the initiative never really addressed the complex problems facing the poor.

During the 1990s, Dr. Ram Cnaan conducted a study, commissioned by the Partners for Sacred Places in Philadelphia. His intention was to illustrate the abundance of community service activities in churches of historical significance within six cities, as well as to suggest a possible strategy for preserving sacred places by linking them to community activities. However, his findings subsequently became the "supporting evidence" for shaping the public discussion led by Dr. John Dilulio, the first director of President Bush's White House Office of Faith-Based and Community Initiatives (FBCI), who alleged that faith-based social services were more effective than government or nonsectarian services.

I was instrumental in helping the Partners for Sacred Places choose Dr. Cnaan to conduct that study. After Cnaan's findings in 1997, a small group of very bright and dedicated people, who had been working with conservative funding groups for years to put the good work of religiously based social services into the public discourse, suddenly had much more ammunition to shape a burgeoning public discussion about the benefits of faith-based social services. One who disagreed was practically labeled a heretic. This book is written from the heretic's perspective.

My account may irritate a number of people, many of whom I like very much. I believe they knew there was no evidence for their claims about the effectiveness of faith-based social services as compared to government or nonsectarian social services. Cnaan's work provided enough information about the effective work of church-based social services nationally that proponents could, and did, link his findings to their broader agenda. Yet, I do not believe they were telling the "big lie"—I call it the "white lie." Their agenda was merely a game of public "word crafting." I believe that, in their hearts, some knew they were referring tacitly to social services that draw people to Jesus. They implied that the faith-based social services about which they spoke in public were more effective than government social services, because government programs do not lure people to Jesus and thus do not change people's hearts.

They were cleverly bilingual when discussing the effectiveness of the faith-based social services they were promoting. To most people, *transformation* means change, but to the circle of people in my focus—the ones who shaped part of the president's Faith-Based Initiative—*transformation* means that when one accepts Jesus, he or she becomes transformed into a new person. I find it to be no accident that *transforming* innocently appears twice on the first page of *Rallying the Armies of Compassion*, the policy document accompanying the executive order establishing the FBCI:

> The indispensable and *transforming* work of faith-based and other charitable service groups must be encouraged.... Without diminishing the important work of government agencies and the wide range of nonprofit service providers, this initiative will support the unique capacity of local faith-based and other community programs to serve people in need, not just by providing services but also by *transforming* lives.[4]

Everyone knows that to *transform* means to change, but the innocent-sounding term also has a different and much richer meaning for evangelical Christians, and I contend it was used quite boldly to send a clear message to right-wing evangelicals that the Faith-Based Initiative was really about *their* faith on two levels: First, the system of social services was going to be transformed by this initiative by encouraging more indispensable work by faith-based and other charitable groups. The planners of this initiative were very smart, so it has not been uncommon for them to throw in a reference to "other charitable service groups" to give the appearance of balance, when they really were focusing on funding their evangelical targets. I will talk later about how the Jews even got thrown into the discussion to mix things up. The president is right back on message a couple of pages later when he states that the "initiative will support the unique capacity of local faith-based and other community programs to serve people in need, not just by providing services but also by transforming lives." There is still no research that supports the notion of "unique capacity," but in Christian terms, transformation is unique.

At its heart is the image of "a way" or "path" of personal transformation. Expressed with many metaphors in the gospels, it is the path to the death to an old identity and way of being, and to being reborn into a new identity and way of being, one centered in God or the Holy Spirit. St. Paul speaks of the same path with the imagery of "dying and rising with Christ" (Rom. 6). Indeed, he speaks of himself as having undergone this process: "I have been crucified with Christ; it is no longer I who live, but Christ who lives in me" (Gal. 2:20). The old Paul is dead, and a new Paul lives. And he invited his communities to the same path: "Let the same mind be in you that was in Christ Jesus ... who emptied himself and humbled himself and became obedient to the point of death, even death on a cross" (Phil. 2:5–8).[5]

Other kinds of evangelical language have filtered into the discourse. Take the "invitational" strategy, which on one level means to be inviting but takes on a completely different meaning in the context of evangelism. Heidi Unruh and Ron Sider, two highly regarded, and fair-minded evangelical Christian scholars, who support the Faith-Based Initiative, define *invitational* and demonstrate how it is used this way in their book *Saving Souls, Serving Society: Understanding the Faith Factor in Church-Based Social Ministry:*

> Invitational strategy beneficiaries are extended the opportunity to connect with religious resources or events outside the parameters of the social service program, including spiritual counseling (such as with a chaplain), regular church activities (such as Sunday worship services), special events (such as an Easter pageant), or religious activities offered in conjunction with the social service (such as a Bible study after program hours). Similar invitations may be extended to unchurched volunteers. These invitational elements are distinct from the program's service methodology, though they may be an important part of the church's plan of evangelism. Church-state restraints led Bethel Temple Community Bible Church to employ an invitational strategy in its outreach to the public middle school across the street. When church staff were invited by the school to conduct workshops on teamwork and problem-solving, they avoided overt religious expressions. Personal invitations and word of mouth, however, drew students into faith-centered youth activities held at the church or on school grounds after hours.[6]

Another strategy is the "relational" approach, which means that beneficiaries encounter "explicitly religious elements through informal interactions with staff or volunteers where staff through such low key interactions, encourage beneficiaries to make religious commitments."[7]

One more "bilingual" term is *winsome*. In common usage, it means "charming," but the way that it is used in bringing someone to Jesus—when an agency receiving public funds is not allowed to proselytize—is the equivalent of the soft sell in marketing as used in this quote from an Internet company: "Businesses on the Internet are finding soft selling very effective. One woman sends a short, friendly note to those who send her e-mail ads. She strikes up a friendship with the other person. In the end she often converts them into customers."[8]

The White House engineers wanted public policy to allocate money to churches that use those intervention strategies. However, they had to veil their intentions of publicly financing evangelical churches in language that kept their true mission covert. They understood that they must muffle any public discussion about using public money to pay for social services that invite recipients of service into the body of Christ as the starting point for change. They have been very clever at verbal sleight of hand.

Jim Towey, former director of the FBCI, was a speaker at the Rockefeller Institute of Government's Conference on Religion and Welfare on December 9, 2004. As in many of his speeches to mixed audiences, he managed to mention how government helped a Jewish group; at this conference, it was Touro Synagogue in Rhode Island.[9] In the same speech he

used the phrase *secular extremist* to characterize those who disagree with
the Faith-Based Initiative: "Quite frankly, I think you'll continue to see
great opposition, and I think that's because there's a continued cry from
the secular extremists who view any presence of religion or faith in the
public square as anathema to them."[10] Towey was asked, "Can you be
more specific as far as the aspects that you think are on sound ground that
should not be challenged any further, and those that would try to are
wasting time and energy unnecessarily?" He answered the question with
an example of an AmeriCorps project where the AmeriCorps participants
(government employees) were teaching religion in parochial schools:

> We were very disappointed in a court decision in the city that had to do with
> an AmeriCorps program. Here are Notre Dame students; they are finishing
> up their schooling and they're going to go get an AmeriCorps grant. This
> was a program started by President Clinton, this particular one. They're
> going to get a grant and they're going to go to some of the poorest schools
> in America, right along the U.S.-Mexico border. And so these Notre Dame
> students, and others that were going, would often get sent to different
> schools, some of which were parochial schools. So they said, well, here are
> the rules if you go to the parochial school. It's a Catholic school. You can-
> not use any of your AmeriCorps grant time—because you've got to have
> 1,800 hours or something like that—can't use any of that time if you're
> teaching religion. You can't use any of it. Now, here are these students
> working for next to nothing—the grant's $5,000.... And working for next
> to nothing, and they're sued because they said—and the court wrote in her
> opinion—she said, well, you know, but the students can't differentiate
> between when you're on the government nickel and when you're off. You
> know what? The kids can't differentiate between English, math and science
> and right and wrong answers.[11]

Towey seemed to indicate that this was a ridiculous lawsuit, in which
the "secular extremist" plaintiffs won the first round, but lost the second
on appeal. What he didn't say was that the secular extremists were the
American Jewish Congress, because he couldn't say it. So the language
game of this initiative is like good ballet—with very few slips.

A major goal of the Faith-Based Initiative, yet not one held by all, has
been getting money to those small evangelical churches. In actually allot-
ting money to churches whose social services start with the development
of a personal relationship to Jesus, the policy analysis and public discussion
had to be credible to the undiscerning. I did not always believe as such,
but subsequent events showed me just how committed the people behind
this initiative have been to winning the culture war.

A BOTTOM-UP ANALYSIS

While compelling, that story is not what influenced me to write this
book. What motivated me is another story. Just about the time I was
involved in the national scene, I became increasingly involved in a local
issue that was, and still is, as intriguing as the national one. The story is

also intricately woven into the national, state, and local religious and political dynamics of the faith-based initiative.

Beginning in 1997, the Rev. Odell Cleveland, a self-described born-again black Baptist preacher, now executive director of the Welfare Reform Liaison Project (WRLP), built a national model for employment training. This idea took shape at the Mt. Zion Baptist Church and in my office in 1997, where we met almost daily to formulate plans for his training project. This partnership occurred about the same time when the national effort to position religious social services to the forefront of the public discourse was forming earnestly, and just after welfare reform of the Clinton years went into effect. I had the opportunity to work with Reverend Cleveland for an entire year planning his program, moving it from an idea through the church, into the mainline social service system of Greensboro, and eventually onto the national scene. We have continued to work together almost every day since our first meeting. The program is a national model in workforce development and training.

In later chapters, I will spend a considerable amount of time illustrating how this agency became a national leader in faith-based social services, determining along the way what works and what does not work in bringing a faith-based organization into the mainstream community social service system. At present, I merely want to explicate the principles Reverend Cleveland followed to move so rapidly. He built the WRLP on four principles: All efforts would:

- be supported by data
- be kept afloat by input from expert consultants
- revolve around building partnerships with the range of community institutions
- rest on the principle that the organization's faith would be expressed through the staff's commitment to its work

Going the "extra mile" in helping people develop new attitudes and concrete skills is the rule, not the exception. Reverend Cleveland can often be heard proclaiming, "Poor people have plenty of religion. They need skills!" He became a certified Covey business trainer. Convincing this Baptist preacher to understand that it was either prayer *or* the "faith works" principle—not both—that would allow him to succeed as a community-based/faith-based organization, even in a Bible Belt community, proved to be an easy endeavor.

It is important to note that the WRLP's success is due to consistently following the principles previously stated. They are the foundation upon which the organization has built and sustained its capacity to thrive. While prayer and the organization's relationship to the religious community are essential to the WRLP's success, voluntary prayer takes place *before* the doors open for business, and all people and organizations representing the range of the community's religions are served by the project without regard to creed.

TESTIMONIAL

Before I complete this introduction with an outline of the chapters, I first want to give a little testimonial. Not as many academics are as fortunate as I have been to collaborate in developing a faith-based program from inside a black church at a time when national policy (of which I had a part) was promoting more social services from these churches. Every day for the last nine-plus years has been invigorating. While I had one eye glued to the national effort, I was entrenched locally in doing what the initiative was promoting—developing faith-based social services—but doing so by seeking community approval all along the way. The task was not always easy; we faced many pitfalls, yet seized many opportunities along the way.

Reverend Cleveland and I recall with humor how the first grant we received, to conduct a needs assessment, was one of "smoke and mirrors" because the "dream organization" was only a plan at the time; finding seed money locally to plan a new agency is difficult. We learned quickly about the business of community ministry, as the leader of Mt. Zion, Bishop George Brooks, ordained "Minister" Cleveland to "Reverend" Cleveland only after Odell brought in that first grant. We were nearly in tears when matters worsened; suddenly we had an opportunity to meet a threatened payroll with a $10,000 contract with the Department of Social Services, but we had to turn it down because it required $75,000 worth of service.

Another memorable occurrence took place when we arrived in Raleigh, North Carolina, to participate in a conference discussing the Faith-Based Initiative and to engage in a fifty-plus-city lunchtime satellite hookup to Washington, D.C., as part of the introduction of H.R. 7 (the broadening of the Faith-Based Initiative)—only to discover that the Rev. Sun Myung Moon's Unification Church was behind the entire endeavor. We quickly realized that this initiative was playing political and religious hardball.

In this book, I share many stories about the development of the Welfare Reform Liaison Project to show the connection between the national and state policies and the local program development. In essence, the real message is that the WRLP is a model of what it takes for a faith-based organization to become a full-fledged member of a local system of services. It serves as a reminder of what the architects and engineers of this initiative *could have* accomplished if they had had a strategy to build community; they had none.

The WRLP is now an institution whose reach extends across corporate America by way of its relationship with Gifts in Kind International, Wal-Mart, CVS, and others. It is the nation's only faith-based community action agency. Statewide, it serves as a mentor to other faith-based North Carolina organizations trying to implement its training model. It consults with other community action agencies and works locally through its various programs. The Ford Foundation has recently sent its second group of organizational leaders to Greensboro to learn from this organizational model. Unlike the first group, which comprised people from around the country, this one is made up of organizational leaders from the Hurricane Katrina–stricken Gulf Coast.

HOPE

This book is hard-hitting at times, but by no means gloomy. I am quite hopeful that one day, when we decide to give our local human service systems the twenty-first-century makeovers they so desperately need, they will tap the exhilarating energy of local faith organizations in ways that regenerate the volunteering spirit upon which they were built and thrive, without turning them into nervous social service bureaucracies. I offer suggestions for how this might be done, because the local Department of Social Services (DSS) asked me to think through how it might work more effectively with the faith community. The heart of the matter is how operations work locally.

What I learned here applies elsewhere. In 2002, DSS officials asked me to conduct a study exploring how it could best work with the churches and faith-based organizations locally. This study, funded by a local foundation, originated when the wife of the foundation's chief program officer was volunteering with her church to help some new refugees find assistance. She sought help from the DSS and found it very frustrating to negotiate with an underfunded and overworked staff. The program officer, a very influential member of the community, hoped to develop easier ways for churches and the DSS to work together effectively. The study yielded some well-grounded suggestions. At last count, about two hundred municipal governments around the country have arranged liaisons with their faith community.[12] I studied eleven faith-community coordinator positions when they first emerged out of county social services departments across North Carolina in 2001. There are now nineteen, so my suggestions are applicable well beyond Greensboro.

SPIRIT AND OUTLINE OF THIS BOOK

Chapter 1 begins this book at President Bush's launch of the White House Office of Faith-Based and Community Initiatives. This made-for-television event was carefully scripted for both the unsuspecting and true believers, seemingly with a cross-section of Americans of different races, different faiths, and political persuasions. The video images were sealed with the president's persuasive and heartfelt oratory about why such an office was necessary. "When we see social needs in America, my administration will look first to faith-based and community groups."[13] This had to be a great day for Don Eberly, the assistant director of the FBCI and author of *The Soul of Civil Society: Voluntary Associations and the Public Value of Moral Habits.*[14] His book provides a blueprint for a society dominated by faith-based and community-based voluntary organizations. He had been working toward this day since he was a Reagan White House staff member.

However, the fact that no one represented Catholic Charities USA, Lutheran Services of America, or Jewish Family Services of North America at the speech is telling. These are three of the largest faith-based social service providers in the country and had been supported with government grants totaling more than three billion dollars the year before.[15] In other words, the country already had a faith-based initiative; but this new one had a different mission. In reality, the event was saturated with "heavy hitters" from the white right-wing evangelical Christian movement, the black religious and nonprofit community, and some Jews with strong ties to the Republican Party. All heard the subtext loudly and clearly: We are going to change who gets what government money around the country. You will be rewarded with power, prestige, and money if you remain compliant.

The chapter untangles the web of surreal motives and complex activities in this newest dimension of the ongoing culture war to capture America's soul. As I separate the warriors—religious extremists, social engineers, and politicos—I weave back and forth, taking readers into the universe of compassionate conservatism. It is an influential world of ambiguous language and inconsistent action, where to the trained secular eye, up is down, down is up, impostors are truth bearers, and opponents of government efforts to fund doggedly sectarian providers are enemies of the state with a special title reserved just for them: secular extremists.

The FBCI launch event was a slice of the politics of "impression management" and a camouflage for a complex political and social agenda that would attempt to increase the black vote, shrink the welfare state, and keep a fragile white evangelical Christian voting block in the thick of Republican politics. Since the 1980s, Republican strategists have increasingly found ways to nationalize strict codes of behavior, thus providing a forum that bonded these once insular and apolitical groups into crusaders to save the whole country. However, the reality that was overlooked, and still is, is that the system of services in the local community is the vehicle through which faith-based partnerships form and thrive. In chapter 2, I step back from the policy analysis and give a detailed picture of a community service system, which is referenced throughout the rest of the book in discussions about the failure to understand the workings of social service delivery against the backdrop of political shenanigans.

Two lesser-known but key figures at the launching of the Faith-Based Initiative were Marvin Olasky, a University of Texas journalism professor, and the Rev. John Castellani, chairman of the board and CEO of Teen Challenge, an international Christ-centered Drug Rehabilitation Program. Both are extremely dedicated to shifting as many federal dollars to faith-based programs as politically feasible. A Christ-centered approach is based on the idea that people cannot free themselves from addiction, domestic violence, habitual crime, or the like unless they publicly declare their acceptance of Jesus as their Personal Savior and Lord. At that instant, they become new human beings, with changed hearts and refurbished souls; they become part of the body of Christ for eternity. This new evangelical Christian then becomes a soldier dedicated to recruiting the fallen into the army of salvation.

For Olasky and Castellani, President Bush's statement about looking first to faith-based groups to address social needs meant that government was now a partner with Christ-centered social services in refurbishing of the soul of America. To them, the Establishment Clause in the First Amendment is but a blip on the road to national salvation.

Olasky, one of the most intriguing and influential evangelical Christians in this movement, is called the "father of compassionate conservatism." He was born and raised Jewish but converted to Christianity as a young man. He has had the ear of George W. Bush since Bush was governor of Texas, and he is a key advisor to the president because he is an important link to a broad section of right-wing evangelical Christians through his influential *World* magazine. Castellani's organization has outposts in most states and overseas. Teen Challenge has been held up as the model Christ-centered substance abuse rehab program by Christian academics, right-wing think tankers, and politicians eager to claim that social science research has demonstrated that accepting Christ can cure addiction. This claim is based on a gross misreading of some extremely tentative findings in a 1999 doctoral dissertation by Aaron Bickness at Northwestern University; Bickness conducted a small study of Teen Challenge that had no statistically significant findings.

Together, Olasky and Castellani's efforts, buoyed by conservative philanthropic dollars and right-wing academics through the Heritage Foundation and Hudson Institute, have shaped the political environment to the point that the administration shifted more than $100 million into a new voucher program called Access to Recovery. In chapter 3, I examine what the research really says.

Who would have guessed that a University of Pennsylvania political scientist, criminologist, and self-described "Big D Democrat" who never conducted a single study on faith-based social services would be tapped to be the first director of the FBCI? As described in chapter 4, when Dr. John Dilulio was at Princeton University, he and prominent conservative Bill Bennett wrote *Body Count*, an influential book detailing the scourge that drug-related killings cast on the inner cities. Dilulio's boundless and convincing efforts to promote the idea that such violence could be turned around by tapping the energy of inner-city black churches caught the attention and earned the respect of both Democratic and Republican policy makers lost for solutions to end the killings.

During the 1990s, Dilulio was driven to get government resources directed to black churches, despite having no data to prove his theory could work. He brilliantly moved the chess pieces to orchestrate a broad-based public discourse about the importance of faith-based social services. Not exactly a self-deprecating guy, he said to me in a recent interview: "I'm Louis B. Mayer of the faith-based movement. I'm in central casting."

In the mid-1990s, to his good fortune, Dilulio learned that the Partners for Sacred Places, an organization in his hometown of Philadelphia, had commissioned University of Pennsylvania professor Ram Cnaan to study social service activities in 111 historic churches in six cities across the country.[16] I was initially asked to conduct that study, as I was a consultant to, and friends with, Bob Jaeger and Diane Cone, the leaders of Partners for Sacred Places. I referred Cnaan because we had been friends since our days as doctoral students, and he is one of the best social science research methodologists in the country. Dilulio learned of the work and befriended Cnaan and the leaders at Partners for Sacred Places. Dilulio would soon take Cnaan's research findings and give them a national stage.

In October 1997, the influential Dilulio produced and directed a National Press Club event where the findings of the six-city study of church-led social services activities were presented by Cnaan. Dilulio had Bennett and Sen. Joe Lieberman (D-Conn.) interpret the virtues of the findings to the press corps. While the study merely said that there are more social services being administered out of 100-plus historic religious buildings than one might imagine, both men made much more out of it than was really there, and the press bit. This carefully staged event started a trend that would become the signature of the promoters of the Faith-Based Initiative—making much ado about next-to-nothing for reasons few really understood.

Bennett and Lieberman became long-term promoters, because, as Dilulio said, "Once an issue gets in the minds of the policy elite community, it stays there for good or for ill."[17] Professor Cnaan's findings didn't exactly prove anything about the effectiveness of social services from faith-based organizations. But they didn't need to. The event, like the initiative itself, was theater. Dilulio got the issue in the minds of the policy elites in both camps and even became an advisor to *both* the Bush and Gore presidential campaigns in 2000. Thus, we had seen *The Birth of an Initiative*, act 1.

Chapter 5 talks about how some lesser-known but very important figures in the faith-based movement shaped how the country was going to perceive and talk about faith-based social services. Essentially, they created an alternative reality that became the centerpiece for discussing such services.

Chapter 6 looks at Jim Towey, a self-described pro-life Democrat and Catholic, who, like Dilulio whom he replaced, was simply a cheerleader for a floundering initiative, but stayed on message all the time. Towey resorted to calling opponents of the initiative "secular extremists," a tenuous strategy at best. The last thing this administration wanted was to look anti-Semitic. Yet, the American Jewish Congress has sued the administration, and prominent Jewish leaders from such organizations as the Religious Action Committee of the Reform Jewish Movement have spoken out vigorously against what they see as blatant church/state violations.

Towey started many of his presentations to lay and academic groups with a vignette about how the initiative helped this or that Jewish group get money, but it was a transparent effort to the trained observer. His strategy attempted to hide the fact that the initiative has floundered legislatively, has been in court much more than its promoters would like, and has earned little support in the 19,000 cities, 16,000 townships, and 3,000 counties where the results of such initiatives are measured. As articulate as he was, the former aide to Mother Teresa could not fool locals into thinking that results abounded when they simply didn't.

In 2000, before George W. Bush was elected president, a gathering of the main strategists who shaped the Faith-Based Initiative was held at Wingspread, the Johnson (of Johnson Wax) Foundation's conference center in Racine, Wisconsin. They were trying to frame a way for faith-based social services to receive government money without losing their religious identity or proselytizing. In chapter 7, I discuss that meeting and tell a personal story of what it was like being the only Jew in the room, especially when they thought it was safe to pray.

In chapter 8, I return to the Rev. Odell Cleveland, born-again black Baptist preacher and executive director of the Welfare Reform Liaison Project. He has a favorite line he likes to use, especially with white soul savers: "Black people have plenty of faith. It helped them survive slavery, Jim Crow, and make it through the civil rights struggles. They need skills!"

Reverend Cleveland was a businessman before becoming a preacher. He uses Stephen Covey's *Seven Habits of Highly Successful People* in the welfare-to-work training classes that he teaches, but before he did so, he became a certified Covey trainer, which cost him $5,000. While at that training, someone asked him why he would make such an investment in women on welfare, especially when the financial returns for him and them were so limited? His response: "Why not?" That, in a nutshell, is the difference between a successful faith-based program and the failed ones in this initiative. Why not do everything humanly possible to position the organization to succeed?

In nine years of operation, one of the WRLP's many noteworthy accomplishments is that the agency has been the largest partner with Gifts in Kind International, the billion-dollar organization that distributes new but discarded corporate goods throughout the nonprofit network nationally and internationally. The WRLP started out like most small faith-based community organizations: as a tiny ministry of a church. These "start-ups" have been the targets of Bush's Faith-Based Initiative. However, Reverend Cleveland's organization thrived so quickly because it developed by doing things exactly the *opposite* of the Bush way. Cleveland mastered the core rules of the local human service cultures, which meant first he had to form numerous personal relationships. Such efforts had to be coupled with a strong business plan.

Local stewardship is heartfelt but monitored with watchful eyes about how other people's resources get used. The hidden agenda of the Faith-Based Initiative has been political, so it has been throwing money at very inexperienced groups, and using outside consultants to help those groups get money, without teaching them the fundamentals of community development. In Reverend Cleveland's case, the organization could not have succeeded without buy-in from prospective employers, church leaders, foundations, public and private agency representatives, and college and university faculty and administrators. His formula of care and concern, supported with a solid business plan and having more breakfast and lunch meetings than one can imagine, is watertight. The politics of this initiative have all but eliminated any ability to achieve the president's mantra: *results.*

George W. Bush set a precedent two years before he landed on the USS *Lincoln* and declared "Mission Accomplished" in the Iraq war: It was January 29, 2001, when he established the White House Office of Faith-Based and Community Initiatives. For insiders like Don Eberly, who had been part of the Reagan White House, or Michael Joyce, who had been funding conservative causes for almost twenty years, the mission was accomplished. The undoing of the welfare state could now begin in earnest from a bunker inside the White House and in the name of God. Imagine their glee.

For those of us who know about local human service delivery and local religious organizations, we wondered whether the Faith-Based Initiative would be an honest attempt to effectively integrate the diverse and marvelous resources of the religious community into a wounded system of local services. The services that make up the bulk of those systems have to be delivered by law, but local governments often lack resources to meet demand. Sadly, we learned early on that the plan was to win the culture war, not win the war on poverty.

There is little question that the thousands of local public human service systems in the United States need drastic makeovers. Most are technologically backwards, have trouble retaining employees, and see increasing demand without corresponding budgets either to plan to meet needs in new ways or to actually do so. It is not an accident that these public systems limp along, nor is it an accident that the culture warriors attack them and want to replace such "Godless bureaucracies" with church-based social services.

A good conservative businessperson, however, might have said that we have an opportunity here to make real change. Let's look carefully at these local systems. After all, they are all affected more or less by the same federal laws and similar state laws. Let's determine what services they are legally required to supply, and then ask whether they are doing so? If not, how can they meet those needs better, and how much might it cost? That same conservative might ask if anyone had taken an accounting of the resources of the religious community. If not, how much might that cost? Once the conservative businessperson knew what the scope of the unmet need was, and what the level of untapped voluntary resources was, a local plan could be developed to begin matching available resources to unmet needs.

With the thousand-plus United Ways in the country, the thousand-plus Catholic Charities, the thousand-plus Salvation Armies, the thousand-plus Lutheran Social Services, and the thousands of active church members working in public agencies across this county, one would think that with some work, it would be easy to get buy-in locally for a faith-based initiative that was going to fight a real war on poverty and proceed in a proud businesslike manner. In the end, the architects of the initiative, like the architects of the war in Iraq, had to implement services. Neither did so intelligently because neither had a plan. Chapter 9 shows the gritty details of what it takes for a start-up church ministry to move from the church to the community and serves as a reality-based reminder of how complex such an effort really is.

Chapter 10 describes how the Welfare Reform Liaison Project became the nation's first Faith-Related Community Service Block Grant designee. The chapter starts out with the headline from the *Greensboro News and Record* the day after the organization received notice that it was selected over five other competitors. While the WRLP had been a separate non-profit corporation for two years, and despite a face-to-face meeting with the editor-in-chief and staff writer, the paper chose to use a lead that said it was Odell's church, Mt. Zion Baptist Church, that received the award. Again this chapter is about the real politics of local service development—something the Faith-Based Initiative ignored.

CHAPTER 1

The Launching

I want to set the parameters of this chapter before I start. This book is about a policy gone sour. As such, both the political infighting under the right-wing political and religious umbrella and the lack of an implementation plan kept effective social service development from happening. Others have and will write more details about right-wing politics and religion in America; I will speak about right-wing religion and politics in the context of social services.

On January 29, 2001, just nine days into his new presidency, President George W. Bush established the White House Office of Faith-Based and Community Initiatives (FBCI)—the official home of Bush's "compassionate conservatism." Its stated mission was to fight society's ills by "rallying the armies of compassion" inside America's churches. Yet beneath the compassionate camouflage lay a five-star war plan to demolish government programs, mobilize and increase the size of the evangelical Christian voting block, shift government money to churches and other Christian faith-based organizations in the conservative-led culture war, and develop a smoke screen of convincing media images and baffling words to confuse detractors. There was little or nothing about effective social service delivery that formed the basis of this launching.

Compassionate conservatism, a concept developed by Prof. Marvin Olasky, sounds like a meaningless banality, but it has actually been a radical scheme that puts supernatural processes at the center of social policy.[1] Compassionate conservatives see conversion to Christianity as the key to social change, which is why this movement is about much more than simply getting good Christian people involved in social service delivery. Olasky's 1992 book *The Tragedy of American Compassion* became the blueprint for faith-based social services with both evangelicals and conservatives.[2] Olasky was born Jewish and even had a Bar Mitzvah. For some time, he was a communist and an atheist. Then he became what is known in evangelical Christian circles as a "Completed Jew," one who, unlike like his recalcitrant brethren, found and accepted Jesus Christ as his Personal Savior.

Interestingly, the year before the FBCI's establishment, Catholic Charities, Lutheran Social Services, Jewish Family and Children's Services, and the Salvation Army—mainstays of religiously based social services in communities everywhere across the country—had received more than four billion dollars in government money to provide a range of services, from assisting pregnant teens to helping people via hospice care.[3] But this is not what Bush had in mind. Reminiscent of Chicago-style politics, part of the Faith-Based Initiative's plan has been to use the instruments of government discretionary grant-making to fund programs central to the Puritan wing of the Republican Party, thus institutionalizing support for a fragile but essential voting bloc. A central part of this book is uncovering the other reasons why President Bush needed another faith-based initiative when he already had one that could have been strengthened.

Had the Founding Fathers been at the launching of the FBCI, they certainly would have stood in disbelief as they witnessed the disintegration of their tireless efforts to separate church and state. In *Federalist* No. 69, Alexander Hamilton distinguished the president of the United States from the king of England: "The one [i.e., the president] has no particle of spiritual jurisdiction; the other [the king] is the supreme head and governor of the national church!"[4] Hamilton laid the foundation for one of the country's most precious principles, set forth in the First Amendment: "Congress shall make no law respecting an establishment of religion."

The Office of Faith-Based and Community Initiatives was not established by Congress, but the Christ-centeredness of that office represented a steady march, at least in the eyes of Bush's evangelical base, toward making their born-again Christian president the head of a national church. Hamilton and other Founding Fathers had feared that a consolidation of power between government and religion would cripple democracy. President Bush has presented himself as the leading promoter of democracy around the world, while at the same time devising a sinister political scheme to institutionalize the growth and strength of evangelical Christianity in his own country.

Compassionate conservatism fundamentally misunderstands social service delivery. Bush's supporters claimed that better social services would prevail in America's urban neighborhoods and rural backlands as a result of the president's Faith-Based Initiative, and that America will be better off because of it. That will not happen. It's important to clear away the smoke that has clouded this initiative and pull the curtain on the false wizards by exposing their naïveté about fixing the serious and complex problems of persistent poverty. I will provide a countermodel and analysis that do not exploit the little churches that have become the targets of the Bush Faith-Based Initiative. It is essential to counter the attempt to replace "The Star Spangled Banner" with "Amazing Grace."

The 141 federal programs on the chopping block in President Bush's 2007 budget and his proposed changes in Social Security reflect a rush to destroy the last vestiges of the New Deal.[5] At the same time, the gutting of the welfare state offers new opportunities to reward the Right's Christian foot soldiers. These soldiers comprise an important part of the conservative political base and are increasingly being compensated for their efforts. Thus, to understand what the Faith-Based Initiative actually stands for, it is important to look at its cast of characters and what they represent. They comprise an interconnected group of religious extremists, social engineering ideologues, and political operatives who will stop at nothing to accomplish their goals. Their ongoing efforts framed the political discussion in "religious and soul terms" so that realistic discussions about how to make social service delivery effective were blurred.

A diverse-looking group of religious and nonprofit dignitaries provided the backdrop at the White House for a carefully staged launching of the FBCI that January morning.[6] While many of them were the leaders in America's Christ-centered social services, an imam and a rabbi were there as well. Two central figures at the event were Professor Olasky and the Rev. John D. Castellani, both of whom had been influential in shaping Governor George W. Bush's Texas Faith-Based Initiative, upon which the national model is based.

Reverend Castellani represented the Texas-based Teen Challenge, a highly touted Christ-centered drug rehabilitation program with affiliates across the country. Such programs claim that drug addiction is caused by a wounded soul and that the only remedy is soothing that wound with Jesus. As governor, Bush used the group as a beacon for his initiative as he stated, "Teen Challenge should view itself as a pioneer in how Texas approaches faith-based programs." The Texas Faith-Based Initiative became an "unregulated" system, "prone to favoritism" and commingling of funds, and even dangerous to the "very people it was supposed to serve."[7]

Olasky, a professor of journalism at the University of Texas, has been a policy advisor to Bush since his tenure as governor of Texas. Olasky's several resurrections make him the perfect trophy for both evangelicals, whose mission is conversion and devotion, and social engineers who are seeking to eliminate the welfare state. In him, they found an articulate university professor to do their bidding in directing money from government into Christ-centered social services. An acknowledgment in *Tragedy of American Compassion* is illuminating: "My greatest thanks are to God who had compassion on me almost two decades ago and pushed me from darkness into light."[8] Unfortunately, Olasky's personal enlightenment has darkened effective social service development nationwide.

Professor Olasky's straightforward instruction about the use of "God talk" in the policy arena is the key to understanding the code of deception underlying President Bush's Faith-Based Initiative. Olasky says, "Conservatives have to be bilingual. They have to speak public policy talk and also Christian talk. Liberals do not have that advantage."[9] Olasky is essentially calling for right-wingers to deceive secularists by using a language whose meaning is really clear only to their base. With their top-down planning model, compassionate conservatives define which issues to fund, maintain control of the purse strings, and direct local operations from Washington. Decentralizing power and yielding to the authority of locals—a requirement for effective social service development and delivery—exposes the faith-based camouflage. Locals know that small churches and pervasively Christian agencies are bit players in their system of services, as I will make very clear in the next chapter. They know that small faith-based organizations cannot deliver what is claimed by the national pronouncements put out by the White House spin machine. If the purse strings were controlled locally, it is unlikely leaders would choose to fund the programs the Bush Faith-Based Initiative promotes, nor would they direct the money to peripheral service providers in the ways the Beltway engineers have been doing it.

The architects of this initiative are vulnerable to the major criticism of this book: This initiative cannot make local services better without an honest commitment from local leaders. However, getting local buy-in means that those homegrown influentials would have a say in which issues to fund and who gets the money to deliver the services. If community leaders nationwide were to decide that their issues are not the same ones Washington wants publicized—for example, substance abuse, abstinence, marriage, or prison reentry—but rather chose to promote worker displacement services, literacy, housing, health care, child abuse prevention, and condom use to stem the explosion in sexually transmitted diseases, the Republican machine in Washington could no longer control the message it sends to its base. There would be neither the stage nor the bankroll to promote and fund the social issues that bind the Christian Right to the White House.

Let me illustrate what is required for effective services—and thereby show just how shallow the political architects of this initiative are when it comes to understanding local social service needs. Before 2003, the Great Depression was the last time that so many people had been out of work at one time in North Carolina. A September 4, 2003, e-mail to the Greensboro Displaced Worker Committee from the director of the Department of Social Services in Greensboro noted that many of the traditional "safety net" programs did not meet the needs of displaced workers whose needs vary greatly, both in extent and timing. "We need a very flexible response system to meet them where they are. We need to work closely with the private sector to be able to anticipate surges in demand and changing needs."[10]

The crisis locally throughout the South has not been about people falling from grace and needing conversion. It has been about what moving textile jobs overseas means to families, and how communities can reconfigure their services to meet the aftermath of economic disaster at the personal, family, and community level. The members of the Displaced Worker Committee were the top leaders in Greensboro's social service and economic development systems: Social Services, the United Way, the Urban Ministry, the Chamber of Commerce, the Worker Investment Council, the Welfare Reform Liaison Project, and the community's largest foundation. These were leaders who know that bit players from small churches have little to offer when a large textile employer moves to China. There has been no critique of President Bush's Faith-Based Initiative that magnifies the important but largely understated relationship between its politics and service delivery.

Four months after the initiative was launched, Reverend Castellani of Teen Challenge appeared before a panel of the House Government Reform Subcommittee exploring the effectiveness of faith-based programs. In this hearing, he failed to distinguish between Christian talk and policy talk, tipping his hand to the real thinking inside this inner circle of warriors. When Mark Souder (R-Ind.) asked Castellani if Teen Challenge accepts clients of other religious persuasions, Castellani commented that some of the Jews who finish the Teen Challenge program become "Completed Jews."[11]

It was thus now on the public record that Jews who do not accept Jesus Christ are incomplete. Even so, Reverend Castellani's comment did not stop President Bush from marching onward. In his 2003 State of the Union Address, Bush told us in thinly veiled code what his soldiers aimed to do:

> Our nation is blessed with recovery programs that do amazing work. One of them is found at the Healing Place Church in Baton Rouge, Louisiana. A man in the program said, "God does miracles in people's lives, and you never think it could be you."[12]

The Christ-centered drug rehabilitation program he was talking about at Healing Place Church is called Set Free Indeed. Its slogan is: "We believe that recovery begins at the Cross. We rely solely on the foundation of the Word of God to break the bands of addiction."[13]

A May 2004 press release from the Substance Abuse Mental Health Service Administration announced a new $100 million discretionary grant program for states, called "Access to Recovery."[14] The new effort allows addicts to use vouchers for programs of their choice, including plans that use the "transforming power of faith" as its treatment. Sadly, there is not a shred of research to substantiate the claim that the "power of faith" is an effective drug treatment.

Nevertheless, right-wing evangelical academics such as Olasky and Stephen Monsma, professor emeritus of Pepperdine University, along with think tank pundits such as Joe Loconte of the Heritage Foundation and Amy Sherman of the Sagamore Institute, have stretched, spun, and repeated the idea that faith is an effective service intervention in hearings, at conferences, in the media, and in journals of all stripes until it turned into $100 million for Christ-centered programs. Vouchers funnel government money to openly sectarian organizations and programs like Teen Challenge and Set Free Indeed, which otherwise cannot receive federal funds because their religious work clearly violates the Constitution's Establishment Clause.

Faith-based extremists also oversee the decision making about who receives grants. The White House now "preordains" reviewers, so what had previously been an independent review process has become tainted politically and religiously. The list of grant reviewers of a recent abstinence grant program forms a Who's Who of the religious right, representing Summit Ministries, Turning Point, the Family Research Council, Concerned Women for America, the Christian Coalition, the Traditional Values Coalition, and the Free Congress Foundation.[15]

The grant review process used to be done by people with academic and programmatic expertise, and they would have to disqualify themselves if they knew an applicant. One would be less likely to suspect shenanigans from people in the organizations just listed if someone of the caliber of a Dr. Susan Philliber headed the review process. She has been the lead evaluator on national projects in youth development, teen pregnancy, school achievement, community development, juvenile crime prevention, and other areas of human service delivery focused on children. However, she was not even invited to participate.

The chief architect and first director of the White House Office of Faith-Based and Community Initiatives was University of Pennsylvania political scientist Dr. John Dilulio. According to a 1999 article in *Christianity Today*, a magazine founded by evangelist Billy Graham, author Tim Stafford shaped the piece to demonstrate that its founder's goal was genuinely realized in the form of Dilulio, a self-described born-again Catholic.[16] Graham wanted to "have the best news coverage of any religious magazine." He wanted it also to be a focal point for the best in evangelical scholarship. Graham said that he knew that "God was already beginning to raise up a generation of highly trained scholars who were deeply committed to Christ and his Word."[17]

Stafford captures some of the impetus behind Dilulio's involvement in pushing what eventually became the faith-based movement forward with the kind of legitimacy few others could have mustered. According to the 1999 article, Dilulio a year earlier at Princeton had taught a seminar in urban at-risk youth, at which he had his guest speakers open each class in prayer. "He was raised to believe that males don't talk about their faith, but he has gotten over that, somewhat aggressively."[18] Stafford goes on to say that Dilulio quit his job directing the Brookings Center for Public Management and wanted to quit Princeton, too, but got talked out of it by his colleagues at Princeton and in his newfound ministry, who "urged him not to throw away such an influential position." Instead, Dilulio took a leave of absence from Princeton, with minimal teaching duties. He briefly returned to regular teaching at Princeton and then moved on to the University of Pennsylvania. Through his connection with the group known as Public/Private Ventures, Dilulio launched a new organization, called Partnership for Research on Religion and At-Risk Youth (PRRAY), devoted to helping inner-city ministries through research, fundraising, and technical assistance. Stafford pointed out that Dilulio wanted to break down the bias against government funding of church programs and favored vouchers for Christian schools. In many blighted neighborhoods, he says, churches are the only positive institutions left.

Dilulio was a central figure in moving the discussion of faith-based social services from the classroom and conservative think tanks to a broader public, hinting in the press and in scholarly journals about the efficacy of such services. There were no studies to back up these intimations, but Dilulio, as I will describe at length later, wanted to put faith-based social services on the radar of the "policy elite" (as he called them in my October 2004 interview with him). Dilulio gave license to other faith-based service trumpeters to contort the truth about how "research" proved the effectiveness of Christ-centered social services, especially in drug treatment. In fact, the research proved no such thing.

Knowing he was headed back to the university sooner rather than later, he eventually backpedaled. After just seven months at FBCI, Dilulio left. Jim Towey, onetime aide to Mother Teresa of the Sisters of Charity, replaced Dilulio. At a June 1, 2004, White House faith-based conference, Towey welcomed the gathering this way: "I'm so honored to be in a room filled with religious fanatics."[19]

Despite Dilulio's reversal, almost four years later, of his earlier claims and still without definitive evidence about the effectiveness of Christ-centered social services anywhere, Marvin Olasky yet again invoked "research" to make his deception look true, saying, "There have been studies that show a high rate of success at Teen Challenge." According to Olasky, such programs fill "holes in our souls."[20] Others with a political or religious agenda, including Loconte of the Heritage Foundation, also tried to convince readers that "research" showed that Teen Challenge was effective.[21] Yet, the only independent evaluation of Teen Challenge that stood the test of rigorous academic scrutiny actually said that *no factual claims* could be made about Teen Challenge's effectiveness.[22] Loconte clearly did not read the study, or if he did, he ignored it or didn't understand it.

The critics of the welfare state in this culture war are religious social engineers. They have scanned the societal landscape and fired off carefully chosen words to shape the public discussion about the causes and solutions for our complex social problems. They often look and sound like academics, and sometimes even wear prestigious titles. Loconte, for example, was the William E. Simon Fellow in Religion and a Free Society. He has never published an academic book or paper subject to independent and expert review, yet he has testified before Congress and appeared on National Public Radio and PBS numerous times. In truth, many of the promoters of this initiative have simply worked for right-wing advertising agencies disguised as academic institutions.

In a winter 2000 article from Manhattan Institute's *City Journal* called "How Catholic Charities Lost Its Soul," Brian C. Anderson clarifies why the Catholics, Jews, and Lutherans were not part of the second Faith-Based Initiative. The conservative social engineer explained, "Catholic Charities has become ... over the last three decades an arm of the welfare state."[23] The Heritage Foundation's Loconte went so far as to use war terminology to characterize long-standing organizations with provable track records like Catholic Charities as being part of the "cavalry of government funding."[24] Anderson also announced that the Association of Jewish Family and Children's Agencies and the Lutheran Services in

America had lost their souls and were similarly indistinguishable from the government. Mainline faith-based service providers had become soulless traitors and needed to be replaced with new Christ-centered reinforcements.

Another social engineer, Don Eberly, an aide in the Reagan White House and former deputy assistant to the president for faith-based and community initiatives, is a leader in fighting the bureaucratic cavalry. In *The Soul of Civil Society*, Eberly railed against the welfare state in the same way Anderson did, but he is much more mean-spirited. "Trained and pedigreed 'social service professionals,'" according to Eberly and his coauthor Ryan Streeter, "are encroaching into nearly every corner of our society," preventing local nonprofessional caregivers from "healing and renewing" the lives of the poor.[25]

In the madcap world where policy talk and Christian talk merge, "healing and renewing" the lives of the poor means filling their hearts with Jesus. As picturesque as the rhetoric is, Loconte's, Eberly's, and Anderson's analysis betrays only a faint understanding of what social service professionals really do. Eberly's rhetoric personifies the enemy and portrays the abstract welfare-state bureaucracy as a human form. "Pedigreed social service professionals are encroaching into nearly every corner of our society" translates to "secular humanist social workers are vermin." Those nonbelievers prevent local faith healers from resurrecting the fallen.

President Bush repeated the God talk at the June 2004 White House faith-based conference and was less "bilingual" than he has been in other speeches: "I can't think of a better place for a prisoner to go than church ... we need to give faith the chance to heal a person's heart." Prisoners, however, do not return to communities with just holes in their hearts; they return without job skills, often broke, and rarely free from their addictions. Increasingly they are afflicted with HIV or hepatitis. Little churches, no matter how faithful, cannot deal with administering AIDS drugs. Citizens all over the nation are now crying foul because their communities lack the resources to do what is needed to deal with the prisoner reentry mess.

Turning social service professionals into metaphorical roaches in one frame, like Eberly did, and making Western Civilization's oldest religions soulless in a paragraph, as Anderson did, does not foster the goodwill necessary to build effective partnerships. Yet it was this kind of thinking that formed the spirit of the Faith-Based Initiative. While the thinking that goes into the rhetoric is dangerous in and of itself, what makes it more irksome is that the discourse that prevailed smothered a discussion of how to make faith-based social services effective partners in social service delivery locally.

While Eberly's use of language may seem clever and even artful, there are other explanations and guidelines for the causes and solutions to our complex problems. Many social service professionals are in fact African American and devout Christians. They staff the mandated children's protection units in public agencies. They are called in at 3:00 A.M. when a drunken parent breaks his child's nose in a fit of rage because the child is screaming in pain, too young to say she has a piercing earache.

Out of the nearly three million reports of abuse or neglect each year, a million and a half of these youngsters show up in hospital emergency rooms of this country. In 2002, more than 1,400 children died as a result of maltreatment.[26] When the child is removed from the home, state and federal laws map out specific follow-up plans to guide social service professionals. The system—to this point, at least—has not sent such children to faith healers, but if we followed down Bush's path that is just where they were headed.

The 1,100 Community Action Programs in the United States receive federal money to develop self-sufficiency programs for people who live in low-income neighborhoods. In subsequent chapters, I will tell stories that revolve around what it takes for a church-based agency to grow and develop inside a complex local system. The case examples will serve as some "dos and don'ts" for the successful integration of faith-based social services into local systems. However, the Bush path is a recipe for doom. Our communities and our religious organizations deserve better.

The Greensboro, North Carolina–based Welfare Reform Liaison Project (WRLP) is the largest partner of Gifts In Kind International, which distributes new but discarded corporate goods to nonprofit agencies across the country and around the world. The WRLP, led by the Rev. Odell Cleveland, redistributes most of those goods to churches, moving $18 million in goods last year.

Since 1997, Reverend Cleveland and I have been involved with the theoretical policy world of the Bush Faith-Based Initiative and the gut-wrenching but rewarding practical work of program development based on building solid partnerships and earning community buy-in. Recently, Reverend Cleveland gave a presentation to the Texas Workforce Development Commission entitled "Building Partnerships between Business and Community Workforce Development Agencies." One would think that a faith-based leader from Texas would be making such a presentation to the state's Workforce Commission, not the leader of an eight-year-old organization from Greensboro. Together we have learned what is behind the president's Faith-Based Initiative and what it really takes to have effective faith-based services in the broader community.

One of the most eye-opening occurrences took place in 2001, when Reverend Cleveland and I arrived in Raleigh, North Carolina, to participate in the American Family Coalition's discussion of the then new Faith-Based Initiative. As a member of the black clergy, he was an invited guest, and he brought me along. Republican politicos are hell-bent on chipping away the traditional African American voter bloc, whose loyalties heavily favor Democrats. Buying off leaders of religious organizations is part of their game of hardball politics, and this event was an invitation to be bought off.

The bonus was participating in a lunchtime satellite hookup to Washington, D.C., with more than fifty other cities. We witnessed live the introduction in Congress of H.R. 7, a bill designed to expand activities that promote more Christ-centered religion in federal programs, thus broadening the Bush administration's Faith-Based Initiative. The carefully scripted event had the feel of the Republican National Convention, with all the trappings—live entertainment, dignitaries, and politicians marching to the podium one after another to praise the president's Faith-Based Initiative and the power of faith in service delivery.

We were astonished that morning to discover that the American Family Coalition was a front for the Unification Church; *the "Moonies" ran the conference*. We were further astounded as we listened to participants, mostly from small black churches, read and discuss meditations of the Rev. Sun Myung Moon. Still more amazing was discovering that the Washington Times Foundation, Moon's organization, had funded the satellite hookups. We quickly realized that this initiative was neither a joke nor a hallucination. It was real, serious—and scary.

We had talked frequently about what it means to be a minority in this society, but until that morning Reverend Cleveland never quite understood how someone like me, a non-Christian Caucasian, could feel out of place in America. Cleveland had an epiphany when he realized that throughout much of the morning session, I had been as quiet as a stone and whiter than a ghost. When we were off in a corner, he looked me in the eye and said, "I am a born-again black Baptist preacher, but now I know what it feels like to be a Jew!"

Dr. Richard "Skip" Moore, the director of the Weaver Foundation of Greensboro, was asked to make a speech at the dedication of the WRLP's new 56,000-square-foot social service, education, training, and distribution center. A couple of lines in the speech capture the fundamental difference between the intervention strategy of President Bush's Faith-Based Initiative and one that can successfully integrate faith-based social services into the web of essential partnerships that must be formed in providing help for the needy.

As Dr. Moore tells the story, he said to Reverend Cleveland, "Odell, the Weaver Foundation is going to give you $100,000 ... to get this training center started." Odell gasped and said, "It's a gift from God!" Then Dr. Moore said, in no uncertain terms, "Yeah, but it is through the Weaver Foundation, and you remember that!"

The safest way for an organization to survive and thrive in social services, even in the Bible Belt South, is to remember that organizations like the Weaver Foundation pay for God's work. God talk in the public square is very trivial compared to the hard work of organizational development that underpins any successful effort to win the souls of community benefactors. This work will contrast the extremely successful strategy the WRLP used to move from the church to the community, leaving God talk at church, with the poorly conceived efforts of President Bush's Faith-Based Initiative, whose goal is to move Christian talk from the White House into the hearts of everyone on Main Street. To do so, we need to understand the local system of services. That is the task of the next chapter.

CHAPTER 2

Changing the System

It is essential to understand that the Bush administration's Faith-Based Initiative was, at least in the mind of one of its original architects—John Dilulio, about whom I will speak in detail in chapter 4—a serious attempt at making a dent in some of the country's broader social ills by using the resources of the country's 350,000 religious congregations. It could have started in Washington as it did, but to work, it would have had to catch fire in the 19,000 cities, 16,000 townships, and 3,000 counties where those problems get tackled. It did not. Religious leaders of all stripes in every community would have had to champion the cause, and they did no such thing. There would have had to be literally a million meetings among the hundreds of thousands of religious leaders, public officials at all levels of government, and the numerous nonprofit organizations that contract with government. Communities everywhere would have had to eventually present plans to overhaul local systems of services nationwide in order to best integrate the resources of the religious community effectively. None of this came to pass.

Each day it becomes clearer that the initiative has been a feeble attempt to gain a victory in the broader culture war and use religious social service providers for political purposes. Before any plans for change could be drawn up, there had to be a broad-scale attempt to get buy-in from the people who actually deliver services—the local agencies. Nothing of the sort happened. Most human service systems have the same structure; some may be big and some small, but they more or less share the same federal programs and block grants—the United Way and the Salvation Army, faith-based organizations and churches, self-help groups and private funders—somehow collaborating to manage and prevent problems in their community.

Buried underneath the surface sloganeering about the Faith-Based Initiative has been a cultural crusade to send sinners back to church, to get
government out of social services, to chip away at the black Democratic
vote, and to reward the religious supporters of the Republican Party. No
matter what the rhetoric says about the wickedness of the welfare state and
those who have fallen from grace, the actuality of American social service
delivery is extremely complex. This reality must be dealt with at the point
of implementation in localities.

For example, as of 2003, there were 523,000 children nationwide in
foster care.[1] Very few of these children caused their own problems, but
the extreme right-wing designers of the Faith-Based Initiative would send
them to church for religious healing because the purists in the faith-based
movement would remove the welfare state. On the other hand, the realists
at the point of implementation, particularly at the state and local level,
have pushed for the laws we now have, and those laws have shaped the
development of services to help protect these youngsters.

Figure 2.1 outlines the responsibilities and the legal authority of the
child protective unit in Guilford County, North Carolina, but the overall
guidelines are similar to those of units anywhere as the federal statute is
backed up by state laws, which also guide implementation.[2] Each year

---

The child protective unit is responsible to:

- Receive reports of abuse, neglect, and dependency
- Make a prompt and thorough investigation to ascertain the facts of the
  situation; the extent of the injury or condition resulting from abuse,
  neglect, or dependency; and the risk of harm to the child to determine
  whether protective services are required or a petition should be
  initiated
- Provide services to prevent removal of children from their homes and
  strengthen family life
- Invoke the jurisdiction of the juvenile court for the child(ren)'s removal
  and placement in a safe home (relatives or foster care) if children are at
  risk of harm

All children and their families are eligible for protective services regardless
of income. The provision of services is based solely on the child's immediate or continuing need. By statute, agencies must provide protective
services twenty-four hours a day, seven days a week. No fees are imposed
for protective services or other services provided to facilitate protective
services.

Legal Authority: North Carolina General Statute 7A-542; 10 NCAC
411.0300; U.S. Public Law 96-272; the Social Security Act.

**Figure 2.1. Mandate of the Child Protective Unit in Guilford County, North
Carolina**

nationwide, more than 1,400 children die from abuse; injuries to children from abuse annually total 140,000.[3] Reports of child abuse number 1.7 million annually: "More than 3 million cases of child abuse and neglect were reported in 2003 in the United States. An estimated 906,000 children were found to be victims, which was approximately 31.7 percent of all children who received an investigation or assessment."[4] According to the Academy of Child and Adolescent Psychiatry, sexual abuse of children has been reported up to 80,000 times a year, but the number of unreported instances is far greater because the children are afraid to tell anyone what has happened and the legal procedure for validating an episode is difficult.[5]

The Welfare Reform Liaison Project (WRLP), the faith-based organization mentioned earlier that I have worked with since its inception nine years ago, helps foster parents make their $390 monthly per-child allotment stretch further. One Church, One Child is an Illinois program that works across that state and with state authorities trying to bolster adoption rates by working with African American congregations. The One Church, One Child program was initiated on a local basis in 1981 by the Rev. George H. Clements in Chicago at the Holy Angels Church, a predominantly black Catholic church. Clements's goal was to recruit black adoptive parents through local churches. The program became a national recruiting effort in 1988, and thirty-two states are using all or portions of its model.[6]

Both the Welfare Reform Liaison Project and One Church, One Child are faith-based efforts; the law limits what they can and cannot do regarding foster care and reflect two different aspects of the kinds of partnerships that make the faith-related community limited, but essential partners in helping the innocent victims of our social ills. When state budgets shrink in poor economic times, social service budgets also decrease, even if the number of foster children grows. Such changes force government workers to "do more with less." Sometimes creativity springs forth, and sometimes it does not. Regardless, budget cuts do not change the laws requiring these vulnerable youngsters to be protected; only a change by the legislature does so. The president's Faith-Based Initiative did not change that basic structure, but it took money away from mainline providers and shifted it to faith-based providers. Therefore, the parsimonious tax-cutter may reduce agency spending, but like springs in a bad couch, the problem pops up somewhere else; by holding down spending, an increase in new problems arises.

Figure 2.1 is a description of the Child Protective Services of Guilford County, my home in North Carolina, including the statutes giving the agency its legal authority. Attempts to cut social service budgets, which happen when the economy tightens up, simply create chaos for the people who must continually do more with less because neither the law nor the need for assistance ceases to exist. This is especially so without any plan to reconfigure the services, something that must be done in hard times.

For example, Figure 2.2 is a glimpse of the daily problems members of my community endure, demonstrating why cooperation is needed among

Every twenty-four hours in Guilford County:

- Three teenagers become pregnant.
- Fourteen children are reported to have been abused or neglected.
- Five children are confirmed to have been abused or neglected.
- Seven teens are arrested for a crime.
- Twenty-six children are treated at one of the three pediatric health clinics.
- Each of the three pediatric health clinics spends $3,179.
- The county mental health system treating mentally ill children spends $40,708.

Every week in Guilford County:

- One premature, low-weight baby dies before its first birthday.
- Two teens are admitted for drug and alcohol abuse.
- Four teen mothers have become pregnant again.
- Eight children are placed in foster homes.
- Eleven teens are treated for sexually transmitted diseases.
- Eighteen children are admitted to the county mental health system.

Source: Maria C. Johnson, "Child Health in Greensboro," *Greensboro News and Record*, September 13, 1998.

Figure 2.2. Social Services Requirements in Guilford County, North Carolina

providers of various sources. Different agencies, including the police and courts, the hospitals and schools, and perhaps the faith community, play important roles. A volunteer component may or may not be a factor in assistance with the problems cited in Figure 2.2, but if there are to be volunteers, they will need solid training to work effectively with such difficulties. Prayers may help, but so will training.

Before putting forth a graphic representation of an entire community's human service system, let me reiterate the following point: A sober approach to integrating resources into the scheme of delivery at the local level rests on five aspects of rational planning and best supports a community's sense of stewardship for its most vulnerable. Inside each step is a series of activities that must take place. For a community to do what I am about to propose, it would have to meet regularly and eventually put forth a plan. In chapter 1, I gave an example of this, noting that when manufacturing jobs started to impact our local service system, community leaders from the public service agency, the Salvation Army, the United Way, the local community college, a major foundation, and other agencies gathered for many planning meetings to address short-term job training needs. Multiply each step by the thousands of communities nationwide, and the scope of any initiative can be seen to be huge.

For a faith-based initiative to grab hold, a community must catalog the scope of all of its social problems. It must also determine the level at which the mandated service agencies are meeting the community's needs. There must be the same level of analysis of the faith community's resources. Once that has been done, leaders must find ways to balance voluntary matching of resources with unmet needs. Once leaders identify the gaps between resources and needs across all social problems, from teen pregnancy to hospice care, they must then search for new and creative resources to fill those gaps. The task is daunting and cannot be done through faith-based rhetoric, divisive lawsuits, shifting a few dollars around in block grants, or developing a set of intermediary organizations nationwide that funnel tidbits of money to ill-equipped churches and small faith-based organizations like the Compassion Capital Fund as President Bush's initiative has done.

First, it is essential to understand exactly what a delivery system looks like. Otherwise, there is simply no way to discuss how to effectively use the resources of the religious community in useful and nonexploitative ways.

SNAPSHOT OF THE SYSTEM

Figure 2.3 shows the four main publicly funded services: social services, mental health, public health, and community action. They are bureaucracies with major responsibilities for protecting vulnerable children, families, seniors, and the disabled. These four agencies alone account for more than $100 million in expenditures in Guilford County. Their funds come from a combination of federal, state, and local resources, but that explanation is somewhat simplified; some of the state money is actually federal block grant money, while other funds come from other state and federal sources, such as contracts and discretionary grant sources.

Those funds, like the block grant money, are passed to local agencies in various ways, sometimes from the state or through the county and city government, and sometimes directly to the agencies. The agencies must comply with the law in regard to delivering the services they have contracted to deliver and must submit financial reports in the format the law mandates. This point is important, because fulfilling these requirements demands a sophistication often lacking in small start-up programs and small churches—the target of this initiative.

To provide some perspective of how intertwined the seemingly differentiated and distinct parts of the system actually are, examine the United Way system and its thirty member agencies, as shown on the top left edge of the large circle in Figure 2.3. These agencies receive about $14 million from the United Way, which holds a community-wide funding campaign that community volunteers run and the United Way staff oversees. While the core agencies in the center of the large circle cover the entire county, the other major city in the county, High Point, has its own United Way that works similarly. The United Way volunteers solicit donations from the

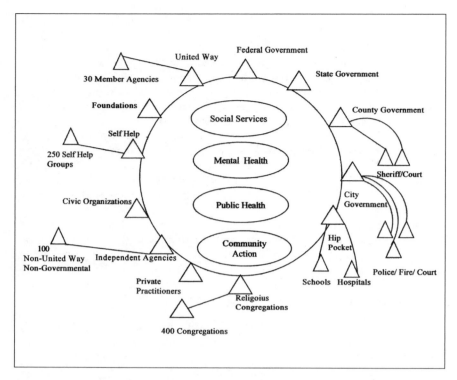

Figure 2.3. Greensboro Community System of Caring for Those in Need

community's 1,600 businesses. That $14 million total covers approximately a third of the overall budget of the thirty United Way agencies, which is about $45 million combined. These agencies, in turn, comprise about one-third of the Greensboro community's nonprofit social service agencies.

To acquire additional funds to meet the demands of their services, these organizations must enter competition for funding—soliciting funds from foundation grants and other sources. The agencies rely upon five major family foundations, a community foundation, a host of small family foundations, and the national and regional foundations to draw resources. Such an endeavor usually requires more effort to meet demand, so they also obtain resources from membership fees, fees for services, and fundraisers. In addition, several faith-based groups received an allocation from *federal revenue* via the City of Greensboro in 2004, as shown in Figure 2.4. The City of Greensboro is a federal Community Development Block Grant and emergency shelter grant recipient, so it can pass federal money to nonprofits. It also uses local funds to help. Some of the agencies in Figure 2.4 are also United Way agencies. It should be noted that the Salvation Army is a church, a United Way agency, *and* a federal Community Development Block Grant recipient.

Organization	Grant Amount
Salvation Army	$153,000
Episcopal Servant Center	$33,630
Jericho House	$62,000
Habitat—Holt's Chapel	$65,000
Christian Counseling/Wellness	$152,500
Interfaith Hospitality Network	$15,000
Malachi House	$56,000
Mary's House	$26,000
Room at the Inn of the Triad	$125,000
Prince of Peace Shelter	$55,000
Greensboro Urban Ministry	$119,600

Source: "Community Development Block Grant: Faith-based Recipients in Greensboro," http://www.ci.greensboro.nc.us/fin/cafr2004.pdf

Figure 2.4. Community Development Block Grants to Faith-Based Recipients in Greensboro, 2004

The other two-thirds of the agencies that are not affiliated with the United Way fall under the Independent triangle at the bottom left side of Figure 2.3 and include large faith-based organizations such as the Greensboro Urban Ministry, whose budget is $4 million, and Malachi House, with a budget of $1.8 million. Malachi House not only receives money from the federal government by way of the city but also contracts with the county, its program's participants cleaning the cages and tending the animals at the Guilford County Animal Shelter. I work extensively with the executive director and staff of Malachi House in program planning and development. Independent religious agencies receive federal funds by way of the city. There are many more agencies that receive money from this block grant that are neither nonprofit United Way nor faith based.

Conservatives and libertarians enjoy arguing that the liberal bleeding hearts, when they were in power, were instrumental in passing the legislation to create these bureaucracies and that the United States would work better without a welfare state at all. Charles Murray said it as clearly as it can be said in the preface of the 1995 paperback edition of Marvin Olasky's *The Tragedy of American Compassion*:

> What is required is no more complicated, and no less revolutionary than recognizing first, that the energy of effective compassion that went into solving the problems of the needy in 1900, deployed in the context of today's national wealth can work wonders; and secondly, that such energy and such compassion cannot be mobilized in a modern welfare state. *The modern welfare state must be dismantled.*[7]

Such sentiments reflect distaste for a theoretical construct of the welfare state that hardly reflects the concerns I have brought up. While the forces of democracy have not allowed the dismantling of the welfare state—which includes the protection of children—the combination of a blind faith in the capabilities of the church to provide social services, belief in a free-market laissez-faire service development policy to address complex problems, and extreme naïveté concerning the realities about social problems and their solutions are what is behind the Faith-Based Initiative. Now in power, conservatives insist on reducing the government bureaucracy and giving the money back to the citizens who were prevented, through taxation, from choosing to contribute as they wished. In this order of things, the "people" would have the freedom to distribute the funds in a way that would make the system leaner and more voluntary in order to preserve lost freedom and thus regain the lost soul of service.[8]

From the information in the figures provided so far, it is clear that the flow of private and government funds allows public, private, and religious agencies to meet needs of the vulnerable community members. If the theorists want to fix things in earnest, then they had best learn how things operate locally. A twist here, a turn there, will accomplish a political agenda perhaps, but it won't put a new paradigm of services in place with the faith-community leading. Murray's paradigm to dismantle the welfare state is cold-hearted and not compassionate at all.

There would be little merit in cutting the block grant on the grounds that private agencies and the faith community could turn to the private sector and acquire the money lost from federal money. The United Way has experienced difficulty meeting its funding goals over the past three years. Why would conservatives want to turn a hundred more agencies loose in an already overextended United Way private solicitation initiative? This complicated situation requires more thought before conservatives decide to simply end the welfare state or cut government funds.

The Bush administration hopes to add as many churches as possible to the funding competition. Yet all one needs to do is walk through, for example, downtown Los Angeles to understand that not only is the public system unable to handle a problem like homelessness but the combined efforts of government, churches, and the private sector fail as well. Furthermore, slashing government funds also means depriving faith-based and private organizations of useful revenue sources; consequently, they must spend more time raising money and less time serving society's needs.

ANOTHER SNAPSHOT

Above, I outlined a snapshot of the relationships among some actors in the network of services, emphasizing the way the system overlaps. Figure 2.5 is a graphic representation of the interconnection among all of the players within the system of services. Located at the bottom left of the illustration are Greensboro's churches. I placed an X in the sectors that rely heavily upon the resources of churches to fulfill their missions. These include:

- Greensboro Urban Ministry, an independent agency, uses resources from about 250 of the community's churches.
- Welfare Reform Liaison Project of Guilford, a faith-based public agency, encompasses more than one hundred churches in its sphere. WRLP works extensively with congregations to help them build their "helping ministries."
- Senior Resources of Guilford, a United Way agency, uses three churches for nutrition sites and volunteers from numerous churches to deliver mobile meals.
- The Red Cross, another United Way agency, depends on thousands of volunteers from the community's congregations.
- A substantial number of Alcoholics Anonymous meetings and other self-help gatherings take place in the community's congregational facilities.

Each and every one of the connections between an agency and resource of the religious community must be planned and monitored: People need to staff the night shelters; seniors need to be fed; and money, goods, and people need to flow from congregation to agency or agency to congregation. Effective implementation of these resources takes time, energy, planning, and people-to-people interaction.

Other independent agencies were not included in Figure 2.5; if they had been, they would show even more exchanges of resources between

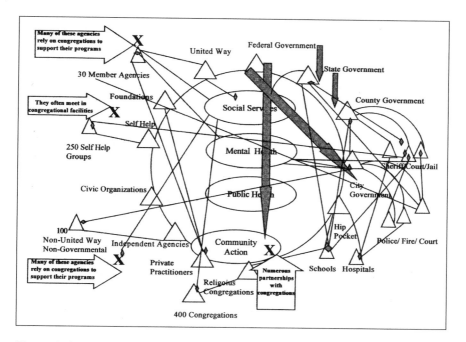

Figure 2.5. Interactions of Participants in the Greensboro Community System

the city, service agencies, and the federal funding cycle through Community Development Block Grants. Each of the core agencies in the middle of the circle receives federal block grant money from different divisions of the state government, thus the thick shaded arrow from the Federal Government triangle to those receiving agencies signifies an important federal relationship. In North Carolina, the state passes the block grant to the county, whose employees administer the programs. The federal government loosely sets the reporting requirements for the state, and the state then sets somewhat more stringent reporting requirements for the counties. County government, however, is not part of the funding scheme in the case of the Community Action Agency, the last entry in the core of the circle for Block Grant recipients. The Community Action Agency—for example, the Welfare Reform Liaison Project—is a separate nonprofit organization. Reexamining Figure 2.2, which cites some of the statistics about child abuse on a daily basis, and noting what sequence of agencies and authorities come into play because of the legalities entailed in this system of exchange, it becomes even more complex. But to those in the know, it is comprehensible. If you are a community leader with these matters facing you squarely, how plausible is it to drop everything and try to bring little congregations into the complex mix just because some politicians and pundits say they would be effective?

For example, when adults in a family fail at parenting for any number of reasons and harm one or more of their children or put them in danger of being harmed, child protection laws enable the state to suspend or terminate the rights of the parents. State law then becomes the guide. The courts handling child protection matters are housed at the local level. The state itself then assumes responsibility as the acting parent. This is the law of every state. However, the process is far from simple, because the states themselves do not assume the parenting role directly; they must find patient, caring people who will provide food, clothing, and shelter to the traumatized children. These foster parents must undergo police background checks and be trained as effective acting parents for children under extreme duress. A local system that cares for children and families in any community is an interconnected assortment of public, private nonprofit, self-help, and religious organizations. Serving one child takes time, and effective help depends on coordinating with many types of providers in the "child rescue system": courts, schools, health care and mental health professionals, and foster parents are just some of the many potential connections.

When I position the arrows from sheriff to hospital, court to schools, and court to a United Way Agency, not only are organizations moving, but so are vulnerable children. A new and similar scenario happens almost daily just in child abuse cases. What is central to making this system operate smoothly is getting people to gain acceptance or approval from others who also care. Such development requires time to form the necessary relationships. The people who accomplish these tasks are not strangers to each other; they have their rules of behavior for completing work as efficiently as possible in an arduous system. Society's needs are so great in number, and the resources available stretched so thin, that the state, as noted in Figure 2.6, started a volunteer program in 1983 called Guardians ad Litem to ensure that children have a voice in this cumbersome and stressful process. In 2003, the 3,824 volunteers served 15,706 children.

This program is yet another component in a procedure of synchronization that protects the rights of the children. With such overwhelming numbers of children in the program and the actors in this process enduring so much strain in trying to do what is best for these children, kids become overlooked when, in fact, the law was designed to help them. State laws also require social workers to develop plans that map strategies for resolving the difficulties within the birth family. Overall, the intention is for the child eventually to return home if that is a viable option. In the end, those involved may simply have to find a temporary home. In severe

---

Visitors to the Guardian ad Litem website (http://www.nccourts.org/citizens/gal/default.asp) are greeted by the following message from Jane Volland, the organization's administrator:

"Welcome to our pages! If you have arrived here, it is because you are at least curious about how you could help an abused or neglected child. . . and you can. Throughout North Carolina, we always need more volunteers to be a voice for the children who find themselves the subject of court cases. We provide training to make sure you are at ease in your role, and as a volunteer Guardian ad Litem you will be in court as a team member with a trained attorney advocate. Since 1983, the North Carolina Guardian ad Litem (GAL) program has served the best interests of thousands of children. Many were able to return home, some now live with other family members, and still others have been adopted. What we try to ensure is that all of the children we represent remain safe and that their homes are permanent.

"In the past fiscal year, 3,824 trained volunteers served 15,706 children. These children were in court because a petition had been filed stating they were abused or neglected. These numbers were a significant increase over the preceding year, and a record number of hearings were scheduled—26,112. We continue to need more volunteer Guardians ad Litem to meet the needs of these growing numbers of children.

"Please take a few minutes to browse our pages. It takes a special person to be a Guardian ad Litem, but being a volunteer GAL will give you the opportunity to make a real difference in the life of a child. Contact the Guardian ad Litem office in your area for information on how you can help. We hope you will decide to join us—a child near you needs you.

"Thank you."

Figure 2.6. Guardian ad Litem: A Child's Advocate in Court

instances, an adoption may be necessary, and in extraordinarily complex cases, those involved may need to seek guardianship through the courts. Returning a child home is an intricate matter, because the issues that caused the child's removal may stem from any combination of child abuse, substance abuse, mental illness, lack of a job, homelessness, and other reasons. Finding counseling for a traumatized child may also be necessary. If adoption is the recommendation, social workers must conduct background checks of prospective adoptive parents and evaluate their home lives to ensure that the child moves to an appropriate living situation. When neither returning a child to his or her home nor adoption is a feasible option, as in cases when the child is too old for adoption or is a teen parent, the social workers must find legal guardians to ensure the safety of such a minor. Each dimension just noted is specified in the state law, and sometimes federal law, and is designed to protect children.

Not only are the outlined dimensions legal, but they also fit into the culture of the community's system of services. Thus, examining this matter by using the model of the system in Figure 2.5, a trained eye, at minimum, would see interconnections among the county Department of Social Services' social workers and attorneys, the police, the hospitals, the schools, the foster family, and Guardian ad Litem, along with its volunteers. While the law requires the involvement of each, the entities that partake in these connections to aid a child are not all government bureaucracies themselves. When other circumstances such as drug abuse, sexual abuse, or physical violence are implicated, private nonprofit and government agencies across other sectors are also called upon for assistance.

In addition to child abuse and neglect, there are the growing problems of homeless families, health problems among the poor, and developmental delays in children of teen mothers and drug users. Conflicts also result from the number of ex-convicts returning to the community with HIV and AIDS. It is inconceivable that our urban poverty policy should be merely a faith-based initiative. The strategy adds more providers to the mix without a plan, simply a vigorous conviction. They add to the confusion and stress at a crucial time when the system needs to focus much more deliberately on planning. Clearly, the direction the initiative has taken is not just unreasonable—it is both careless and dishonorable when examined against the backdrop of thoughtful program planning at the community level!

If the planners of the president's Faith-Based Initiative were genuinely concerned about the poor and were grounded outside of their theoretical and spiritual idealism, and thus grasped the reality of how difficult it is to get an effective level of service delivery in the present system, they could have contributed with a more thoughtful and possibly more effective intervention system. They also could have avoided the dozen or so church *vs.* state lawsuits and the associated controversy.[9] Instead, this initiative focuses on winning a culture war, sending the fallen to church, and finally directing God to where He is needed most: the hearts of the fallen. What follows is an outline of the Bush administration's intervention strategy as it relates to the system.

ADMINISTRATIVE RULE CHANGES

Figure 2.7 shows the system of services as envisioned by the Bush administration. In this third model, a series of shapes—an arrow, a rectangle, a cross, and an oval—appear either on the periphery of the system or entering into the system of services at various points. Administrative policy has changed the rules specifically to include faith-based organizations in the groups deemed eligible for discretionary grants. These grants come from different agencies of the federal government, such as the departments of Health and Human Services, Housing and Urban Development, and Labor and Education, among others. With these rule changes and as a result of legislation, churches are now eligible to receive funds from one or more of these departments. The "bully pulpit" effort was also used as a "civil rights" strategy in public discussions to gain widespread approval for the initiative.

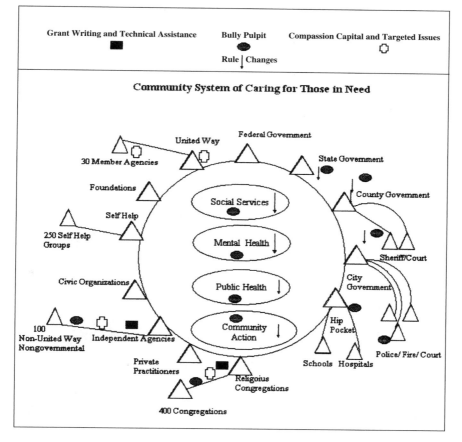

Figure 2.7. Bush Faith-Based Intervention Strategy at the Community Level

Suffice it to say for now, the legal suits brought against the Faith-Based Initiative have challenged the legality of awarding money to programs that fund specific religious activities such as teaching religious classes or using government money to hire people of only a specific religion. The Bush administration also altered the rules in block grants to states that enabled, though not necessarily compelled, the states to use some of their block grants to fund faith-based organizations. These rule changes did not really get beyond the surface and go deeply into the service sector, given the broad range and severity of the problems with which the people in this system must work. As one can see in Figure 2.7, the churches are on the border of the system. Simply revising some rules so the churches in the community can obtain some money did not rouse them to apply for federal money, nor did it stir up the other actors to collaborate with churches. The difficulties in such partnerships could fill several volumes.

Bully Pulpit

Another of President Bush's intervention strategies is the bully pulpit—using the power of his office to speak out and be heard on matters of the Faith-Based Initiative. The attempt has been to support the system via the airwaves and media. But the bully pulpit was not simply used to promote the Faith-Based Initiative. The president has given more than fifty speeches on issues related directly to his Faith-Based Initiative, to legislation his initiative targeted, or to some of the black churches where the pastors were chief supporters of his initiative.[10] These venues were his focus for increased awareness. There is much more to this political manipulation than merely seeking approval for making local changes.

Grant-Writing Conferences and Technical Assistance

Government planners realized early on that while it was politically savvy for the president to be seen in black churches, their strategy and rhetoric were also targeting small black churches to receive funding even though most did not have the skills to access it. Approximately 350,000 churches span the country. According to Mark Chaves, the vast majority of congregations are involved in social services in a peripheral way; only 6 percent of them have a staff person devoting at least a quarter of his or her time to social service projects.[11] From a broad perspective, there are very few congregations with people in place and possessing the appropriate skills to plan a federal grant-based program, to implement that program, to manage the funding and matching requirements, and then to conduct the evaluation and submit the necessary reports that accompany government grants.

I teach grant writing and program administration to graduate students and have conducted numerous one- and two-day grant-writing workshops. I have also received numerous federal, state, and privately funded grants and contracts. From my experience, the *basics* of grant writing might be grasped in a three-day workshop, but there is no doubt whatsoever that the essence of grant writing—defining the problem, research, program planning, goal setting, development of implementation strategies, building of key partnerships, budgeting, and learning essential evaluation skills—requires long-term and concerted efforts to master.

To the administration's credit, it has addressed these deficits by conducting regional conferences with a focus on grant writing and technical assistance, such as learning how to develop outcome measures. Figure 2.8 is an announcement of technical assistance events found on the Office of Faith-Based and Community Initiatives web page. But even if thousands

---

The following is a sample of some of the technical assistance events and resources promoted on the website of the White House Office of Faith-Based and Community Initiatives (http://www.whitehouse.gov/government/fbci/technical-assistance.html).

Training for Grassroots Faith-Based & Community Organizations
The Substance Abuse and Mental Health Services Administration is holding a series of workshops around the country. These workshops help grassroots organizations with grant writing and capacity building. For a schedule of upcoming workshops, ...

Upcoming Supplemental Educational Services Workshops
Supplemental Services provide extra academic help for low-income students in low performing schools. The workshops are free but require pre-registration. . . .

Housing and Community Development Seminars, Workshops, Conferences
The Department of Housing and Urban Development is conducting FREE, two-day, intensive Grant-Writing Training Workshops for Faith-Based & Community-Based Organizations to teach them how to secure Federal funding. The sessions include Organizational Development, Legal Do's & Don'ts, Five Factors for Awards, The Art & Science of Grant Writing, as well as a sample YouthBuild Application. . . .

Office of Justice Programs Technical Assistance Opportunities
The Office of Justice Programs at the Department of Justice offers a range of technical assistance options for organizations involved in community-based crime prevention and which serve young offenders, ex-offenders, and victims of crime. . . .

Online Technical Assistance for Supplemental Educational Services
In an effort to provide technical assistance to faith-based and community organizations, the Office of Innovation and Improvement and the Center for Faith-Based and Community Initiatives have produced a webcast that is intended to help faith-based and community organizations apply to become approved providers of supplemental services. . . .

Figure 2.8. Technical Assistance Events and Resources

were to attend, they would not gain the skills to be major competitors in the sophisticated grants game.

Recognizing this, the Bush administration has put out a twenty-page booklet called "Guidance to Faith-Based and Community Organizations on Partnering with the Federal Government."[12] The clearest message in the document is that if one does not know the answer to a question, he or she should call the number listed for free help with an organization the government has hired to provide technical assistance. However, it would appear that this guide might have been an afterthought, as it was developed in November 2003. Having taught members of the groups this initiative is targeting, I would evaluate the booklet as a less-than-average intervention strategy.

The twenty-page brochure would work well as a supplement for my graduate course in social service administration, as it provides a framework for the novice federal grant seeker, but its language is too sophisticated for members of small organizations, who may not have an answering machine let alone a computer or a bookkeeper familiar with auditing principles.

Even if each little church were successful, since there is no "new" money as of yet in the faith-based initiative, more serious contenders would compete for the same amount of money in the community system. Such an intervention strategy does little to develop the kind of goodwill an organization needs as it enters into the local system, because that organization depends upon more than learning how to win a government grant. In the local culture of service delivery, resources are exchanged not merely through grants and contracts but also through people networking. Therefore, based upon the first four intervention strategies of the Bush administration in Figure 2.7, the president's planners are still at the starting gate in regard to successful intervention into the community.

Capital Compassion Fund and Targeted Issues

The Capital Compassion Fund is a pool of money designated to go to intermediary organizations to mentor small churches and community-based organizations in developing programs that mainly address self-sufficiency, family issues, children of prisoners, prison reentry, and child care. To understand the issues regarding the Capital Compassion Fund, some context is necessary (much more detail is provided in the next chapter).

The majority of congregations in the United States (57%), comprising 75 percent of the total number of people who attend congregations, provide some type of social service. Food programs rank as the most common social service activity, being provided by 32 percent. Clothing programs come in second, at 18 percent. Fewer than 10 percent of the congregations are engaged in the kinds of social service activities that are the target of the president's Faith-Based Initiative—substance abuse, tutoring/ mentoring, prison-related programs, and the like.[13]

The administration understood that most of the congregations and organizations intended to receive federal money were too small to become even little service agencies. As a result, the government provided ways to disburse money to small churches that, for the most part, were under the radar of the local community service systems. However, one of Chaves's major findings is:

> The rare congregations that engage more intensively in social services do so mainly in collaboration with a wide range of religious organizations, secular nonprofit organizations, and government agencies. It is more accurate to say congregation based social services depend on secular social service agencies than to say they constitute an alternative to those agencies.[14]

The federal plan had to be conducted in such a way that all recipients would be at least somewhat accountable for the funds, and a real learning curve in planning, budgeting, and other skills for these new organizations would be in place. Thus, the initiative could extend to additional organizations more thoroughly than through the traditional grant and technical assistance workshops. The initiative also targeted specific issues—not uncommon behavior for federal or private agencies distributing funds. However, when the government at the federal level guides an entire intervention strategy, instead of allowing each community to decide what issues it is facing are most important, what happens is that organizations chase money and tailor programs to the needs of the funding entity instead of the requests of the community.

In 1996 I wanted to understand how agencies planned for, implemented, and evaluated the resources of the religious community. I reported the following in the *Journal of Community Practice* based on the survey responses of 147 agency directors (out of the 193 surveyed):

> This study shows that the strength of the religious community lies in the supportive role it assumes in service delivery at the local level. I feel that there are three assumptions beneath politician's proposals for more religious involvement in service delivery that need closer scrutiny: (1) the religious community has the capacity to shift from a minor to major social service provider, (2) the religious community wants to expand its service role; and (3) the religious community will provide better services than the public sector.[15]

This piggybacks on what Chaves noted and bolsters the broader point that an intervention strategy must understand the system in which changes are going to occur.

Ten years after I made those points, the religious community still does not have the capacity to shift from minor to major provider. It was never asked if it wanted a broader role, and there is not a shred of real evidence that the religious community will provide better services than the public sector. The principle behind the Compassion Capital Fund has been to work with small faith-based organizations nationwide through a mentoring system, the assumption of some being that they will make better providers. The federal government offered a competitive request for federal dollars, with its target group being larger, mainly private, nonprofit, intermediary organizations. Those larger groups, in turn, had to develop a comprehensive three-year proposal wherein plans would help small ministries grow and learn, through "guided development" by the intermediary, how to strengthen their own programs. The incentive to accomplish this goal was for intermediary organizations to use some of the money from its larger grant to award developmental start-up grants to the smaller ministries.

The larger organizations were to serve as mentors to the smaller groups. On one level, this concept is marvelous; however, many of the intermediary organizations worked with sets of groups either on a nationwide or statewide basis. Consequently, the focus was teaching organizations how to attain grants, to develop program plans, and to gain other programming skills, but little occurred in terms of intervention to *become a partner* in solving local problems in partnerships with the agencies and organizations in the local system. Therefore, when one examines the model in Figure 2.7, the arrow positioned next to the Independent Agencies and Churches is there to show that the intervention was performed outside the main system of services and is not an intervention at all with regard to playing a supportive role.

In Raleigh, North Carolina, a for-profit organization initially named Mission Tree (now Educational Grant Services, Inc.) received a $1.5 million Compassion Capital grant, the first step in becoming an intermediary. Recently, the grant was renewed. Nine recipients of the subawardees resided in the home city of the intermediary, but fourteen other recipients were spread across North Carolina and one was located in Virginia. The $70,000 spent on the two organizations in Greensboro who received subawards had no impact whatsoever on the local system.

From a community intervention perspective, it is clear that the intermediary's focus is certainly not helping these organizations become part of their local systems of service; instead, these organizations are merely learning how to become self-sufficient agencies so that they can compete for federal money. Again, as part of the tactic to gain acceptance in the culture of community services, the Capital Compassion Fund strategy, while creative, does very little in solving the problems at broader community level and creates no avenues for creating partnership with local stakeholders.

The arrows in Figure 2.7 are purposefully placed outside of the core of the community system, with the exception of the four arrows down the center of the figure. Had the plan been thoughtful, there would be numerous arrows on the inside of the system and pointing at the key actors and stakeholders. Furthermore, arrows would also have been coming from the inside of the system toward the actors and stakeholders on the outside. But this was a top-down effort and it hit the wrong targets.

My Intervention Strategy

As a community analyst determining whether or not the faith-based initiative planners' intervention strategy could make a positive change in how any sector, or the system itself, solves, manages, or prevents problems,

I would initially make an assessment of the intervention by seeking answers to three basic questions:

1. How is the overall issue being marketed to the community in general and particularly to the leaders in the complex and interconnected sectors that comprise the system?
2. What role have key stakeholders in the community played in shaping how the issue will be presented to the community?
3. Are the issues that the policy is addressing important to the stakeholders?

Overall Marketing

The arrows in Figure 2.7 represent not only administrative rule changes but also the central flaw in the intervention strategy. The arrows are positioned vertically because this represents a top-down intervention strategy, meaning that the effort was not really shaped, influenced, or refined by the stakeholders in the service systems of the 50 states, 19,000 cities, 16,000 townships, or 3,000 counties in the country. From this view, it must be called a Beltway and bureaucratic initiative that has ignored the grass roots because the planners did not understand the basics of this system. Almost five years after this initiative began, the key stakeholders at the community level in Greensboro still look puzzled when asked how the Faith-Based Initiative has influenced their operations.

A Model Example

Mothers Against Drunk Driving (MADD) serves as an example of a grassroots movement that successfully took hold. Not only is MADD a household word, but the organization was influential in changing drunk driving laws in almost all of the states, reducing fatalities, and even creating a new term: the designated driver.

Every community in our country continues to have a stake in what MADD has already achieved and continues to accomplish—a goal of saving lives and sparing families the incomprehensible grief of burying a child because of drunk driving—a behavioral choice that can be prevented. Every community in this country has a stake, maybe not personal but certainly moral, in insuring that children have a place to sleep at night, that they are not beaten or psychologically damaged, and that their caretakers have the resources to insure that the wounded spirits of these damaged youngsters are healed in the quickest and healthiest manner; these kids have done nothing to deserve such a fate.

MADD's work conducted at both the personal and systemic levels was magical. The architects of this movement framed the issue as a "victims' assistance concern" and made an impact on sentencing laws for drunk driving. More than 2,300 anti–drunk driving laws have been passed. But more importantly, they changed behavior not by moralizing about the sin of drinking but by focusing on the sin of drinking and driving. Since MADD has been in existence, the percentage of alcohol-related fatalities has decreased from 60 percent to 40 percent, which translates to an estimated 290,675 lives saved.[16]

This important issue remains personal to me on two levels, as my brother-in-law was killed because of drinking and driving, and for the last eight years one or the other of my children has been a teen driver in an alcohol culture where peer influence sometimes is stronger than parental demands. MADD gave our family a language emphasizing life over lies. My wife and I repeatedly reminded our son and daughter that if there were no designated drivers, no matter what time, what distance they were from home, or what condition they were in, they could call and we would pick them up without sanction. We "bought in," our children bought in, and the society has bought in.

Critics might say this comparison is unfair or that it is invalid because it describes two different things. But there are some similarities. Both movements had legislative agendas and national advertising campaigns, and both have intervened locally. However, the differences demonstrate the distinction between the success of one effort and the failure of the other: On the one hand, MADD has strong involvement of grassroots mothers, boasts six hundred local chapters that keep this issue alive through legislation, and its advertising helps gain buy-in at the family level and in the community institutions. On the other hand, the Faith-Based Initiative has had little involvement from local religious leaders and even less by the social service community.

Simply stated, the faith-based architects made their case nationally, but it is vague and lacks genuine state and local focuses; thus, local advocates are few in number. Bush's arrangement is a top-down, liberal model of wasteful government spending; not only was it denied major buy-in from the community, but it also failed the following six-question test:

1. Was there a cataloguing of the scope of the community's problems? *No.*
2. Do we now know the exact level to which the mandated services are meeting that need? *No.*
3. After this intervention by the Faith-Based Initiative architects, do we have some semblance of an understanding of the resources of the faith community? *No.*
4. Did the architects figure out ways to match resources with need? *No.*
5. Did anyone figure out where the gaps exist between resources and need? *No.*
6. Has there been any groundswell from local faith-based leaders or community leaders? *No.*

As an administration that enjoys giving report cards, Bush and his faith-based architects would not take kindly to my giving them a failing grade for not providing a coherent, local intervention strategy.

CHAPTER 3

The Research Shows ...

Studying faith-based social services is no simple matter. Before any researcher can make definite claims about the effectiveness of this or that faith-based approach, there has to be an understanding of religious congregations as organizations; knowledge about the system of services where those organizations deliver their programs; a working understanding of the interventions under scrutiny; an understanding of the strengths and limitations of the research employed to clarify the interplay of these elements; and a clear knowledge of the policy environment that bears down on service delivery systems. Unless all five of these elements are a clearly defined part of a research project, it is very difficult to make supportable claims.

In his 2004 book *Congregations in America*, Professor Mark Chaves, one of the world's leading authorities on social services and religious congregations, addresses the question of whether faith-based social services are more effective than nonfaith-based ones:

> Comprehensively assessing the relative effectiveness of religiously based social services requires attention to organizations other than congregations. A full discussion of this issue is beyond the scope of this book *but it is worth noting that there is no empirical basis for concluding that religious organizations are in general more effective than secular organizations in delivering social services.*[1]

Chaves is right on both counts, despite what those with a policy agenda might have said about the Teen Challenge work and other research. The story, as he aptly noted, is too complex to be included in his groundbreaking book that examines faith-based social services nationally.

Some of the most important studies on the topic of faith-based social services are those by Jean-Philippe Laurenceau, Aaron Todd Bicknese, Stephen Monsma, and Wolfgang Bielefeld. Laurenceau's study is a marriage intervention program. Current social policy emphasizes the importance of marriage and promotes using religious resources to support it, hoping to increase the number of couples who choose marriage and to decrease the number of divorces among those partners who do marry. Bicknese's study, noted previously in chapter 1, is a drug intervention program. Policy advocates also envision untapped resources in the religious community for expanding drug intervention programs.

Monsma and Bielefeld's studies examine both religious and nonreligious providers of welfare-to-work training services, another policy area faith-based social services advocates deem important. To understand fully the problems in the Monsma and Bielefeld studies requires some understanding of survey research, local service systems, and policy environment. While social policymakers have already been promoting the use of religious organizations as important groups for helping people make the transition from welfare to work, no research substantiates such an endorsement. Monsma and Bielefeld focus on welfare-to-work programs only offhandedly, attempting to compare them to their nonreligious counterparts on different dimensions in the broad realm of social service delivery. Some scholars claim that holistic services are central components of service delivery exclusive to faith-based organizations. These services are too complicated to measure by themselves, let alone in the context of the organizational and service delivery environments, a changing policy environment, and challenging conceptualization of what is being measured. The Monsma and Bielefeld surveys need to be included here for these very reasons.

While Bielefeld's latest study (with Sheila Suess Kennedy) was a survey,[2] he had more than four thousand people who were assigned by caseworkers in Indiana to either government or faith-based welfare-to-work programs. He created a statistical comparison after researchers collected the data that allowed him to create a computerized version of a quasi-experiment. Bielefeld made no apologies; rather, he appropriately called this creative bit of research a "beginning." To understand his findings, I placed the work in what it was originally, a survey.

Without more interdisciplinary research and better language to define service organizations with a religious connection, we will never grasp the reality of social services and the system through which they serve. Consequently, our scientific understanding will remain at its current primitive level.

EXPERIMENTAL, QUASI-EXPERIMENTAL, AND SURVEY RESEARCH

As this discussion proceeds, I cannot overemphasize how important it is to understand the organizational and community contexts from which social services are delivered. However, it is also important to view those matters against the backdrop of the complexities of the social science research enterprise.

Experimental Research

In the world of experimental research, the most scientifically valid studies are double-blind, experimental studies. In a double-blind study, neither the researchers nor the participants know which participants are assigned to what program. All involved have an equal chance at being in one or another program. Double-blind studies are almost impossible to conduct in the real world of social programs and are thus better suited to laboratories. Social scientists, however, have determined ways to conduct research to better understand social programs and still have "best-guess" estimates of whether a program's success, or parts of its success, could in fact be attributed to a "faith component."

One may consider a double-blind experimental study as the top rung of a twelve-rung ladder of assurance that what might be learned would be applicable or valid anywhere. The rungs on this ladder of understanding descend from the top levels, which acquire the most knowledge and are valid virtually anywhere, to the bottom rung, where the findings are not applicable at all.

Experimental studies range from the best double-blind studies to simple experimental studies. In the latter, people are randomly assigned to a program, but both they and the researcher know which program they are in. Thus they are weaker than double-blind experiments, because once people know to what kind of program they have been assigned, their behavior might change and affect the outcome. Experimental studies of all types, however, would take up the top three or four rungs of a ladder of true knowledge acquisition.

Quasi-Experimentation

As one goes down the ladder from perfect experimentation to quasi-experimentation, different kinds of events threaten the assurances that the program would work if administered elsewhere to a similar population. (This point is the major drawback of the Bielefeld study, and he says so.) The closer the study remains to the top of the ladder, the better chance the findings will be valid and thus applicable to a larger population. Quasi-experimental studies range from just above the middle of the ladder of potential for gaining true knowledge to the bottom rung, representing a total inability to make any valid claims about the effects of a program.

The Laurenceau study is an example of a quasi-experimental study, because the names of the participants were not assigned randomly to receive one particular training over another. Instead, they were already attending a religious organization for the training. The trainings, not the people, were randomly assigned to the organizations, or "cluster" as it is termed in social science. As a result, the findings of the study are probably on the middle rung of the ladder of validity. As Laurenceau notes correctly, much more research needs must occur to determine the full truth.

Survey Research

Imagine five people attending a lunch meeting. The server asks what each person wants to eat. If she gives each person the opportunity to choose any lunch, she might hear six different choices. However, if she asks them whether they want turkey or tuna sandwiches, only three choices are available: turkey, tuna, or no lunch. The first example would be an open-ended survey of lunch participants; the second would be a closed-ended survey, meaning that the choices are limited.

The survey in our example is called a *total population survey* because the server asks *everyone* what he or she wants for lunch. If everyone responded, the server would know with 100 percent accuracy what everyone at that meeting *wanted* for lunch at the time of the survey. Thus a total population survey is the best form of survey research. Surveys diminish in accuracy the further they move away from measuring the responses of everyone in a group—be it a lunch group, a community, or the country.

Even though the server might know what everyone desires to eat, she would not know whether people actually *ate* what they chose, or perhaps made a trade, unless she observed them during or surveyed them after lunch. And even a small lunch survey can grow increasingly more complex if the order taker allows choices for types of bread, garnishes, drinks, and dessert.

Survey researchers have developed means for staying close to the top rung of the ladder of knowledge by using the same principles that underlie experimental research: randomization. In the case of surveys, random selection replaces random assignment, but the quality of measurement is essential.

Suppose one hundred people were coming to lunch. It might then be too cumbersome to ask *each person* what he or she wanted. The server might then randomly ask fifty people what they want to eat and use this information to make a "best guess" of what everyone wanted for lunch. Still, she may still become overwhelmed by all the choices fifty people could select. However, if the choices were limited to just tuna or turkey, it might be more accurate at arriving at a best guess of what the whole lunch group wanted by asking fifty people randomly to choose between tuna and turkey.

Now, instead of lunches, consider trying to find out the difference in services provided by faith-based organizations versus nonreligious organizations. We may be able to conduct a total population survey in one small community, but it would be impossible to do so for an entire state or the nation. In order to determine a best guess, therefore, we would do what we did for our 100 lunch attendees: randomly select enough faith-based and nonfaith-based organizations in whatever place we are studying and limit the choices of interventions we have to compare. To do so, however, one would have to know the kinds of services both categories of organizations are likely to provide, in order to determine the most accurate measure as possible. Since both types of organizations are often partners with each other in the real world of service delivery, gaining a clearer picture of what they do, and then comparing them, would require determining the different mixes of who does what before we could draw any conclusions about the faith-based service provision as compared to its secular counterpart. Sadly, the members of the social science community are not good at this step.[3]

Trying to draw any major conclusions about the Monsma or Bielefeld study beyond simple guesswork is impossible, because Monsma looked at organizations in only four cities and really did not compare organizations in ways that yielded measures that compare effectiveness; Bielefeld tried to make such comparisons in three states, but even when he zeroed in on just one, he noted he had too many problems with the permutations to build knowledge much beyond a rung or two above the bottom of the ladder, making the answer about comparative effectiveness extremely elusive. However, Bielefeld's work stands above Monsma's bottom-rung analysis in the eyes of the social science research community.

THE LAURENCEAU QUASI-EXPERIMENTAL FINDINGS

Jean-Philippe Laurenceau and his team were determined to find out if a scientifically tested, premarital communication training called PREP would increase communication among couples considering marriage. If proven totally effective, such training would provide a useful way for couples to communicate upon entering into marriage. In fact, the study found no change in communication among the men in the study fourteen months into their marriage, but there was one small and significant finding that is important regarding our discussion: Women who attended PREP training administered by clergy were likely to communicate *less negatively* with their partners than either the women who took the same PREP training administered by university clinicians or the women who did not take the PREP training yet completed a traditional premarital counseling program at the congregation of their own choosing instead. What made the study both compelling and pertinent to this discussion is the trainings were administered at religious organizations, and the group of women who had the *most positive* communication patterns after the training was the one trained by clergy.

The Laurenceau study was not a true experimental study of the highest order, but rather a quasi-experimental study. It did, however, include some of the major elements of a pure experiment—randomization and testing before and after the training. The subjects of the study were *not* randomly assigned to receive the PREP training, though. A random assignment would have made the research project a true experimental study. Instead, the PREP training and the traditional training were randomly assigned to the different religious organizations, but the trainees were free to choose from which religious organizations they wished to take the training. Even so, all of the participants were tested before the training and again fourteen months later when they were married.

The authors concluded:

> We believe that couple intervention researchers can benefit especially well given the role that any community organizations, such as ROs [Religious Organizations], play in supporting functional marriages. Findings from the present study indicate that not only does PREP [the scientifically tested program] seem transportable, but it also demonstrates powerful intervention effects when *integrated into existing community systems*. Future work should focus on evaluation of longer-term effects and putative mechanisms that explain how premarital intervention programs, such as PREP, might be more effective *from within* the community.[4]

The Laurenceau study possibly adds one small brick to a tall building of understanding called faith-based social services, yet by no means does it answer whether faith-based social services are more effective than non-faith-based social services.

TEEN CHALLENGE

The study drawing the most attention from scholars conducting research and advocating social service policy positions from the think-tank world, and somewhat so in the academy, is Aaron Bicknese's 1999 doctoral dissertation, entitled "The Teen Challenge Drug Treatment Program in Comparative Perspective." Bicknese explains that one reason he took on this work was because the subjects of the first Teen Challenge Study, performed by the National Institute on Drug Abuse (NIDA),[5] were 1968 graduates of a Teen Challenge program, and it has not been known whether the program has had a similar effect in more recent years. Second, the fourteen-page NIDA study provided no rigorous analysis of results. While the effect size was provided, the report lacked a calculation of statistical significance as well as a thorough explanation of variance between the treatment group and control group (in that study, early dropouts); Bicknese's project does endeavor to analyze variance and show statistical significance. Third, the NIDA study did not explicitly compare the Teen Challenge results with those of publicly funded programs. The comparison group for Bicknese's study is a sample of publicly funded program graduates.[6]

Teen Challenge is a national organization with local residential treatment facilities spread across the nation. The central tenet for reducing addictions in the yearlong program is that its residents make a commitment to Jesus Christ as their Personal Savior and Lord. Sometimes this recognition happens instantly, sometimes it occurs through the relationships one develops in this sort of program, and sometimes it arises through the connections one starts to build with other Christ-centered people who lead the change-oriented or Christ-focused setting. The program teaches that whenever the ex-addict genuinely accepts Christ, he or she becomes a new human being and that *only through this acceptance* can he or she shed the immoral life of the past. It does not matter whether one was an addict, unemployed, unemployable, or burdened by any human plague. From this perspective, a person's problems all spring forth from a hole in his or her spiritual life. The repair, first and foremost, is letting the love of Jesus into one's heart, which is a pathway to correcting the problem in the soul.

This type of intervention carries different names and several dimensions, but for the purpose of my discussion, four significant terms regarding this intervention are:

- *Christ-centered*, including bible study and prayer
- *relational*, the formation of personal relationships in ways that demonstrate Christ's love through care and concern
- *holistic*, the combination of the religious and the personal expressions of care and concern through the conscious effort to influence the behavior, attitudes, and values of program participants by means of activities focused on life skills and mentoring
- *transformational*, the process of change through any or all combinations of the above

I have personal experience with the Teen Challenge model, as I have consulted with the staff and board of Malachi House in Greensboro, North Carolina, and I have been an executive coach for Cliff Lovick, Malachi House's director for more than three years. Elder Lovick is an ordained minister and a graduate of a Teen Challenge program himself; he is now drug free and a consultant to the national Teen Challenge organization, speaking frequently at national Teen Challenge events. His program is one of the more successful programs using the Teen Challenge model, boasting nearly a 50 percent success rate. No research has been done on this particular program, but it is questionable whether or not the Christ-centeredness of the program is the cause for success. It is probably some combination of faith, the director's charisma, his leadership, and the board of directors' close watch over the program administration.[7]

In short, Teen Challenge is a Christ-centered, relational, holistic, and transformational intervention model for which success in becoming free from addiction rests first and foremost on program participants maintaining a personal relationship with Jesus. Unfortunately, with regard to a true understanding of the wide range of social services, this kind of intervention approach has often become interchangeable in the public discourse with faith-based social services in general. The conservative evangelical branch of the Christian faith, which uses this model more than either liberal Christians or non-Christians, seems to hold the first mortgage on the behavioral elements they term "holistic." In social scientific terms, the independent variable, or the cause of cessation of substance abuse, is one's commitment to Christ, and the dependent variables, or the results of this acceptance, are cessation of substance abuse and commitment to work, family, and community. What these kinds of providers often claim is that the relationships, bible study, and loving community form a holistic service that brings one to Christ-centeredness and freedom from addiction.

The Bicknese study was a quasi-experimental case study comparing participants from three Teen Challenge programs—one in Rehrersburg, Pennsylvania; one in Cape Girardeau, Missouri; and one in Riverside, California—with participants in one Short Term Intervention (STI) program, which had no religious intervention strategy whatsoever. If the Bicknese study were the perfect double-blind study, participants would have been randomly assigned to either Teen Challenge or STI, but they were not. Furthermore, the programs would have been more similar in characteristics other than religion; for example, STI was a thirty day program, while Teen Challenge lasted a year. Ideally, all of the participants would have answered the questions regarding the changes they made as a result of the program, but in Bicknese's study, only 39 percent of the Teen Challenge participants answered questions about their lifestyle changes after the program, and only 31 percent of the STI participants did so.

In essence, the Bicknese study was a doctoral dissertation that taught the researcher how and how not to conduct research. It also taught Bicknese how to use the language of research to explain findings, or the lack thereof. In his own words, Aaron Bicknese tells the real story of his research findings, unable to make any claims that the program worked:

> The findings to be presented here represent flaws which the present study cannot correct. One such flaw, as has been explained, is limited external validity due to low response rates in both the Teen Challenge dataset and the comparison group (39.3% and 30.7%, respectively). We can compare the two datasets with one another reliably enough, but much caution is in order before extending these results to compare with other studies. Furthermore, much variation in outcome variables remains yet to be explained.[8]

Bicknese proceeds in the language of research to inform his doctoral committee, and anyone else who reads his dissertation, that much more work must completed to determine if Teen Challenge is more effective than its government-funded counterpart: "The best solution to this problem is to compile a bigger dataset, a task I leave to those who will address this question in the future."[9] So far, no one has taken on the Bicknese challenge.

MONSMA STUDY

In this analysis, I have included Stephen Monsma's 2004 book *Putting Faith in Partnerships*,[10] not because it compares whether social services are more effective than nonsocial services—it does not—but rather because its findings, along with the author's earlier report with Carolyn Mounts entitled "Working Faith: How Religious Organizations Provide Welfare-to-Work Services,"[11] are confused in policy circles and the academic community for research that *does* make this comparison. If Monsma's surveys and interviews of faith-based and nonfaith-based providers in Philadelphia, Dallas, Chicago, and Los Angeles *were* making such comparisons, the research would have examined differences between faith-based and non-faith-based providers with regard to which placed more clients in jobs; how long the trainees, once hired, stayed in their jobs; how wages, benefits, career ladders, and other outcomes related to employment compared; and so forth. No such comparisons took place.

Monsma, a respected scholar, has advocated alongside the other scholars I mentioned previously and will mention later, and who mainly conduct their work from right-leaning think tanks and who have advocated for over a decade to shift government funds toward the holistic and Christ-centered programs such as Teen Challenge. Since no research provides a platform to substantiate the claims of the supporters of this policy position, Monsma's survey of 500 faith-based and secular organizations in four cities provides an empirical framework to continue to shape the policy discussion.

It is not until page 36 of his book that Monsma clearly states what the work is *not* about:

> *Are nongovernmental entities more effective in delivering social services?* It is often claimed that for-profit, and community-based social service programs have higher success rates than do government programs and large, professionalized nonprofit programs. This study, however, does not seek to address the question of whether or not this is in fact the case. Doing so would raise an entire set of methodological issues and concerns that the current study was not designed to meet. Exploration of this issue area must await future studies.[12]

I have known Professor Monsma for almost a decade and recognize both his public and private voices. He is a cautious scholar, and one would not ordinarily decipher the nuances in his work. However, his speech at the Sixth Annual Henry Lecture at Calvin College—"Myths, Lies, and Soundbites: Reactions to President Bush's Initiative"—was not just a rebuke to critics of President Bush's faith-based policies but was uncharacteristically vocal with claims about the effectiveness of existing studies, especially Teen Challenge research. In his speech, he noted, "There is some empirical evidence in support of the greater effectiveness of programs: two studies of Teen Challenge have demonstrated its higher success levels than comparable secular drug-treatment programs."[13] Bicknese conducted his study partly because no such claims could be substantiated, and he wanted to recognize Teen Challenge's effectiveness. However, even his research was unable to build any base of knowledge along such lines.

Thus, a fair question to ask of the Monsma study is what the survey *did* try to measure if it did not compare faith-based and nonfaith-based welfare-to-work programs on outcome measures as noted: job placement, job retention, wages, and so forth. Monsma genuinely sought the appropriate role for government and nongovernmental service providers by trying to understand what each does in the provision of services in welfare to work. However, a creeping bias seemed to exist toward confirming that holistic service providers are more effective at influencing behavior than government providers. As such, he was looking to demonstrate that point with some evidence through his four-city, nonrandom survey.

In making his comparison, Monsma did have to ask whether nonfaith-based providers offer holistic service—without the prayer, of course. Chaves describes the findings of Monsma's study on this concern as follows:

> In addition to the standard job-oriented services, such as GED (General Educational Development) test preparation, vocational training, and job placement services, for each provider they measured the extent to which they also attempted to influence "the behavior, attitudes, and values of welfare recipients" through activities focused on "work preparedness, life skills, and mentoring." The key result in the current context is that the religious organizations did no more of this activity than the secular non-government, or even for-profit providers. This null result holds even when religion-based programs that integrate explicitly religious elements into their programming are isolated. At least among providers of welfare-to-work services, there is no evidence that religious organizations are more likely to do things "holistically."[14]

What advocates for Christ-centered social services believe, as I have alluded to but the Monsma research was unable to confirm, is that providing holistic services in a spirit of Christ has the advantage over secular service provision. One needs to acquire full knowledge of religious organizations, which must be coupled with an understanding of the system of services where those organizations deliver their programs. Additionally, there must be an understanding of the interventions themselves and knowledge of the policy environment that bears down on service delivery systems. Even with such data, it is difficult to understand the interplay of these elements to gain some insight into effective social service delivery, be it faith-based or secular, without knowing the kind of research employed to ascertain the information.

Monsma's research did not fully offer an understanding of the complexities of the range of interconnections that undergird local social services. Though his survey was not a random sample, he found no difference in holistic services when looking at faith-based and secular providers, and he did not even measure comparative outcomes between different welfare-to-work programs to determine differences in employment outcomes. His work remains an important discussion piece, but it never climbs off the first rung on the ladder of knowledge.

The study still warrants a bit more attention, however. I have taught in the Bible Belt South for more than twenty-five years and have instructed close to two thousand Christian students, many of whom are self-declared born-again Christians who fall under the umbrella of conservative Christianity by any definition. My former students staff public agencies, private non-profit agencies, and faith-based and private for-profit service organizations. While they may not trumpet their declarations of religious commitment in the public square, they do bring their obligation to energetic, committed, and caring service—a holistic approach—to their work life regardless of where they are employed. Monsma compared different kinds of organizations, assuming that the holistic approach would be more pronounced in faith-based organizations. Therefore, he measured the type of organization instead of the commitment of the people in those organizations and found no difference.

Chaves's research brings up another factor that may explain why Monsma was unable to show that religious organizations provide any greater degree of holistic services than secular providers.

> It just may be that people who staff non-religious social service organizations breed from a liberal faith tradition but do not abandon their care and concern in the workplace.
>
> Whatever their denominational affiliations, congregations in denominations that are described by their leaders as theologically liberal report participating in or supporting two more social service programs on average than congregations that are described as theologically conservative. This might not sound like a substantial difference, but consider this comparison: the difference in social service involvement between self-described liberal and self-described conservative congregations is about the same as the difference between a seventy-five-person congregation and a thousand-person congregation. This pattern is consistent with previous research on both congregations and individuals, showing that theologically liberal individuals and congregations are, in a variety of ways, more connected to their surrounding communities than individuals and congregations associated with more evangelical or conservative traditions.[15]

My point here is not to undermine the Monsma study but rather to demonstrate the complexities of conducting social science research so as to illustrate why there are no scientifically valid studies showing how faith-based social services compare in effectiveness with nonfaith-based services. The next study makes that point better than the rest.

SHEILA KENNEDY AND WOLFGANG BIELEFELD'S STUDY

Kennedy and Bielefeld's study compared three different state policies regarding welfare-to-work. They wanted to see if there were differences in the states and the kinds of organizations they used in providing job-training services funded by the welfare-to-work Temporary Assistance to Needy Families (TANF) program in North Carolina, Indiana, and Massachusetts. The study found that there were wide variations in state-level initiatives, making comparisons of results difficult. In Indiana, however, Bielefeld (he ran the statistics) interviewed job-training providers and obtained client outcome data. It is important to quote Kennedy and Bielefeld at length because they eloquently capture the spirit of this chapter:

> We began with a deceptively simple question: do faith-based job training and placement providers do a better job than secular job training and placement providers? We defined "better job" only by objective, measurable criteria: i.e., placement rates, and wages and benefits paid. And we limited that inquiry to the organizations providing those services as part of the IMPACT program in Indiana. That we chose to work with so narrow a sample, coming from one state and one type of social service, meant that our findings would not necessarily be generalizable; but it also meant that we should be able to produce statistical analyses that would be both meaningful and credible. It would, in short, be a beginning.[16]

They conclude as one might expect from patient scientists:

> In this study, we attempted to determine whether the measurable, labor market outcomes of job training programs differed depending upon whether the provider was faith-based or secular. We controlled, to the extent possible, for the possibilities of caseworker selection and assignment bias, and we controlled for size, age and contracting experience. We found that faith-based and secular providers placed clients into jobs at essentially the same rates, and those jobs paid similar hourly wages. However, we also found that clients who received their training and placement from more strongly faith-based providers were substantially less likely to be placed into full-time jobs, and substantially less likely to be employed in positions providing health insurance coverage.[17]

Kennedy and Bielefeld's study tried to determine an answer to the focus of this chapter: Do faith-based job training and placement providers do a better job than secular job training and placement providers? Gallant as the effort was, it suffered from many of the problems one might expect but often have little control over in real-world research. State caseworkers assigned people to the faith-based or government program in ways that were not scientific; in the best of all worlds, the researchers would have done so randomly. Other concerns—for example, how to determine whether an organization was faith based and to what degree—also limited the project. The combination of unanticipated political issues and the changing funding environment disabled the researchers from obtaining the kinds of measures that would have put this study on the higher rungs of the ladder of social science knowledge.

OVERVIEW OF SOCIAL SERVICES STUDIES

The study of faith-based social services did not begin in earnest until the early 1980s, and at that time, hardly any scholarship existed that examined their effectiveness or compared them to secular social services. Today, there are hundreds of books and tens of thousands of journal, magazine, and newspaper articles touching on one or another aspect of social service.

Even so, the social science community cannot say with assurance that even one study adds to the body of knowledge to shed light on whether social services are more effective than nonfaith-based social services. Three good reasons for so few comparative studies are:

1. The subject matter is so complex that it would take many interdisciplinary teams to unravel its dimensions.
2. The academy is not equipped to conduct the interdisciplinary research needed to yield clear-cut answers.
3. There are few incentives driving the academy to change.

Such research is lengthy, complex, and costly and would require interdisciplinary expertise. Faith-based social services, as the studies in this chapter illustrate, are about religion, social services, organizational and community development, federal, state, and local governmental policy, and much more. Those policy realms touch on everything from neonatal services to workforce development and tap multiple dimensions of every social issue in between, straight through to end-of-life programs like hospice care for the frail elderly. Not only does one have to know about religion and congregational life, but it is also essential to understand the interaction of those general topics with other broad and narrow concerns, such as policy development and program implementation.

The academy is arranged in such a way that the study of religion is cordoned off into gated-like communities, with seminaries, divinity schools, religion departments, and sociology departments claiming one or another aspect of religion and congregational life as their academic territory. Regardless of where the study of religion is situated, its scholars have not been concerned with matters of social service provision until recently. Such an area of inquiry is most often housed inside the gated community of social work, which historically has not been much concerned with religion. Even though that disinterest is changing somewhat, gaps exist in the knowledge of one or another form of service and organizational and community mechanisms for delivery.

The Reagan budget cuts of the 1980s; the promotion of voluntary service promoted by George H. W. Bush, captured in his famous "Thousand Points of Light" speech in the late 1980s; Bill Clinton's "changing welfare as we know it" in the 1990s; and George W. Bush's Faith-Based Initiative in 2001 were all policy initiatives that directly or indirectly pressed for more social services at the local level. Public policy is political science's gated community, and it traditionally has not opened its doors to policy and implementation themes that take place below the radar of local governmental services where social services are actually delivered.

Since the 1980s, a new reality has emerged in urban and rural communities across the United States. Religiously affiliated social services are an integral part of community life. To understand the development of the new reality at the community level from an academic perspective, one would need to know something about history, theology, sociology of religion, organizational development, social work, community development, political science, child development, aging, health, criminology, community psychology, and more. Yet, we do not have the interdisciplinary lenses to study the in-between spaces—where one gated academic discipline ends and another begins. As I have shown, studies consequently take on some aspect of social service delivery—and there are many aspects, so quite often the work misses the mark about the complexity of the intersection of that social service realm and the other domains with which it interacts.

In the pure sciences, when an occurrence requires a combined set of lenses, perhaps to understand the interaction of biological and chemical processes, a new field like biochemistry emerges. This transformation has not happened in social sciences. Disciplinary boundaries primarily constrain each branch of social science or the related professional fields, and thus research lacks the cross-fertilization that could strengthen lines of inquiry around faith-based social service. As I showed through the discussion of the four studies above, current scholarship tackles many concerns in such small increments that the interdisciplinary perspective is often omitted from the inquiry. We need a common language and an understanding of the complexities of faith-based social services from many perspectives, along with a commitment to interdisciplinary research.

Many newcomers to this discussion, including media representatives and academicians, view the social services emanating from congregations and sectarian organizations with lenses that primarily magnify the degree of their religiosity in relationship to providing service. Consequently, the analysis and discussion become bogged down in the age-old question of whether one can measure faith—something that by definition does not need measurement and detracts from the more important matters of developing the best services possible. Accordingly, much of the recent discussion regarding the effectiveness of organizations is wedged in the quicksand of politics and religion, which is not where such an important discussion should be heading. The much more important discussion is nowhere to be found, focusing on how congregations function as organizations in and of themselves; what roles they assume in community-based partnerships with sectarian, interdenominational, and secular agencies; and what factors make the organizations and partnerships effective.

Faith-Based or Faith-Related?

The Welfare Reform Liaison Project (WRLP) of Greensboro, North Carolina, is the nation's only *faith-based* Community Service Block Grant designee, or what is commonly referred to as a Community Action Agency. But what does it mean to be faith based?

Even though the agency started as a ministry of Mt. Zion Baptist Church in Greensboro, a visitor walking into the 56,000-square-foot agency would find no one praying, no religious icons, and no biblical passages used in any of its other programs. The agency receives no cash from its founding church, and there are no contracts binding it to Mt. Zion in any fashion. Some may conclude that it is not a faith-based agency at all and may point out that it is a rather large workforce development and training agency, whose executive director and CEO happens to be a Baptist minister. The only other hint that the WRLP is faith based is on its stationery, which quotes Matt. 25:35–36 in small print at the bottom: "For I was hungered and ye gave me meat: I was thirsty and ye gave me drink: I was a stranger, and ye took me in: Naked and ye clothed me: I was sick, and ye visited me, I was in prison and ye came unto me."

The term *faith-based* has come to mean the display of icons, using scripture in service-related programs, and some form of prayer and holistic services. However, Steven Rathgeb Smith and Michael R. Sosin propose a variation on the term that solves the conundrum about classifying the WRLP and many others that claim to be—or disavow being—faith based.[18] Smith and Sosin change the term to *faith-related*. This simple change broadens the universe and provides a clearer picture of what may or may not be obvious.

> Faith-related agencies may be defined as social service organizations that have any of the following: a formal funding or administrative arrangement with a religious authority or authorities; a historical tie of this kind; a specific commitment to act within the dictates of a particular established faith; or a commitment to work together that stems from a common religion.[19]

Mark Chaves takes the definition a step further by noting that these agencies have some link to religion at the institutional level, either directly or because some individuals act on the basis of their relation to a religious institution, not simply on the basis of their personal belief system.[20]

Therefore, while the casual observer may not recognize many overt signs of religion such as prayer, religious icons, or bible study, and might thus conclude that the Welfare Reform Liaison Project is not a faith-based agency, a thorough understanding of the WRLP makes it indisputably a *faith-related* agency:

- The executive director of the organization is a minister in the founding church, and while the church does not pay his salary now, it once did.
- Currently, he is able to claim a ministerial housing allotment on his federal income tax even though his organization is a separate 501(c)(3) nonprofit organization distinct from the church in finances and governance.
- Some members of the board of directors are members of the founding church, as are several employees of the agency.
- The bishop of the founding church is an ex officio member of the board.
- Many of the agency's community-wide activities take place in the facilities of the founding church.

Thus, it is clearly faith-*related*, while not necessarily appearing faith-*based* as the term has come to mean. Until we move away from "faith-based" as the common denominator and study organizations from a faith-related perspective, we will remain mired in a political debate that does not allow for the proper conceptualization of good studies.

Congregational Context

It is important not only to use a terminology that captures the realm of religious services but also to understand the organizations that provide faith-related services and the kinds of services they provide. Congregations, the main venues through which most faith-related social services are delivered, are extremely busy providing help for their membership and surrounding neighborhoods as well as faith-related social service organizations, both nonsectarian and public agencies in their communities.[21] The number and scope of services stemming from the nation's 350,000 congregations vary depending upon the researcher,[22] but more important than haggling over the number and types of service is grasping the idea that congregations are *limited but essential* organizations in a set of complex partnerships within a broader community of care.

To understand research about the nature and scope of their service provision, and consequently, whether they are or are not more effective than secular organizations, it is important to recognize several dimensions of services that emerge from congregations, not just what services they provide or how they provide them. These institutions need to be viewed like their secular partners—as nonprofit organizations with a special history, possibly relating to a "special mission" but serving in an intertwined set of complex partnerships as a broader system of care.

That system looks like a spider web. It is comprised of secular public, nonprofit, and for-profit organizations, ranging from the largest welfare agency that must serve anyone and everyone who falls under the mandate for which it receives public funds, to the smallest cancer support group that is completely voluntary but may be housed in a for-profit hospital. The system also comprises religious congregations and faith-related nonprofit organizations. Thus, to understand service provisions from congregations, it is important to understand them as both organizations and partners in a system of complex partnerships. So what do scholars tell us about social services and our nation's congregations?

First and foremost, congregations are based in places of worship. But while worship is first, members are often intricately involved in the provision of a range of social services. Only a fraction of the congregational activities are social service related.[23] What is confusing is that there is no clear distinction between service provisions coming from "faith-related" organizations and from congregations, because quite often Catholics, Lutherans, Baptists, Jews, Methodists, and Salvationists (members of the Salvation Army) have vast networks of social service organizations in communities throughout this country. They operate somewhat like the ministerial alliances springing up nationwide to pool resources in communities for addressing homelessness, hunger, transportation, work, and the like.

Such organizations are, in fact, 501(c)(3) nonprofit corporations that have professional staff and multiple funding streams. Yet, they also tap into congregations for volunteers, space, and money, sometimes making it difficult to distinguish between the congregation and the denomination's community-based organization.

There are also numerous community development corporations spawned by and intricately tied to the African American churches. The Eisenhower Foundation in Washington, D.C., has been instrumental in expanding the growth of a movement boasting close to two thousand such organizations, 14 percent of which emerged from congregations, according to Chaves.[24]

There is more. Congregations themselves may have programs through which members visit the sick or shut-ins, provide child care or after-school care, house an Alcoholics Anonymous program, or serve as a meal site for senior citizens. They may host a blood drive, shelter the homeless through national networks like the Hospitality Network, or have a team of volunteers who work at soup kitchens. Volunteers may build a house through Habitat for Humanity, help flood victims, or provide space for a nonprofit organization. They may help resettle refugees or provide grants to community-based organizations. Interestingly, the research indicates that they have three such programs, on average. Also, they are spawning ponds for new community organizations, which address problems ranging from teen pregnancy to hospice care. My own research shows that 18 percent of Greensboro's agencies were born out of congregational efforts.[25]

The religious community's spirit is not housed in a vacuum. On the one hand, this intricate system of services is staffed heavily by volunteers and fueled by an unyielding faith. On the other, that volunteer spirit works in tandem with, and is often inseparable from, the professional service efforts of other faith-related, private nonprofit, and even government agencies. A Red Cross blood drive at a local congregation characterizes how a private nonprofit organization uses a congregation's resources to accomplish a public health mission. The organizations in the broader system of care in any community in the United States, as noted in chapter 2, are dominated by public agencies in the fields of social services, public health, and mental health.

Increasing social problems and decreasing public funds have compelled community leaders to rely upon people from the faith community for volunteers and funding. The faith community has responded reliably with the best of intentions. Those individuals who deliver or oversee mandated services, such as our parole officers, foster-care social workers, or comptrollers, demonstrate how congregations and organizations can be important partners; however, they are limited by law as to what services they can provide and how they can spend public money.

If we are going to work effectively and begin to conduct research that positions us into twenty-first-century understanding, we must create a common language that strips the politics from faith, and we must form well financed, interdisciplinary research teams. These teams must understand what they are studying and what their purpose is. There can be no better intention than conducting research to find the best ways to solve, manage, or prevent human suffering. Until we change our ways, the social scientific enterprise concerned with religion and service will remain on the bottom rung of the ladder of knowledge, which is a waste of marvelous talent.

CHAPTER 4

The Director

John Dilulio, a brilliant professor, a Democrat, and the first director of the White House Office of Faith-Based and Community Initiatives (FBCI), probably left his job—or was nudged out by White House insiders—because he was smart, inquisitive, and a challenger of weak ideas. Plus, he more than likely miscalculated how important the Religious Right was to the Republican political agenda. It is unimaginable that the well-versed, self-described "Louis B. Mayer of the Faith-Based Initiative"[1] could sit tongue-tied and watch lightweight intellects inside the White House undermine his dream of bringing the power of neighborhood churches into the fight against poverty and urban crime. What ultimately weighed against Dilulio had little to do with his brains or a serious push for more faith-based social services. He made two tactical errors in miscalculating Republican power, control, and greed—perturbing academics who could have been allies and leading the evangelical intelligentsia into the promised land of research.

More than a year after Dilulio left the White House, he exposed the Bush Faith-Based Initiative for the political swindle it really is. In an October 24, 2002, letter to Ron Suskind of *Esquire* magazine, who later published some excerpts from it, Dilulio slammed both senior and junior White House staff three times in the letter, calling them "Mayberry Machiavellians." He claimed they "consistently talked and acted as if the height of political sophistication consisted in reducing every issue to its simplest, black-and-white terms for public consumption, then steering legislative initiatives or policy proposals as far right as possible."[2]

Soon after Suskind's article, Dilulio recanted, but did so as if his lips were stitched shut. *Esquire* stood by its story. Dilulio may have been the first ex–Bush White House official to be silenced. Karl Rove and his subordinates inside the White House did not take kindly to being painted in an unflattering light. The research grant Dilulio received,[3] perhaps as his golden parachute, may have been vulnerable. Dilulio wouldn't tell me what happened.

Toward the end of an hour-plus interview I had with Dilulio, I asked him about the "Mayberry Machiavellians" quote. From what started as an otherwise energetic, somewhat self-aggrandizing, and at times academic session, he suddenly switched gears and became concise and contrite. He told me that someone like himself, who was on the inside, knows that government servants have criticisms gushing at them at them twenty-four hours a day. As such, he said he should have been the last person to criticize, let alone to do so in "a smart-ass way." He went on to note that he should have been respectful or kept his big mouth shut. "I didn't keep mine shut and said things that were either wrong or exaggerated."[4] His tone seemed sickly, and his words seemed disingenuous in what was an otherwise upbeat and forthright interview. Had he been threatened?

Dilulio was a brilliant spokesperson for his cause. He was indeed like Louis B. Mayer, the famous Hollywood studio mogul, in that he was also clever, energetic, talented, and strongly committed to his ideals. The professor could have created a forceful movement at the local level, spearheaded by clergy in the nation's 350,000 congregations. Certainly there are enough dreadful concerns across the country that need immediate action. With some imagination and new money, it was very possible that Dilulio would have crafted numerous church and state partnerships in communities throughout the nation, galvanizing both local clergy and civil servants into constructive assaults on a range of social problems. Today they might be playing their proper role in a continuum of evolving partnerships—had there only been a plan.

Every community in this country has a tremendous stake in ensuring that its children are well taken care of. It *does* take a community to raise a child—just take a look at a community's public school or child protective services budget. Failing to work together to raise them will eventually allow the wayward ones to raise hell. Out of the nearly three million reports of abuse or neglect each year, an estimated 872,000 children were determined to be victims of child abuse or neglect in 2004.[5] Such battered and neglected children resume life with irreparable physical and psychological wounds.

Nearly a million black children live in extreme poverty, which takes into account food and housing benefits their parents receive. The number of extremely poor black children is now at its highest level in twenty-three years.[6] Of the more than 500,000 children in foster care in 2003, 35 percent were non-Hispanic black children.[7] Of 100,000 kids awaiting adoption in 2003, 53,000 were black.[8] Some were beaten, others neglected, and each was then abandoned in a psychological purgatory. In any of the nation's prisons where the two million murderers, rapists, drug dealers, and thieves reside, a disproportionate number of blacks and minorities fill the cells.[9] Three common threads exist among nearly all of them: They come from impoverished households, they were abused or neglected as children, and they cannot read.[10]

The situation described above bothers tax-conscious citizens because quite often they do not think their tax dollars are working effectively. The money is spent on increasingly costly jail construction when it should be spent on schools and other services. These citizens throw up their hands and ask, "When is enough *enough*?" Over the years, increased problems and decreased spending have forced local public health, mental health, and social service systems to do more with less. It does not take too much imagination to guess what life will look like for a "crack baby" who spends three months in an incubator in detox before being carried off to a state-run foster care agency or, as is increasingly becoming the case, handed over to one of the two million grandmothers who is tending to her children's children. The situation continues to grow more complicated.

Dilulio, a political scientist and criminologist, expanded his original idea to use churches to fight urban crime. He saw a relatively inexpensive way to bring in new resources to assist with numerous problems. He wanted to bring small black churches into the service fold. Dilulio knew that the right effort could at least hold such monstrous social problems at bay, but to achieve his goal would require real imagination and a true understanding of how to translate ideas into action. The churches needed professional guidance in learning how to support the overworked and exasperated professionals in foster care, schools, and prison systems. Local religious groups needed to unite, and the whole enterprise had to start with buy-in from all segments of local systems, especially the local pulpit.

To his credit, Dilulio had already brought liberal and conservative policy-making elite together at the national level to support this issue. Given enough time, he may have earned the backing from those in the trenches across the country and started a faith-based initiative that would actually have made a difference. If there ever were a person who could have guided this daunting remake of local service systems, it was Dilulio, flaws and all. However, his rhetoric was stolen for political and religious purposes.

The politics surrounding the Bush Faith-Based Initiative took precedence over a marvelous opportunity to create change. Dilulio came from the academy with unassailable credentials—a Harvard Ph.D. and full professorships, first at Princeton and then the University of Pennsylvania. He is hard to dislike because he is down-to-earth, has a Philadelphia working-class genuineness, and is unpretentious most of the time. It is next to impossible to earn respectability in the academy and in both liberal and conservative policy circles. Dilulio was respected, though maybe too much so and by the wrong crowd.

When at Princeton, Dilulio wrote *Body Count* with prominent conservative Bill Bennett.[11] This influential book detailed the scourge that drug-related killings cast on people of the country's inner cities. Even though the academic and political Left criticized the book for repackaging the traditional conservative solutions to crime by emphasizing personal responsibility and the need for two-parent families, it also introduced the new idea that neighborhood-based churches could be enlisted in a wide-scale assault on crime.

Dilulio's boundless and convincing efforts promoted the idea that this violence could be turned around by tapping the energy of inner-city black churches, drawing the interest of both Democratic and Republican policy makers who were lost for solutions to end the killings. Dilulio was so influential that he advised both the Bush and Gore 2000 presidential campaigns. Dilulio's desire to address real social concerns with a new source of energy drove this prolific writer and extremely talented social entrepreneur to work tirelessly to put a faith-based initiative on the public radar screen.

Early on, some problems developed that essentially undermined Dilulio's idea for a genuine and workable faith-based initiative. The superb scholar switched hats and became the full-time social entrepreneur. In looking outside academia to find a sales force dedicated to promoting church-based social services, his ideas took on a life of their own.

During the mid- to late 1990s, there was simply no large-scale social science research demonstrating that churches would heed the call to service or that they could be successful in a national social service initiative. Had there been the least bit of broad-based evidence for either, he would have found academic backing. But the ivory tower is stuffy. It is simply not a place where new and untested ideas are bandied about like cheerleaders waving pompoms. Academics are cynical and hardly ever play the cheerleading role. Even if an idea is intellectually worthy, academics don't champion a cause without evidence.

To promote his ideas into the mainstream, Dilulio made sure he had the backing of elite policy makers. At the same time, he lost sight of what needed to be said repeatedly about the ultimate need for local buy-in. In his heart, he also knew success hinged on academic respectability. In late 1996 and into 1997, he recognized what he thought was the break he was looking for—a way to bring together the academy and the policy elite to champion a broad-based faith-based initiative. He befriended University of Pennsylvania social scientist Professor Ram Cnaan.

Cnaan was commissioned to conduct a study on the social service activities taking place in historical religious buildings nationwide by Partners for Sacred Places of Philadelphia, an organization dedicated to preserving historic religious buildings. A fledgling national organization at the time, Partners heard from its major benefactor, the Lilly Endowment, that it ought to consider reframing its storyline about the importance of preserving historical religious buildings for their architectural significance to include the social service activities that were taking place in those buildings.

Dr. James Wind, a program officer in the Religion Division of the Lilly Endowment, who oversaw millions of dollars of research money that went into the study of and programs in American religion, worked with Partners. He knew that the philanthropic world would not continually fund an organization whose sole emphasis was the preservation of historical religious structures for beauty's sake alone, so to win the other money that would sustain Partners over the long haul, Wind suggested that Partners broaden its focus. He had a bit of data to serve as the basis for making this request.

Wind was instrumental in the Endowment's funding of my work in 1992, a local study that found an unexpected and extraordinary amount of social service activity coming from the religious congregations of Greensboro, North Carolina. A power broker and risk taker, Wind surmised that if church-based social service was thriving in Greensboro, it would be worth the $70,000 he allocated to Partners to see if the same level of service provision might be happening inside historic church buildings nationally. If so, then the Lilly Endowment and other philanthropies would have a stronger case for funding Partners.

Therefore, in 1993 Wind brokered a relationship between Bob Jaeger and Diane Cone, the codirectors of Partners for Sacred Places, and me, which led to Cnaan's groundbreaking study. Cone and Jaeger first asked if I would conduct the study for them. I declined, but referred them to Cnaan because I knew that he was one of the best research methodologists nationally and was also based in Philadelphia, which would make the logistics smoother. Ram Cnaan and I had been office mates as doctoral students and have maintained a long friendship. On all accounts, I believed he could do a better job of conducting a national study than I could.

The real kickoff for the protracted and serious national discussion about the values of faith-based social services was launched at the National Press Club on October 30, 1997. Partners for Sacred Places of Philadelphia introduced the findings of Cnaan's six-city study examining the social service activities taking place in historic religious buildings. Cnaan found vast social service activity in just about every one of the 111 historic religious buildings he examined. What had begun as Wind's gamble became national headlines.

A thrilled Dilulio, with Cnaan's data in hand, was behind the scenes directing the event. Dilulio's friend, conservative Republican William Bennett, who had been Ronald Reagan's secretary of education and the first President Bush's "drug czar," and moderate Democratic senator and eventual vice presidential candidate Joe Lieberman of Connecticut were the main panelists. After the discussion, Cnaan took questions from the press. Dilulio found enough legitimacy in Cnaan's research findings to direct Bennett and Lieberman to spearhead the national discussion. On that day, Professor John Dilulio essentially became the first director of the White House Office of Faith-Based and Community Initiatives, although he would not actually land in the White House until three years later. Unfortunately, he would not stay on his feet for long after he got there.

Dilulio made two miscalculations in putting the discussion of church-based social services on the national agenda. First, he rankled academicians instead of winning their full support. Second, he became too cozy with the right-wing evangelicals who eventually narrowed the meaning of *faith-based* social services to mean specifically *Christ-centered* social services; in their world, no service effort can be effective unless the recipient has been saved. Both actions turned Dilulio, the social entrepreneur and most articulate spokesperson for harnessing the energy of little churches to wage war on poverty through government partnerships, into a defensive lineman fighting an onrush of attacks from all sides. By the time Dilulio made it to the White House, he was losing important allies, control of his message, and his chance for making local buy-in the lynchpin of this policy initiative.

That skid started on March 12, 1999, when, in a *Wall Street Journal* article, Dilulio claimed that "scientific studies testify to the efficacy of faith-based efforts."[12] Cnaan's research had in fact said *no such thing*, and the academy knew it. The findings merely emphasized that there were more-than-expected service activities taking place in historic religious buildings; not a word was uttered about their *effectiveness*. While Dilulio earned the support of policy and corporate elites whom he was targeting, he alienated some of the more notable academicians in the field of religion.

Once an idea enters the minds of the policy elite, according to Dilulio, "it stays there for good or for ill."[13] What Dilulio meant to say by using "efficacy" was merely to tell an audience unfamiliar with research lingo that emerging research showed there was much more social service activity coming from the nation's churches than one might expect or even imagine. But the tactic backfired. To academicians, Dilulio overstated his case; they are as serious about their science as evangelicals are about Jesus. He was not lying, yet in the eyes of academicians, he had "spun a yarn," which was on the fringe of lying, the academy's biggest sin.

Dilulio's unassigned surrogates in the evangelical intelligentsia were not telling the truth, either. As noted in the previous chapters, not a single study in 1999—or to date, for that matter—proved anything about faith-based social services being more effective than any other kind of program, yet the right-wing pundits claimed this farce to be fact. By the time Dilulio arrived at the White House in January 2001, policy elites had indeed bought in, but so did a herd of right-wing scholars, who, by and large, made their homes in conservative think tanks, where ironically Dilulio became both a guru and a pawn in a much bigger game than he imagined.

The evangelical thinkers turned his *Wall Street Journal* claim into a doctrine, using it to substantiate their notion that research had once and for all proved that Christ-centered social services were more effective than all other services. In their universe, where quite often up is down and down is up, faith and fact became indisputably one and the same. Dilulio and the *Wall Street Journal* provided the proof, broad-based legitimacy, and an opening for them to speak publicly about what they had "known" privately all along—that being saved should be the basis for all service provision.

In September 1999, Dr. Amy Sherman of the Hudson Institute, second only to Dilulio in her influence in both the evangelical social service world and mainline conservative policy and philanthropic circles and a frequent expert witness at congressional hearings on faith-based matters, published an article entitled "Seven Habits of Highly Effective Charities."[14] Her third "habit" for effective faith-based organizations emphasizes transformation, not rehabilitation. *Transformation*, in the world of evangelicals, is code for being saved.

Sherman pointed out that religious organizations are not interested in "returning people to the state they were in before they fell into the pit of drug abuse or welfare dependency or gang membership." In Sherman's eyes, those people had fallen from grace; they were sinners. To her, reha- bilitation is inadequate because it is not Christ-centered. It merely pulls the person out of the pit, only to set him up for another fall. According to Sherman, religious transformation means that "we've got to make you a new person so that when you're back in the old environment, when you're standing in front of the pit, you won't fall in again."[15] That new person has been transformed or born again.

Using the same strategy they had after Dilulio's *Wall Street Journal* arti- cle, the confident evangelical elite found other "research" to prove that, indeed, the supernatural interventions of Christ-centered programs work. It was Aaron Bicknese who conducted the research this time. He wrote his 1999 doctoral dissertation comparing a single Teen Challenge intervention program to a government-funded program. A careful reading of that dis- sertation shows that Bicknese's study proved absolutely nothing about the effectiveness of Teen Challenge, and Bicknese said so. In fact, in his chap- ter 4, Bicknese walked the reader through a laundry list of factors that prevented him, or anyone else, from claiming that Teen Challenge is an effective treatment when compared to short-term, government-funded programs. Nevertheless, Sherman and others in evangelical think tanks were making bogus claims about Teen Challenge's effectiveness.

In social science research, after scholars use clearly defined research pro- tocols for their study but simply don't find what they were looking for and don't have much to talk about, they then sometimes suspend the rules of scientific inquiry and enter an imaginary "what-if" world. From the moment the researchers enter this world, they cannot make any reliable claim whatsoever! A fishing line of inquiry is now cast into the pool of data in ways that strict research protocols would never allow. The research is no longer about scientific fact finding, but about guessing, speculating, and surmising.

Bicknese did what many researchers do when they don't find anything statistically significant—he went fishing. When budding researchers con- ducting their doctoral research go on the kind of fishing trip Bicknese did, they are performing an academic ritual designed to help them gain more experience in data analysis and theory development. Turning the imaginary findings of an academic exercise into the springboard for broad-based social policy change is an academic sin of the first order. But Bicknese wasn't the culprit.

He found some imaginary things on his fishing trip that were statisti- cally significant. Yet, because the rules of scientific inquiry were suspended and he said so, his findings were, at best, extremely speculative and neither valid nor important—except to people like Sherman who needed some- thing, anything, to link their faith to research fact. The evangelical intelli- gentsia seized on Bicknese's imaginary findings and made them bigger than life. To Professor Dilulio's dismay, the national discussion became even more polarized, devolving into a bizarre debate between academics and right-wing evangelicals. The larger worry about fixing some of the nation's social ills got reduced to debates about whether research really demonstrated that Christ-centered programs are effective. Dilulio was in quicksand even before he landed in the White House.

Meanwhile, President George W. Bush came into office on the promise that he would be a "uniter not a divider." Because members of the mighty evangelical Christian Right comprise close to 25 percent of the Republican voting bloc, he systematically pandered to them on religious and social issues. He placed the politics of religion prominently ahead of developing a coherent urban policy. Since the 1980s, Republican strategists have increasingly found ways to nationalize strict codes of behavior. They have provided a forum that bonded these once insular and apolitical groups into crusaders on a mission to save the whole country.

Now, a driving force motivating these once disparate Christian groups has become saving the national soul for the next life. A stimulus for Republican strategists is therefore to institutionalize efforts that help these evangelicals achieve their aims. They both are in trouble without each other. The FBCI became a central command post to communicate with these crusaders, and Dilulio became a sideshow in a political carnival.

The politicos took this route despite being sued regularly. The Roundtable on Religion and Social Welfare Policy, a nonpartisan research center, monitors lawsuits brought against Bush's Faith-Based Initiative and lists at least a dozen federal cases.[16] It is hard to get an exact number because of the number of appeals, according to Robert Tuttle of George Washington University Law School, who has been following these cases.[17] The cases range from challenges over the use of federal money to allow AmeriCorps employees to teach catechism as part of tutoring in a Texas Catholic school, to requiring a long-term Jewish employee of the Salvation Army in New York City to sign an oath of religious allegiance even though the program in which she works is federally funded.

These lawsuits hardly make national news with the same fanfare that teaching creationism versus evolution does. Nevertheless, these suits perplex and polarize local social service providers throughout the country. They also stymie comprehensive community service development. The lawsuits divide, not unite. They started almost immediately after the onset of the Faith-Based Initiative. At a December 2004 presentation in Washington, D.C., Dilulio's replacement, Jim Towey, went so far as to label the plaintiffs in what he considered ridiculous lawsuits "secular extremists" (although when members of the American Jewish Congress's legal team brought suit against AmeriCorps, Towey had enough political savvy not to claim outright that Jews are secular extremists).

It is not difficult to imagine the frustration an eminent social scientist of Dilulio's caliber must have experienced, knowing that his vision was vanishing. Instead of moving the country to talk about how to gain local support to help small neighborhood churches play stronger roles in supporting police, school, health officials, and other civil servants as they battle poverty, the Bush administration's efforts dissolved into a chorus of side issues that the soul savers cherish: Christ-centered drug and abstinence programs, marriage initiatives, and support for discrimination in religious hiring. Bush divided and Dilulio's ideas were conquered.

There is still no research that demonstrates the effectiveness of Christ-centered programs. However, the claims of their effectiveness lace the pages of right-wing periodicals and trumpet from the lips of pundits at right-wing think tanks. This political sleight of hand was not just about inaccurate research claims. It is also about patronage. Just look who got the money: Pat Robertson's Operation Blessing; John Castellani's Teen Challenge, the Christ-centered drug rehab program; and Franklin Graham's (Billy's son) Samaritan's Purse are among the most notable recipients of government money in the right-wing Christian evangelical movement.[18] And there is no way these leaders would accept government money and promise *not* to evangelize, unless they did so while crossing their fingers.

To date, the most flagrant trampling of our constitutional principles was not the false claim suggesting that the Christ-centered Teen Challenge was more effective than government-funded drug rehab programs, though. It was the shifting of $100 million of discretionary grant funds to Christ-centered programs through Access to Recovery, an experimental program that provides vouchers for drug addicts, who can then use them to buy services from either pervasively sectarian or secular programs. The voucher allows an addict to manage his own recovery by making a rational business decision. He uses "his money," given in the form of a government voucher, to purchase religious help. This is a creative end run around the Establishment Clause. Transferring taxpayer dollars to a strung-out addict so he can make a rational business decision in the name of "choice" might seem like a crazy waste of money to the average citizen—because it is.

For Dilulio, a national policy initiative with the magnitude of the Faith-Based Initiative was about more than just money. He had a system in mind that had to have local buy-in. This acceptance is the most conservative and yet most democratic of forces because it is controlled by the people themselves, not a distant government. Its momentum must evolve from pulpits of the 350,000 religious congregations in this country.

Such an initiative would also have to weave its way through 19,000 mayors' and city managers' offices, generating along the way a groundswell of support from the thousands of directors of local public health, mental health, and social services agencies and their colleagues in police departments and probation offices that mark the nation's local human service landscape. After Dilulio got the issue on the national radar, he wanted to move it to the grass roots.

The administration higher-ups had no plans for a grassroots effort, however. The FBCI launched a new phase of the culture war. Noticeably absent from the carefully scripted launching of the Faith-Based Initiative on January 29, 2001, were representatives from Catholic Charities USA, Lutheran Social Services, and Jewish Family Services, three of the four largest recipients of government grants and contracts at the time, accounting for more than three billion dollars annually; the fourth, the Salvation Army, was present.

Leaving the mainline Catholic, Lutheran, and Jewish social service representatives out of the celebration was an act of war that doomed any chance at successful local buy-in. Those groups not only provide social

services in thousands of communities around the country but also connect
to tens of thousands of congregations where buy-in begins. Robertson's,
Castellani's, and Graham's organizations are not connected to the congregations that support local social services.

Bush's people chose a top-down effort to control the national discussion and funnel money through such surrogates as Robertson, Graham,
Castellani, and others who enjoy great media exposure and have great
influence over what their followers think. Robertson's television show, the
700 Club, for example, has nearly a million weekly viewers.[19] These are
national political arms of the Bush administration and huge fundraising
operations, not local social service providers.

"Rallying the Armies of Compassion," the document establishing the
FBCI, was filled with the divisive language that eventually characterized
this deception. In one breath, it called for government partnerships with
new neighborhood churches and community "healers," while in another,
it claimed that these little churches were in fact "out-manned and out-
flanked" by government. Who would want to forge partnerships with an
adversarial government, unless cultural crusaders who infiltrated government waved a coded flag that sent a clear message to the faithful that *this*
White House is now out of enemy hands?

By February 19, 2001, sensing that his meteoric rise was over and he
was headed back to the academy sooner than later, Dilulio embedded a
mea culpa of sorts in a long *Wall Street Journal* essay: "There are, as yet,
no suitably scientific studies that 'prove' the efficacy or cost-effectiveness of
faith-based approaches to social ills, or that support the success claims of
certain well-known national faith-based programs."[20]

Sadly, the "Louis B. Mayer of the Faith-Based Initiative" never
achieved complete buy-in from his academic colleagues, the one group
that could have contributed the clout necessary to support his efforts.
Instead, he gained buy-in from a group of evangelical thinkers and politicos who turned what could have been a successful policy into faith-based
follies. In less than seven months, Dilulio left—looking more like Barney
Fife than Louis B. Mayer. And tragically, nothing more is being done to
address the scourge of poverty than when Bush came into office.

CHAPTER 5

Shaping the Discourse: The Marathoners

To appreciate how George W. Bush's Faith-Based Initiative took hold as part of public discourse, it is important to understand the ideas and the underlying message of key people who shaped its direction. I have a unique vantage point on this because I have been studying faith-based social services since the early 1980s with an eye on my specialty—trying to comprehend the connection between social policy and the design and implementation of social services. There really was no body of research knowledge about faith-based social services in the early 1980s, nor had there been any policy initiatives from Washington that enlisted the faith community like we see today. However, Ronald Reagan dropped some early hints that policy was heading toward more involvement of the black church and the mainline religious community. When the Reagan budget cuts hit Greensboro in the early 1980s, I found myself in many community meetings at local churches, digging in, trying to help those individuals most affected.[1]

As part of my master's degree, I was trained in community organization, and at the doctoral level, I studied social welfare policy. As a young scholar watching this huge policy change hit my community, I began to question whether what was happening in Greensboro—the way churches were responding to the Reagan budget cuts—was also occurring elsewhere. I was puzzled on another question as well: Why had we never previously recognized churches as community-based organizations? Hardly any scholarship from that time could answer either concern, but this changed somewhat with the publication of the *Newer Deal* (1999).[2]

Prof. Roy Lubove, my policy mentor, always said that news stories are primary documents, first drafts of what will later appear in the scholarly literature and will eventually be polished and prepared for scholarly consumption. Not having the luxury of Google in the early 1980s, I was relegated to long stretches at the library where I conducted microfiche searches for news articles. I discovered that changes on the ground were developing rapidly, and churches elsewhere were springing into action; therefore, broader implications were expanding the policy realm outside of mere news stories.

Two important articles appeared in the *Washington Post* within less than three weeks of each other in March and April 1982. From the onset, what seemed just below the surface of the articles was an emerging policy agenda designed to reshape the welfare state by cutting programs, altering discourse from the language of "entitlement" that had characterized the New Deal, and sharpening up a moral language of "personal responsibility," thus implying the notion that social ills were the results of a fall from grace. Such rhetoric made it easier to encourage churches of all denominations into service. An added benefit to shaping the discussion about poverty into religious terms was the opportunity to set in motion a strategy to invite more blacks under the Republican umbrella through a courtship of black ministers. Conspiratorial? Maybe. A plan? More likely. These two *Washington Post* news stories may have also initiated what we now know as the Faith-Based Initiative.

On March 26, 1982, the headline of the first article read: "Reagan Is Host to Black Ministers; Reagan Defends His Policies to Black Ministers."[3] The article stated that President Reagan had played host to seventy-five friendly black ministers from across the country, including a dozen recent "converts" to the Republican party from nearby Prince George's County, Maryland. To this group, Reagan defended charges that his administration did not care about minorities and the poor. He also used the occasion to welcome the newcomers to the GOP. White House press spokesman Larry Speakes said, in what has become fashionable political doublespeak, that no connection existed between the invitations to the Prince George's ministers and any expectations of the party increasing its showing among blacks for the fall 1982 elections. "I don't link it to a strategy for the elections," Speakes said. "Certainly we welcome Republicans from wherever they come—and we'll welcome their votes in the fall."[4]

The second article was titled "Reagan Urges More Church Aid for Needy." It described President Reagan speaking to a group of more than one hundred religious leaders, the majority of them white. In this venue, Reagan further crafted the discussion now so central to current social policy: "Churches and voluntary groups should accept more responsibility for the needy rather than leaving it to the bureaucracy."[5] In addition, he told his version of the story of the Good Samaritan. His vignette provided a caricature of what would soon become the not-so-veiled subtext that positions itself directly below the surface of the language that shaped the discourse of faith-based policy—that voluntarism and religious self-help are Godly, and government social services are demonlike.

> The story of the Good Samaritan has always illustrated to me what God's challenge really is.... He didn't go running into town and look for a case-worker to tell him that there was a fellow out there that needed help. He took it upon himself.[6]

By the mid-1990s, when the Republicans had gained control of both houses of Congress and thus acquired more influence in the policy-making sphere, former senator Dan Coats (R-Ind.), a very instrumental figure in the early development of the Faith-Based Initiative, influenced the discussion with a story that certainly grabbed public attention. He, like Reagan, enjoyed telling a story, but his was of the Gospel Mission, a drug-treatment center for homeless men not far from the Capitol. Under the leadership of John Woods, the mission successfully rehabilitated two-thirds of those individuals who sought treatment there. Just three blocks away was a government-operated shelter with similar goals, but even though it spent twenty times money more per person, that shelter boasted only a 10 percent success rate. Senator Coats explained the disparity as follows: "The Gospel Mission succeeds because it provides more than a meal, more than a drug treatment. It is in the business of spreading the grace of God."[7] Such language has become so commonplace that it substitutes for the sheer lack of any reliable data to support claims for the success of faith-based social services.

More than likely, the Gospel Mission chose which clients it would accept, or the clients self-selected, therefore increasing the chance for success in the Gospel Mission's programs. The government shelter, on the contrary, was probably more diverse. Comparing the success of a program that in some way selects its clients to one that assists any client in need is not necessarily a valid basis for policy development. Nevertheless, like President Reagan with his story of the Good Samaritan, Senator Coats makes the comparison between the small, religiously based service provider and the large government-financed program, leaving behind the scent of good versus evil. Instead of developing a broad-based discussion on how to solve our complex problems, the discourse became just another means of attributing to faith-based programs the status of a real solution for these problems, implying that government programs were wasteful and ineffective.

Don Eberly was both a part of the Reagan White House and one of the participants at the important Wingspread Conference, which shaped the Faith-Based Initiative. Eberly also served as deputy director of the White House Office of Faith-Based and Community Initiatives under its first director, John Dilulio. Founder of the National Fatherhood Initiative, Eberly was the director of the Civil Society Project and the former deputy assistant to the president for faith-based and community initiatives as well. In his 2002 book *The Soul of Civil Society*, coauthored with Ryan Streeter, Eberly and Streeter note:

> The drive against the central welfare state in recent years has been driven by much more than concern over rising costs. It has been fueled by a desire to push back against the bureaucratization of America. The encroachment of trained and pedigreed "social service professionals" into nearly every corner of our society suffocates citizenship and discourages local nonprofessional caregivers from getting involved in healing and renewing the lives of the poor.[8]

I did not realize it then, but I am certain of it now: Reagan's speeches, as well as the budget cuts of the 1980s that sent local human service systems into a tizzy, were the conservative movement's early steps in executing a twenty-plus-year business plan to realign the discussion of the problems of the poor as ones basically caused by the lack of personal responsibility and to focus a large part of the blame on the liberal establishment for expanding an impersonal, uncaring welfare state that accomplished nothing but created more indolence. In the minds of those shaping the discussion, the afflicted and those individuals who serve them are the cause and perpetuation of immoral behavior.

One can sense how much Eberly, who has been advising Republican administrations since Reagan's, dislikes social workers. I would guess he probably has met few social workers or recipients of welfare. What concerns me is not only the mean-spiritedness and self-righteous attitude expressed in the early budget cuts but also the superficiality regarding a true understanding of how social services really work. The Right created a thoughtfully constructed "devil" and simply kills it again and again with its channel of communication. In this black-and-white linguistic world, one exorcises society's individual demons by leading the fallen to church. A broader policy aimed at reducing the welfare state starves the welfare devil and shifts money to churches. The real truth is not just pushed further from the public's ear; disputing such rhetoric traps one into defending evil at the expense of unraveling a complex truth.

First of all, Eberly's metaphor—encroachment of "trained and pedigreed social service professionals into nearly every corner of our society"—to me, is debasing. He seems to suggest that social workers are "dog show like" and "roach like" in the same breath. What I infer is that these elite professionals have crawled into every corner of society like roaches and have choked the genuine healers of society—volunteers and the religious community. Eberly recites this rhetoric repeatedly with different degrees of rancor, as do the works of other key figures in the faith-based movement.

While Eberly's use of language may seem clever or artful, the truth is that hardworking, caring human beings staff the mandated foster care units in public and private agencies. State and federal laws require that social workers who perform mandated service follow procedure: conducting home studies for public and private adoption agencies; coordinating services for families of hospice patients; testifying in child abuse and neglect cases; trying to place people in nursing homes or coordinate home health services after patients are released from hospitals; counseling rape victims and drug addicts; and sitting on the other end of crisis hotlines, unceremoniously convincing youngsters not to commit suicide. In addition to following the law, they also manage drop-in centers and group homes for the mentally ill; operate support groups for children of divorcees; and organize and supervise support groups for the caregivers who work with people with AIDS or cancer, as well as victims of incest.

Unfortunately, the only truth to the "roach-like" metaphor is that social service professionals, like insects, crawl in the deepest corners of social compost. They try to do their best with oversized caseloads in large, underfunded, and scorned bureaucracies and yet serve as the target of every ideological tax cutter who buys the uncomplicated theories, neither understanding the system's nuances nor its laws. Employees in this system do not earn much money, yet they have become scapegoats of right-wing analysts like Eberly. They visit some of society's darkest corners and conduct some of the most soul-wrenching work on the planet—where the rubber hits the road. That road is in the complex system of local services that has been the target of the religious Right and conservative politicos.

I know from both my formal research and from my experience as an educator and advisor that social workers use the resources of their own churches and any others they can muster when public aid is exhausted.[9] I also recognize from my research that welfare recipients often have one or more of the following complications in their lives:

• learning disabilities never addressed when they attended school
• victimization of sexual and physical abuse
• responsibility as caregivers for their sick parents
• lack of decent transportation and suitable housing

Despite these barriers, many of the recipients I have met want to work, attain jobs after decent training, and work hard when given the opportunity. However, the spokespeople for the faith-based movement do not want the public to consider or acknowledge such information.

What follows is a journey through the language of three influential people whom I refer to as the "marathoners" of the faith-based movement: Amy Sherman, Marvin Olasky, and Joe Loconte. They have been tireless and instrumental not only in shaping President Bush's Faith-Based Initiative but also in creating a jargon that shrouds a comprehensive discussion on how to fit faith-based social services into the complex system of local care. This language of faith-masking is their proven intervention.

While each marathoner has spoken, written, or testified before Congress about a number of issues related to faith-based social services, the message remains the same—a position that advocates for Christ-centered social services to play an increasingly important role in social policy. Each marathoner subtly or not so subtly has promoted the same faith-based program much in the spirit of Ronald Reagan, Dan Coats, and Don Eberly. This program is Teen Challenge, which boasts 130 organizations nationwide and applies Christ-centeredness and holistic services as its main intervention approaches.

AMY SHERMAN

Before President Bush's Faith-Based Initiative received national exposure, Amy Sherman wrote an article for *Philanthropy* magazine called "Implementing 'Charitable Choice': Transcending the Separation between

Church and State."[10] In this piece, she advocated Charitable Choice, the provision in the 1996 welfare reform legislation that allows government to fund churches—specifically the kind of churches Sherman believes do the best kind of work: the ones that convert people to Christ.

In making her case promoting the benefits of Christ-centered services, Dr. Sherman, like Senator Coats before her, tells a story to make her major point, beginning the article with a tale involving a Texas regulatory agency and the faith-based drug rehabilitation agency Teen Challenge. She recounts the story of how the Rev. James Heurich "recalls being hounded by the demons of drug and alcohol addiction before 'getting clean' 28 years ago."[11] In a contrast between good and evil less spirited than but similar to that devised by Eberly, Sherman continues, saying that in late 1995, a different kind of demon, which she calls an "antagonist," was harassing Reverend Heurich, who was running the San Antonio chapter of Teen Challenge. This so-called antagonist was the Texas Commission on Alcohol and Drug Abuse, which was attempting to shut down the facility for operating without credentialed chemical-dependency counselors. Teen Challenge does not employ credentialed counselors. According to Sherman:

> It runs its rehab programs with "homegrown" leaders, former addicts who've transformed their lives through conversion to Christianity. Teen Challenge's success rates—which hover between 70 and 86 percent compared to the single-digit rates seen by more expensive, secular programs—apparently made no difference to John D. Cooke, the Commission's assistant deputy director. "Outcomes and outputs are not an issue for us," he told reporters. "If they want to call it treatment, then state law says they must be licensed."[12]

The legerdemain is not in the portrayal of Christians as the unjust victims of nitpicking government regulations, though that is certainly a subtext, nor is it the use of the same rhetorical device Coats employed in his analogy of the Gospel Mission. What Sherman and others who follow such thinking do, in more or less confusing ways, is to misrepresent the real research about the effectiveness of Teen Challenge (described in chapter 3) in order to cheerlead for their more broad-based position.

John Dilulio, who was also instrumental in shaping the discourse about the initiative (see chapter 4), was correct in saying that the successes and failures of Teen Challenge are largely unexamined. He was also more guarded about trumpeting the success of the program when he made the following remarks about Teen Challenge:

> Teen Challenge features a two-part process in which program participants spend several months at a reception center getting clean and sober before officially beginning the program. The program is explicitly Christ-centered and predicated on the belief that drug addiction can be cured only by total reliance on God's grace. Teen Challenge reports tremendous (over 80 percent) success rates in curing young adult drug abusers. A few decent studies of Teen Challenge have been completed, and their results are generally

positive, but none of these studies meets the most rigorous evaluation research standards. Selection bias, a lack of data over an extended time period, and other problems plague the extant documentation on the program's efficacy.[13]

I think Dr. Dilulio was stretching it somewhat when he said a "few decent studies," but as a careful academic, he was safe in the social scientific community by noting the limitations of those studies. What was left unsaid is that the readership of both *Philanthropy* and *Public Interest* is probably not as familiar with the finer points of research, so what might hold more weight is the larger seed planted: that these programs are effective. Nonetheless, the translation of "Selection bias, a lack of data over an extended time period, and other problems plague the extant documentation on the program's efficacy" is that no credible claims can be made regarding the program's effectiveness.

Four years after Sherman's *Philanthropy* article, when suspicions in the academic community continued regarding the strength of the research on Teen Challenge, Sherman was still tossing around Teen Challenge success figures.[14] She was much more measured in her words, but still carefully invoked the 86 percent success rate found in 1976 by the National Institute on Drug Abuse (NIDA).[15] She then introduced two new studies, a 1994 follow-up to the 1976 study she cited originally, and Aaron Todd Bicknese's dissertation findings.[16] Sherman exemplified the rhetorical style employed continually to plant the seeds of effectiveness when, in fact, there is a continual recycling of the subtext that faith-based services are effective, and research is beginning to show as much:

> A handful of studies have also been conducted on the effectiveness of Teen Challenge, a faith-based drug rehabilitation program. An early study (1976) by the National Institute on Drug Abuse found that an astonishing 86 percent of Teen Challenge graduates remained drug free seven years after their graduation from the program. This compared to a success rate in the single digits for government-run, secular programs. A follow-up study in 1994 surveyed alumni of Teen Challenge over a 13-year period and documented again very high numbers of graduates who had remained drug free. Even though 72 percent of the participants in the study had failed in other drug rehabilitation programs before entering Teen Challenge, 67 percent of those who graduated were continuing to abstain from drug and alcohol use. The most recent assessment of the ministry was conducted by a Northwestern University Ph.D. candidate. His dissertation showed that 86 percent of those who complete the Teen Challenge program have remained drug free and that nearly all had escaped the "revolving door phenomenon" of substance abuse treatment.

> The anecdotal and limited empirical evidence gives plausibility to the idea that some faith-based approaches do indeed work well, though additional rigorous empirical studies are needed before any broad-ranging claims about the superiority of faith-based approaches over others can be justified. After all, in Dilulio's witticism, the plural of anecdote does not equal data. Nonetheless, a body of evidence suggesting the power of [faith-based organizations] appears to be gradually accumulating.[17]

Taking some liberty, Sherman's last paragraph carries the exact same lack of truthful meaning as the following: "The anecdotal and limited empirical evidence gives plausibility as well to the idea that the cow jumped over the moon, though rigorous empirical studies are needed before any broad-ranging claims about the cow jumping over the moon can be justified. Nonetheless, a body of evidence suggesting that the cow jumped over the moon appears to be gradually accumulating." Sadly, the same body of evidence found in Senator Coats's claim is gradually accumulating, but it is bit of stretch and spin.

MARVIN OLASKY

Promoters of faith-based social services—some more shamelessly than others—continued to spread the same message as Sherman. On December 20, 2004, the Roundtable on Religion and Social Welfare Policy interviewed Marvin Olasky, who made the following remarks about Teen Challenge:

> The Teen Challenge counselors are people who have been alcoholics or addicts themselves and have come out of it through a *religious transformation*. The model taught at the institutions where they are to be trained was the therapeutic model, which is basically treating alcoholism or addiction almost like a physical illness, whereas the Teen Challenge people said it is a spiritual illness.
>
> My summary of their teaching is that we all have holes in our souls. A person is going to fill that hole with something. Some people fill it by searching for more money. Some people fill it by searching for power. Some use alcohol or drugs. In any case, they will continue to try filling that hole unless it is filled with Jesus Christ. There have been studies that show a high rate of success at Teen Challenge, and anecdotally it also showed success.[18]

Olasky is technically correct. Studies do show a high rate of success at Teen Challenge and, anecdotally, it has shown success. What must be noted, though, is that Olasky is not just a Christian; he is also an academic who has gained rights and privileges by earning a doctorate and admission into an institution supposedly dedicated to seeking and speaking the truth. Olasky has participated on the faith-based circuit a long time and knows, or should know, that the Teen Challenge studies have come under great suspicion in the academy. In somewhat of a contrast, he, and others as well, seem to work diligently to keep the notion alive that research demonstrates the effectiveness of what they believe, rather than to tell their audience the work that they cite is actually faulty.

As a researcher, I have yet to see evidence that faith-based social services in any broad sense—in particular, ones coming from congregations or Christ-centered programs—are more effective than nonfaith-based ones. I have the deepest respect for the work religious congregations and religiously related service organizations of all faiths are now doing, but I believe the efforts of these promoters border on a self-serving presentation to cast them as anything other than "boutique" social service providers, especially when their main mission is to provide gathering sites for a community of like-minded worshipers. It appears to me that neither Dr. Sherman nor Professor Olasky understands social science research to the degree necessary for them to separate their desire for Christ-centered, faith-based social services to rule the day from what the data actually determine about their effectiveness. I find that they see only what they believe in the research.

JOE LOCONTE

In a 2004 article in *Public Interest*, Joe Loconte and William E. Simon, scholar in Religion at the Heritage Foundation at the time, capped what appeared to be bubbling enthusiasm over the seeming effectiveness of Teen Challenge. He veiled his enthusiasm in academic-sounding neutrality while attempting to explain the Bicknese findings, using the very academic, even cult-like language that social science researchers use, as was the case in Bicknese's dissertation, to promote the right-wing cause.

> More important, however, is a recent comparative study of Teen Challenge graduates completed by Aaron Bicknese as his doctoral dissertation at Northwestern University. It is one of the most methodologically rigorous studies to date of faith-based treatment programs. Bicknese collected hour-long interviews with 59 program graduates, drawing on post-treatment cohorts of twelve months, eighteen months, and twenty-four months. He minimized the problem of selection bias by including questions about the participants' church backgrounds. His comparison group was a short-term secular program that also made abstinence from drug use its primary goal. The two groups were matched based on five variables: gender, ethnicity, age, severity of pretreatment addiction, and court-referral status. Dropout rates were also about equal. Bicknese admits that low-response rates from Teen Challenge and the comparison group (39% and 30%, respectively) indicate the need for a larger data set before broad conclusions can be drawn, but his findings are still significant.[19]

After closely reading the Bicknese study myself, I concluded that Loconte, like my students when they are not really sure what they are talking about, made little sense, but tried desperately to persuade the uninformed that science and religion had become one through Teen Challenge. He even feigned that the study was recent, when in fact it was conducted in 1995 and presented in 1999. He further deemed the study significant even after he cited the major threat to the validity making the study insignificant, which Dr. Bicknese so appropriately pointed out.

Paid by the Heritage Foundation, Loconte used the title of an academic to convince people of his objectivity when he was actually selling a point of view. His job may have been to slant the data in a way that makes his argument sound like science, so it could be perceived as persuasive. If so, he did it well.

In the United States, if organizations wish to market their product in an unregulated arena like the Internet or think tanks and they stretch the truth, then such is business. For example, I grew up *knowing* that the Wonder Bread I was eating built my body in twelve different ways. I never questioned how it might also be hurting me or whether my grand-mother's homemade bread might build my body in twenty ways. I bought into the advertising. *But advertising is not scholarship.* What is more vital to me is it seems that conservative Christian scholars like Olasky, Sherman, and Loconte want so desperately for there to be hardcore evidence that Christ-centered programs are the path to personal and policy salvation that their pitch sounds more like advertising than what I would have expected from people who are otherwise so cautious and thoughtful.

Just because results are statistically significant does not mean they are important from a research view. If one makes less than important research findings significant for political purposes that promote conservative poli-cies, which these people seem to have done, then the findings in the Bicknese and other studies are politically significant at the expense of demeaning the academic research enterprise. All of the people I focused on in this chapter wear scholarly titles and use academic legitimacy to cre-ate a very weak set of research findings that have become the "truth" in terms of Beltway political capital. Hans Christian Andersen's fairy tale "The Emperor's New Clothes" captures the heart of the Teen Challenge marathon: "How well they look! How well they fit!" said all. "What a beautiful pattern! What fine colors! That is a magnificent suit of clothes!"

CHAPTER 6

Blacks and Jews

One has to marvel at how clever Republican strategists were in inter-twining religion, blacks, Jews, social services, and politics into its formula for political triumph in 2004. One part of the battle plan for the 2004 presidential campaign was designed to chip away at the traditional black and Jewish Democratic voting blocs—in an election in which a few thousand votes in key states would make the difference between winning and losing—by promoting the Faith-Based Initiative. On one level such a plan could be praised because its choreography added to some of the highest quality theater imaginable. Yet the effort was a folly because once again the show had nothing to do with effective service delivery. When one thinks about the values that underlie helping the most vulnerable elements of society, the recklessness goes to a new low in Machiavellian politics.

One reason Republicans have been perennial winners is that they turned respectful debate and discussion, the glue of civil society, into vicious verbal gunfights, making unsuspecting opponents into timid hedgehogs. They portrayed John Kerry as a traitor in the 2004 election and have mastered the subtleties of language with laserlike precision, moving images around the media with a magician's sleight of hand. And they seem to have quieted John Dilulio, someone who had the talent to make a difference. On another front they framed the terms of debate such that real issues seemed like small talk.

To win more votes from relatively small but important constituencies in 2004, Republicans targeted conservative-leaning black ministers, a strategy that began in 1982, as well as Orthodox and hawkish Jews. The effort included trumpeting the sins of gay marriage, promoting school vouchers, hammering away at terrorism, and connecting Jews and right-wing evangelical Christians in a bizarre bond to the administration's Israel policy.[1]

Republicans create a fiction, rally their troops around it, push fence-sitters to their side, confuse their detractors, and make elections into war games in which winning is everything. They even mass-marketed a new rendition of Affirmative Action and wove it into the broader civil rights movement. They claimed that the government had been withholding money from important faith-based groups because such groups are more religious than others. This deceptive tactic morally justified the Faith-Based Initiative, using a fictitious civil rights issue to fend off critics. The moral plea was to end the liberal conspiracy that allowed government to deny public financing to their kind of religious organizations, which a vote for President Bush would ultimately fix.

The discharge also diffused critics by discrediting them as enemies of civil rights. Once the academy started to question the lack of research and challenged the effectiveness of the Teen Challenge claims and the effectiveness of faith-based organizations compared to secular organizations, that is, once there wasn't any proof—boom! A new "stretch and trumpet" language took hold. An August 2001 government document entitled "Unlevel Playing Field: Barriers to Participation by Faith-Based and Community Organizations in Federal Social Service Programs" finally justified the need to fund faith-based organizations on civil rights grounds—Affirmative Action for the Christian Right.[2]

The document is packed with civil rights jargon. Its subtext is on the unfairness hindering small church-based social services from acquiring government money. There is no reference to the ravages of poverty nor to linking services nor about measuring need, and there is nothing in it about building community. Instead, the document complains about small churches not being welcomed into the government's circle of spending. This handbook serves the faith-based proponents, like Joe Loconte, who allude to it to legitimize all the discrimination ever cast on pervasively sectarian churches and agencies seeking public funds. In an e-mail exchange I had with Loconte, he wrote:

> One obvious problem with the status quo is that the thousands of smaller, lesser-known, but spiritually robust organizations have been ignored—or bullied—by government for years. The Catholic Charities model, though useful and appropriate in some ways, is simply not a model endorsed by many (if not most) of the faith-based charities doing the best work.[3]

Loconte says it all in one broad sweep. The big religious charities are bad and the little Christian ones are the best—case closed.

What I find so disheartening about using civil rights language to justify funding faith-based social services is that it puts our government discretionary grant-making mechanism and the people who make those grants on the same field as the segregationists responsible for lynchings, cross burnings, repeated denials of basic rights, and dehumanization of U.S. citizens. With that kind of strategy serving to justify why money ought to be given to churches, casting opponents of faith-based funding as being against civil rights, it is no wonder that Jim Towey easily called church–state separationists "secular extremists." Being against their ideas, be they war or faith-based social service, is simply anti-American, warranting harsh consequences from self-appointed defenders of American values.

Figure 6.1 shows the summary of the report's main findings, from the introduction of "Unlevel Playing Field." The five subpoints under point 2 form the core of the civil rights violations the government was said to have committed against religious organizations. Keep in mind that Catholic Charities, Salvation Army, Lutheran Social Services, and Jewish Family Services had been receiving federal funds for years, so this hastily thrown together report is not talking about violations to the civil rights denied to those religious organizations but only the supposed violations cast on small, mainly Christ-centered, black, Hispanic, and white evangelical churches.

Here is what the author of the document said about its report's specificity:

> This report provides an overview of problems uncovered by the first ever audit of Federal programs undertaken by the newly-created Centers for Faith-Based & Community Initiatives at HHS, HUD, Education, Labor, and Justice. Because of the Centers' recent vintage and limited staff, the shortened turnaround time for the report, and the extensive range of affected agency programs, the audit could not cover every potentially affected program in depth. Thus, the Centers emphasized programs that receive major funding, programs that are covered by existing Charitable Choice laws, programs characteristic of the respective departments, and programs in which participation by faith-based and other community-serving groups would be natural or especially fruitful.[4]

I took this to really mean: We will put something in here to make it look like an official report, give it an official-sounding title, and run with it.

Seven uses of the word *discrimination* appear in the twenty-five-page document, three of which are about employment discrimination. The purpose is to suggest that faith-based providers are victims of discrimination because they cannot use federal money to hire members of only their religion. Not one verified case of discrimination against a small faith-based organization was in there; there is only one statistical chart that serves to give the report an appearance of legitimacy. The document is weak in substance but nevertheless serves as a framework for the Right to base its arguments and programs. It is a language trap the proponents of the initiative set up to hold critics at bay.

To demonstrate the architects' basic lack of understanding of how community systems really work, I will devote a good part of two later chapters to addressing how details of just one point play out at the local level: "Imposing anti-competitive mandates on some programs, such as requiring applicants to demonstrate support from government agencies or others that might also be competing for the same funds."[5] For now, I want to challenge the linking of government's denial to fund pervasively sectarian agencies to civil rights violations implied in the first bullet.

Among the findings of the five centers' reports are the following:

1. A funding gap exists between the government and the grassroots. Smaller groups, faith-based and secular, receive very little federal support relative to the size and scope of the social services they provide.
2. There exists a widespread bias against faith- and community-based organizations in federal social service programs:

   - Restricting some kinds of religious organizations from applying for funding
   - Restricting religious activities that are not prohibited by the Constitution
   - Not honoring rights that religious organizations have in federal law
   - Burdening small organizations with cumbersome regulations and requirements
   - Imposing anti-competitive mandates on some programs, such as requiring applicants to demonstrate support from government agencies or others that might also be competing for the same funds

3. Legislation requires some restrictions on the full participation of faith-based organizations, but many of the regulations are needlessly burdensome administrative creations.
4. Congress's remedy to barriers to faith-based organizations—the federal law known as "Charitable Choice"—has been almost entirely ignored by federal administrators, who have done little to help or require state and local governments to comply with the new rules for involving faith-based providers.
5. Despite these obstacles, some faith-based and community-based service groups receive financial support from the federal government, either by winning federal discretionary grants or gaining a share of federal formula grants used by state and local governments to deliver social services.

Source: Centers for Faith-Based and Community Initiatives, introduction to "Unlevel Playing Field: Barriers to Participation by Faith-Based and Community organizations in Federal Social Service Programs," August 2001, http://www.whitehouse.gov/news/releases/2001/08/unlevelfield1.html.

Figure 6.1. The Case for Funding Faith-Based Organizations on Civil Rights Grounds

As I read that charge, I tried to compare the alleged civil rights violation in the bullet to the 1963 March on Washington; the 1964 murders of civil rights workers Michael Schwerner, Andrew Goodman, and James Chaney in Mississippi; or the 1965 March on Washington or the march from Birmingham to Selma, Alabama. No matter how I twisted and turned it, I didn't feel the same pain over a requirement to coordinate services or gain support from a potential competitor that I feel when I think of suffering that led to our nation's real civil rights changes. If, however, the government manufactures a civil rights violation that has been supposedly cast on small churches, it then has justification for giving them money without having them play by the same rules as everyone else. That is a slick but unsightly strategy.

In one of my classes where I require a grant proposal, I demand that my students gain support from potential competitors, for two reasons. First, they develop programs and seek funding for at least partial solutions to problems. By seeking support from prospective competitors, they learn what others are doing and possibly reshape their ideas based on what they find in seeking support. Helping kids in a complex system of services depends on coordination, communication, and cooperation, not reckless, dynamic competition—which seems to be the assumption embedded in the supposed civil rights violation. Second, gaining support for a program idea requires making connections in the system of services and brokering relationships. The only way to thrive in the community system is to work and plan together in this complex culture of service delivery. So while this theoretical civil rights violation isn't really one at all, the Compassion Capital Fund mentioned in chapter 2 actually "fixes" this violation at the expense of thoughtful entry into the broader system of services.

It is clear that the Compassion Capital Fund, which gives money to larger intermediary organizations who then help smaller, primarily religious organizations, administers the money from this framework. No one can possibly get behind the veil to see if such groups are violating the Establishment Clause. The justification, however, relies upon the use of civil rights and Affirmative Action language to argue that small faith-based and community organizations have been omitted from the federal funding mix because they were too religious. The Compassion Capital strategy fixes this manufactured violation.

While "Unlevel Playing Field" is less than convincing with actual cases of discrimination, it set the terms in the run-up to the 2004 election for the president and his spokesmen, Jim Towey and John Ashcroft, to continue the same kind of "stretch and trumpet" that was seen with the Teen Challenge research. While this initiative is really about funding Christ-centered services and keeping the base happy, the administration had to find a way to deal with the Jews and thus make it look like it was the new champion of civil rights for all the oppressed religions.

The Faith-Based Initiative and the courtship of blacks started in the Reagan era. So did the complex strategies that were employed so seamlessly in the 2004 election. Ronald Reagan kicked off the 1980 campaign on August 3 in Philadelphia, Mississippi. It was no coincidence that he did so just one day before the sixteenth anniversary of the discovery of the bodies of civil rights workers Chaney, Schwerner, and Goodman, one black and two Jewish, who were murdered there in 1964. Speechwriters brilliantly resurrected the ghost of the Confederacy when Reagan invoked what his audience considered an endearing allusion to "states' rights."[6] His handlers were not dimwitted. Reagan never said exactly what he meant, but to gain ground with Southern whites, he distanced himself and his party from Lincoln's emancipation of slaves. Instead, he associated himself, in a veiled but shady way, with the racist party of George Lincoln Rockwell.

Reagan complained that the federal government had stolen the rights of western states by forbidding cattle farmers from letting their cattle graze on federal land. Ironically, the same federal government that had ended slavery, instituted voting rights for blacks, eradicated Jim Crow laws, and brought down the Confederacy was prohibiting western farmers from doing what they wanted with their property. Slavery was a "states' rights" issue, and so was grazing. While Reagan addressed states' rights in the name of grazing, he was actually signaling his white Southern listeners that under his presidency, there would be less federal intrusion into their affairs. Everyone in Dixie knew exactly what ringing a "states' rights" cowbell meant in Philadelphia, Mississippi, in August 1980.

Before opponents could cry foul, Reagan was in New York City, the bastion of Jewish liberalism and a large black population. By August 5, he was delivering a speech to the Urban League. Douglas Kneeland of the *New York Times* reported that Reagan declared, "I am committed to the protection of the civil rights of black Americans. That commitment is interwoven into every phase of the programs I will propose."[7] One can only imagine what would have happened if Reagan had reversed the two speeches, talking instead about civil rights to the "good old boys" in Mississippi and about states' rights to blacks in New York.

From Reagan on, Republican politics have centered on winning at all costs. Razzle-dazzle is simply central to their game plan. Twenty-one years later, Republican pollster Frank Luntz offered advice to strategists preparing the game plan for the 2004 election. In the 2000 election, blacks had given Bush between 8 and 9 percent of their vote. Bush had lost the popular vote, yet squeaked by with an Electoral College win after a controversial victory in Florida. Luntz said in a March 11, 2001, story in the *Boston Globe* that the Faith-Based Initiative was President Bush's best outreach tool: "If he continues on this road, that becomes the first successful effort I have seen to penetrate the black mind-set."[8] In fact his strategists used the veil of his Faith-Based Initiative to penetrate the black and even the Jewish mindset.

A January 18, 2005, *Los Angeles Times* story explained how Bush's faith-based team had penetrated the black state of mind. One of Milwaukee's most prominent black pastors, Bishop Sedgwick Daniels of Holy Redeemer Institutional Church of God in Christ, had backed Democrats Bill Clinton and Al Gore in the previous three presidential elections.[9] Gore won Wisconsin in 2000 by 5,708 votes of nearly three million votes cast, or .02 percent, which is a razor-thin victory in politics. Not only was Wisconsin up for grabs in the 2004 election, but so too were Florida, Pennsylvania, Missouri, Ohio, and possibly New Jersey, states with high concentrations of blacks and Jews in their urban and suburban centers. In July 2002, President Bush visited Bishop Daniels in Milwaukee. Bush strategists did not just pull a rabbit out of their hat. The Milwaukee-based Bradley Foundation and its director at the time, Michael Joyce, had been instrumental in funding many conservative causes both nationally and locally for years and had funded Daniels's youth center to the tune of more than a million dollars between 1998 and 2001.[10] It appeared that the Bush team would sign Daniels to a long-term contract if he cooperated.

The next stop for Daniels was the Housing and Community Opportunity Subcommittee of the House Financial Services Committee, which held a hearing on March 25, 2003. The topic was faith-based social services. In opening the hearing, Subcommittee Chair Bob Ney (R-Ohio) and Rep. Mark Green (R-Wis.) both praised the administration's goal of increasing the involvement of faith-based groups in providing housing and other services. Appearing before that committee, Bishop Daniels presented a written statement in which he clarified what services his organization provided and praised faith-based efforts.[11] In spoken testimony, Daniels noted that he had encountered obstacles in accessing Housing and Urban Development (HUD) funding for low-income housing in various communities, leaving the impression that the barriers connected to Holy Redeemer Institutional Church of God in Christ's housing entity might have been faith-related.[12] Daniels was playing ball in what was not a backyard pick-up game; this was rough-and-tumble Republican football.

In September 2003, Daniels's Holy Redeemer Institutional Church of God in Christ received an award of $626,598, the first installment of a $1.5 million Compassion Capital grant; he received the second installment of $824,471 in 2004.[13] In the fall of 2004, right before election time, Bishop Daniels's picture appeared on Republican Party fliers in the battleground state of Wisconsin, endorsing President Bush as the candidate who "shares our views." Undoubtedly, Daniels knows how to win grants; he demonstrated as much with the Bradley Foundation's support. His church comprises more than twenty spin-off organizations, or "entities" as he referred to them in his congressional testimony. Therefore, it is certain he supported them through grants, contracts, and other traditional means of fundraising used in the nonprofit world. There were probably no guarantees of winning the $1.5 million grant, but perhaps his mindset was first penetrated with a wink and a nod and then some money.

The Bush administration also used this process to penetrate the defenses of other high-profile African American organizations whose leaders were linked directly or indirectly to the GOP. The Rev. Herb Lusk's church in Philadelphia, a key city in Pennsylvania, another battleground state, received $1 million in federal funds for a program to help low-income Philadelphians. Lusk gave the invocation at the 2000 Republican convention and has remained an outspoken Bush supporter. Another beneficiary was a South Florida–based organization headed by Bishop Harold Ray, a longtime Bush acquaintance who gave an invocation for Vice President Dick Cheney at a West Palm Beach, Florida, gathering. Ray's group received a stunning $1.7 million in government funding.[14]

Republican strategists know that money turns not only blacks into supporters; it does the same for Jews as well. In President Bush's speech in Milwaukee in July 2002, he slipped in the first hint of how his staff would penetrate the Jewish mindset. Jews posed a different problem for the schemers behind the Faith-Based Initiative. Mainline Jewish organizations were openly opposed to President Bush's initiative because they knew intuitively that it was really a means of communicating with his base of evangelical Christians to buy their votes while appearing to be even-handed. The American Jewish Congress had even brought a lawsuit against the administration,[15] so the Bush strategists needed a tactic to neutralize that criticism immediately. On the broader political side, they blunted some of the force of the criticism when veteran Christian Right leaders and Republican Party power brokers joined forces in 2002 with Jewish leaders to launch a couple of pro-Israel organizations.[16]

Even before those relationships were fostered, the faith-based flank was gearing up for battle. The use of civil rights language in the "Unlevel Playing Field" to justify widening federal funding opportunities for pervasively sectarian black churches and white evangelical churches now served to work the Jews into the equation. It is no wonder that President Bush subtly identified Jews as victims of discrimination in his July 2, 2002, speech in Milwaukee when he visited Daniels. Bush claimed that faith-based groups are prohibited or discouraged from even applying for federal grants. He then pointed out that during the previous week, Jim Towey, his then new director of the White House Office of Faith-Based and Community Initiatives, had met with the Metropolitan Council on Jewish Poverty out of New York and learned that "because of their name and their identity, federal officials have repeatedly discouraged them from applying for federal funds."[17] As he spoke further about expanding federal legislation to assist religious organizations, Bush again identified Jews as victims of new civil rights violations: "One of the key principles is there's equal treatment. Organizations that have a religious name or religious icons on the wall like a cross or Star of David should be welcomed partners in providing for the poor."[18] As early as July 2002, the Faith-Based Initiative was chipping away at the black and Jewish voting bloc.

A serious game plan was formulated to lure more Jews under the Republican tent, especially since none of the scandals that later plagued Bush and the Republican Party was choking the public in 2002 and 2003. Quite the opposite, the president enjoyed tremendous public support, so the time was right for strategists to lure in some of the Jewish vote. At the Rockefeller Institute of Government Roundtable on Religion panel at the National Press Club in Washington on October 23, 2002, panelist Towey continued with the well-orchestrated battle cry about the victimization of

Jews. He, too, brought up the Metropolitan Council on Jewish Poverty to champion the broader cause for a new justice:

> Just because you have [a] religious name, you can be denied opportunities to compete.... I went and toured their programs in New York City, and they said: "When we went to HHS [the Department of Health and Human Services] to try to apply, we were told, no, you've got Jewish in your name. You can't apply. You can't apply."[19]

Towey was not merely touring the agency; he was paving the way for a public relations blitz that would appear to rectify the injustices cast upon the Jews. Some serious political speculation took place behind the scenes that the Jewish vote might be up for grabs.

Though barely publicized, an exit poll in the 2002 New York governor's race determined that close to 50 percent of Jews might consider voting for Bush, who was then riding high in the approval ratings because of his post-9/11 leadership that briefly unified the country.[20] Did this little bit of data provide the ammunition for pursuing the Jewish vote? Two months later, in a December 12, 2002, speech in Philadelphia, President Bush restated, "A few years ago in New York, the Metropolitan Council on Jewish Poverty was discouraged from even applying for federal funds because it had the word 'Jewish' in its name."[21] The Republicans were not finished with this blitz just yet.

On Christmas Day 2002, Jewish Democrat William E. "Willie" Rapfogel of the Metropolitan Council on Jewish Poverty received a signal that Santa was a Republican. Naughty or nice, he had to play ball, and when he did, the council would be rewarded like Bishop Daniels's Holy Redeemer Church. All would appear to be on the up-and-up, but Rapfogel would have to deliver a clear message to the Jewish community, as Daniels did with blacks in Wisconsin, that he and President Bush "shared similar views."

Jim Towey was interviewed on PBS's *News Hour with Jim Lehrer* that Christmas.[22] Towey shifted his words ever so slightly, but he stayed on course, again using the Metropolitan Council on Jewish Poverty in New York City as the example of how Jews had been victims. This time, however, it was a national audience to whom he was speaking, not just one in a battleground state or a conference at a National Press Club event: "They were denied the ability to apply for a grant just because the word 'Jewish' was in their name," he stated. Towey went on to say that President Bush wanted the benchmark for success to be a program's effectiveness, not its faith. Then he invoked what later turned out to be a bogus charge of government immorality. Nevertheless, the advertising campaign portrayed the Bush administration as one for truth, justice, and the American way and a friend of the Jews. What could be more convincing than saying so on Christmas Day? If only it were the truth.

In the interview, Towey continued, "I think we found in our country so many groups that have been stiff-armed by the government and kept away from being able to address these urgent needs in our communities, and I think President Bush wants to put an end to that because there is a moral necessity."[23] White House strategists had Towey placing George W. Bush in the same pasture where Ronald Reagan had stood twenty-three years earlier: He, too, would end the injustice the government cast on the victims of a made-for-politics injustice.

By the end of 2003, Rapfogel's Metropolitan Council not only was beginning to look more and more like Daniels's Holy Redeemer Church but was also becoming the Bush administration's national Jewish faith-based poster child. Even Attorney General John Ashcroft got into the promotion in Florida, a key battleground state, proclaiming:

> For many years, faith-based and other community groups were prohibited from competing for federal funding. New York's Metropolitan Council on Jewish Poverty has for many years provided social services in the City of New York. The federal government told the Council that it *could not apply* for federal grants because the word "Jewish" appeared in its title.[24]

This poster child, moreover, appeared in the Metropolitan New York media market, one of the largest in the world. On December 26, 2003, a personal check from President and Mrs. Bush arrived at the Metropolitan Council on Poverty. By January 2, 2004, news of the president's gift appeared in *Forward*, a Jewish weekly newspaper. "I was truly shocked to see President Bush's check," said Rapfogel, who mentioned that Bush also had sent him a letter recently, praising "the wonderful work that you and your team are doing." Rapfogel added, "It's an honor to be included among the charities he believes in."[25] Appendix B contains the full text of a letter from Rapfogel that appeared in the *Jewish Press* on January 7 telling of the Bushes' private contribution.[26]

In August 2004, the Metropolitan Council on Jewish Poverty received a $525,645 Federal Compassion Capital grant.[27] Just one and a half months later, in another article published in the *Forward*, Rapfogel was quoted as saying: "President Bush was truly shocked to learn that Met Council had been *denied opportunities* to serve needy people because we had 'Jewish' in our name."[28] Rapfogel, a Democrat, said, "The President recognized an injustice, said he would end it, and kept his word. Previous administrations of both parties allowed it to stand, so George W. Bush deserves credit and our gratitude for doing the right thing."[29] Did Willie Rapfogel get bought? As Mark Twain said in his autobiography, "If we would learn what the human race really is at bottom, we need only observe it in election times."

On December 18, 2004, I spoke with Adena Kaplan of the Metropolitan Council on Jewish Poverty and asked her if she could tell me (1) when the grant request that was supposedly denied was actually submitted; (2) to which office in government the application was sent; (3) what kind of grant it was; and (4) who the person was who denied it. She told me that a self-sufficiency grant had been submitted to the Department of Health and Human Services (HHS) in *1994*. An unidentified source at HHS *discouraged* the agency from applying because "Jewish" was in its name. The agency applied anyway, and the grant was denied. Kaplan verified for me that the Metropolitan Council had received both federal and state money before that particular grant request was rejected and had continued to receive both federal and state money right up to the time of receiving the Compassion Capital award. Actually, the agency has a $120 million budget, with more than 90 percent of it coming from federal and state funds.[30]

It must be a fairytale-like event when the president of the United States, undoubtedly the most powerful human being on the planet, who oversees a three-trillion-plus-dollar budget, takes the time to visit a social service agency of any kind. Agency leaders work tirelessly to keep the spotlight on their organizations, whether they are in small towns or big cities. Public relations is an essential ingredient in the competitive game of human service funding. If organizational leaders do not attend dinners, meet with the business community, and broker grants and contracts regularly, then someone may lose a meal, live without heat, miss a prescription, be denied a job opportunity, or lose a ride to religious services where they find community and inner peace. A breakfast meeting with a business leader might mean a bicycle for a child whose mother cannot afford it. Delivering a speech at a synagogue could result in increasing the pool of volunteers who make agencies work better than they would without them. The people served by such organizations are mothers and fathers, brothers and sisters; they are quite often those who need a helping hand to regain some balance and security in a vulnerable existence.

Social service employees at every organizational tier work diligently to deal with all aspects of human misery. They have little time to shape the national discussion of what might be required to solve, manage, or prevent the range of problems they struggle to contain daily. Bishop Daniels's and Willie Rapfogel's programs confront a slew of human problems that come with poverty. Their organizations are about doing the good deed. In a way, Daniels and Rapfogel are like the helicopter pilots who plucked Hurricane Katrina victims off of rooftops—without them or someone like them in the pilot's seat, people would drown. If their broader mission is to position their organizations so they can better help those sitting on the rooftops of poverty, how can they tell the president of the United States, be he a Democrat or Republican, "I don't want to play ball with you"? Even when playing ball, the funding game is a gamble.

A barely publicized memo in May 2004 foreshadowed the real thinking in Republican circles and put government agencies on notice that if President Bush were reelected, his budget for 2006 might include spending cuts for virtually all agencies in charge of domestic programs—the very same ones that fund Daniels's and Rapfogel's organizations, including education, homeland security, and others that the president had backed in the 2004 campaign. In other words, what was given in 2004 would be taken away in 2006 if Bush had his way.[31] In the upside-down world of the Faith-Based Initiative and in the world of Republican politics, where winning is of primary concern, the message is more important than the truth. Despite the truth that the Metropolitan Council would stand to lose more federal aid in 2006 than it was getting by playing ball in 2004, an e-mail for the Jewish community was sent from the White House Office of Public Liaison (see appendix C) to Jewish leaders around the country on August 25, 2004, with the subject "President Bush's Initiative Helps Jewish Faith-Based Institutions."[32] One particular line in the e-mail apparently refers to the same Metropolitan Council on Jewish Poverty story: "One charity was told not to apply for a grant because it had the word 'Jewish' in its name, even though it served both gentiles and Jews." Less than one hour later, the majority of that same e-mail's contents were word for word on a Jewish website called *Kesher Talk*,[33] which describes itself as "news and views from a hawkish liberal Jewish perspective." I e-mailed the editor, Judith Weiss, five times and asked her about the direct quote but I received no response.

Nationwide, blacks increased their vote for Bush from 9 percent in 2000 to 11 percent in 2004; in the crucial state of Ohio, their Republican vote rose from 9 percent to 16 percent. Similarly, Jews increased their nationwide vote for Bush from 19 percent in 2000 to 24 percent in 2004; in Florida, Bush received 12 percent of the Jewish vote in 2000 and 20 percent in 2004.[34] In the trench warfare of political football, it is safe to say that Sedgwick Daniels and Willie Rapfogel helped gain some important yardage in the 2004 victory even though it was gained with tax dollars; Rapfogel's letter to the entire Jewish world in February 2004 says as much.

Unfortunately, Bush tried to take the money back two years later. While not completely successful, it is not difficult to see why Daniels and Rapfogel were important. What was missing from the stories that these shenanigans represent was a sober national discussion about the role faith-based organizations could and should assume in the wider effort to help the poor. Yet, the Faith-Based Initiative, the core of compassionate conservatism, has never been about helping the poor; its focus has been winning votes and using the kind of razzle-dazzle that in football would make Vince Lombardi—who coined the phrase "winning isn't everything, it's the only thing"—proud. Straight shooters like Lombardi don't cheat to win however, be it politics or football.

CHAPTER 7

Wingspread

Much of this work thus far has focused on how the architects and politicos behind the Faith-Based Initiative used the rhetoric of exaggerated research findings to create a new, unsubstantiated, and demeaning "civil rights" movement and a broad public relations campaign to control the discussion. Control of the political agenda was emphasized at the expense of laying out a clear plan of how to get buy-in at the community level and effectively use the resources of the religious community to tackle some of our country's most complicated social ills. I illustrated in chapter 2 that the Faith-Based Initiative's strategy of trying to intervene at the community level, unlike the upbeat, convincing rhetoric, was an afterthought and resulted in a flimsy intervention plan. Compassionate conservatism is something like left-handed scissors; they exist, but they are hard to find. Sadly, slogans like "filling holes in souls" or "making Jews complete through conversion" don't substitute for well-planned programs. Even worse is that the conservative Faith-Based Initiative has been top-down, as "anti-local" as any liberal social program in history, making local intervention on an equal footing impossible.

I have tried not to become disoriented monitoring the rhetoric and actions of this initiative, but at times, I have felt the way the fictitious Dorothy must have felt in *The Wizard of Oz* as she spun in her dream from Kansas and suddenly found herself with hordes of Munchkins. I have had to pinch myself more than once. I have spent literally my entire adult life in some type of community service, and even though I have held an academic position for the past twenty-six years, I have been rooted in the community service trenches. For the last nine years, I have worked daily with the Rev. Odell Cleveland and the Welfare Reform Liaison Project in Greensboro, North Carolina; it is this relationship that takes up much of the rest of this book. But before I move on with that, it is worthwhile to talk a bit about Wingspread, the conference that spawned the Faith-Based Initiative. It provides a window into the construction of the alternative reality that has shaped the initiative and shows how blind faith and inattention to other voices has shepherded the Faith-Based Initiative to its failure locally.

As one who has spent so many years studying this subject, in one way or another I have come to know many of the people who have shaped this initiative but haven't been as visible as the "marathoners" I discussed in chapter 5. There has been a cast of smart, thoughtful, and influential people shaping the agenda for years. This by and large white, evangelical, right-leaning group of Christians rapidly built a rainbow coalition. Supporters of their efforts increasingly reflected the different hues and faiths on the spectrum. These people are neither mean nor wicked—just driven. They care about the plight of the poor. They have been very skilled in organizing and especially competent at framing the terms of the discussion. They play hardball because their mission requires it, and they do it intelligently and perform well—except in getting their agenda to produce real results locally. They have been on a mission for quite some time. Their ranks include Democrats, or at least former Democrats, as well as Republicans. However, it has been extremely hard to tell at times what their push is really all about because they have been skillful at never clearly stating in public what they want. What is clear, though, is that they got it all wrong when it came to developing social service partnerships that could demonstrate results in solving major social problems.

I have mentioned some members of this interconnected group throughout this book. Because I had been studying faith-based social services long before the 2001 official launching, and was one of the few scholars doing so, I got to meet many of the proponents of more faith-based social services at conferences and smaller gatherings. I was, and still am, a proponent of government efforts to use religious resources more effectively. I ran away from most of the crowd at Wingspread after Bush was elected because they were not promoting a more effective use of faith-related resources. They were promoting a religious and political agenda. They, too, ran away from me because I never failed to remind them that their efforts would not accomplish the goal of helping "the least of these" without a focus on building effective partnerships with members of community service systems in localities across the country.

I have believed from the get-go that the best way to influence the direction of this movement would be to focus on its workability, not to alter the consciousness of the country legislatively and create church–state tensions through fighting over civil rights issues in court, as the two sides have been doing for a long time. They have had deep pockets in fighting on this front. However, most (there are some exceptions) have demonstrated only a vague understanding about how social services operate locally, except to say over and over that public services are huge, inefficient, and unresponsive bureaucracies in one breath, while calling for partnerships between those same bureaucracies and the faith community in another. I have also told them that any group or coalition of groups that merely fights for the expansion of the Charitable Choice Initiative simply on the church-and-state side of the argument will ultimately lose, whether or not the initiative gets stopped in court.

According to John Dilulio, "there's nothing about poverty that isn't solvable"[1]—a sentiment with which I agree, even though our means take different paths. He had in mind something like a coalition of Christians "meeting three times a year to solidify its commitment and to coordinate practical support." It would be

> broadly based—Protestant, Catholic, and Orthodox; Pentecostal, mainline, and white evangelicals taking the lead. They have a sense of mission in America. They most closely share the spiritual heritage of those working effectively in the inner city. And they are the ones inner-city ministers feel most abandoned by.[2]

I bring Dilulio back into this discussion because he is no "religious fanatic," and it would make little to no sense to engage him or any of the people behind this initiative on that level. He was the director. I liken the energy and spirit that fueled this initiative to that which I had when I was a VISTA volunteer close to thirty years ago. I was going to fight the War on Poverty and win. Nothing was going to get in my way! These poverty fighters are older than I was when I started at age 23, but their sense of mission and solutions have been no less spirited than mine were thirty-three years ago. One difference, however, is that most of them spent the last twenty years studying things *other than* the complex issues and the intricate systems of service that try to solve, manage, and prevent some of our most perplexing social problems.

The architects of the Faith-Based Initiative needed to focus on what the details of this initiative would be and what it would really take to make the religious community more effective service providers. I have noted that congregations are already partners—*limited* ones, but partners nevertheless—and that they are not going away unless faith-based policies and practices become so bad as to drive them away. This initiative has never talked about the details of the necessary kinds of service provision that ought to come from mainline faith-based service providers, which already are part of service delivery systems and were at the time of Wingspread. The faith-based efforts we talked about at Wingspread were about getting money to small neighborhood congregations, mainly in African American communities, and they were to be increasingly shifted in that direction by a white conservative political and evangelical leadership who would try to do so from the top of the policy chain. My major concern has always been about the naïveté that formed the core of their game plan.

THE WINGSPREAD CONFERENCE

On April 25–26, 2000, I attended a gathering at Wingspread Conference Center in Racine, Wisconsin, called "The Future of Government Partnerships with the Faith Community." It was sponsored by the Welfare

Policy Center, Hudson Institute, and the Johnson Foundation. The mainly right-wing evangelical Christians and conservative think tank leaders in attendance tilted the conference rightward, for the most part. The tone was one of hope that George W. Bush would win the White House in 2000. Several of the conference participants would later play visible or behind-the-scenes roles in the White House Office of Faith-Based and Community Initiatives (FBCI) and have been pushing for Charitable Choice and its expansion for years. In its simplest terms, Charitable Choice is section 104 of the 1996 welfare reform legislation that allows government to fund church social services directly and explicitly protects the religious character of such organizations that accept public funds.

While the conference was heavily stacked with mostly right-leaning, white, evangelical Christians and was led by right-wing think tankers, there were exceptions, which demonstrated at least an attempt at the appearance of balance. The featured speaker was to be John Dilulio, the head of this initiative. He couldn't make it, however, due to an illness in the family, I believe. He nevertheless wrote the preface to the proceedings of the conference; he went a bit over the top with what the research actually showed about faith-based social services, but, given the spirit of the conference, the preface was appropriate.[3]

A major presenter at the conference was E. J. Dionne—a professed liberal, a *Washington Post* columnist who doesn't shy away from his Catholicism, a friend of Dilulio, and, it seemed then at least, more a detached observer of the initiative than a cheerleader. Thus, the movement had a prominent liberal columnist balancing the agenda along with a host of conservative leaders and cheerleaders.

Another major presenter was Stanley Carlson Thies, then head of social policy at the Center for Public Justice, a Christian think tank, part of whose mission is to "transform public life."[4] Thies is one of the nation's strongest proponents of Charitable Choice. I like Stanley and know him fairly well professionally and have a deep respect for him. There was also Carl Esbeck, then director of the Law Center Christian Legal Society and chief legal strategist for Charitable Choice; former Republican senator Dan Coats, a supporter of John Ashcroft's Charitable Choice provision in the welfare law of 1996; and Don Eberly, who wrote *The Soul of Civil Society* along with Ryan Streeter, a conference organizer.

Amy Sherman, spoke, too. Then a senior Fellow at the Welfare Policy Center, Hudson Institute, she had previously laid out a role for the church in the community in a 1999 speech at the Alban Institute that I believe underscores what is never really said in public about what is behind the Faith-Based Initiative. She had several propositions in that 1999 speech that were about Christian ministry. In Proposition II, she talked about the church moving from one that did simple random acts of kindness to a more planned role, so that onlookers might catch the spirit of their actions and ask:

"Why are they doing that? How do they find the strength to do that? What's going on over there is, well, it's supernatural! And, wow, isn't it marvelous that those abused children are being healed through that, and the drug addicts are becoming clean through that, and the welfare moms are finding jobs through that!" We must be conducting ministries of mercy that have the smell of God about them. They have to give off a beautiful aroma that brings about wonder, amazement, and rejoicing in the city.[5]

I can't imagine her saying that at a public forum with people of other faiths present. It is just not the architects' style unless they slip up.

I was the only self-proclaimed Jew in attendance at the conference. I knew this was a serious conference of insiders.

Don Willett, the research and special projects director of the Policy Division of the Office of the Governor under then Texas governor George W. Bush, sat next to me; like many others at the conference, he later ended up in the FBCI. Willett and Marvin Olasky, the architect of compassionate conservatism, went to England together in June, less than two months after the Wingspread Conference, and, according to Elena Curti of the Catholic publication *The Tablet*, were the featured speakers at England's Christian Conservative Fellowship's Conference on Religion and Welfare. At that event, according to Curti's article, Willett told the British audience he had come from the Lone Star State, which was rallying the armies of compassion and unleashing the best of Texas, and that

faith-based groups were aggressive champions conquering social ills. The facts showed that they produced better results than government programmes: they did it better and more cheaply. Governor Bush did not care whether they were Christian, Jewish or secular projects: all he cared about was "results, results, results."[6]

On the second day of the Wingspread conference, I announced in the general discussion that I was Jewish and that I like to look at community involvement of congregations from the perspective of Tikkun Olam—a framework for change that is different from *personal transformation*, which is a public code phrase for accepting Jesus Christ as one's Personal Savior and Lord and which was used at the conference and interestingly on pages 1 and 6 of "Rallying the Armies of Compassion," the twenty-six-page document introducing the country to this initiative and the document that houses the president's executive orders establishing the FBCI and associated centers in the cabinet offices.[7] My promotion of Tikkun Olam didn't generate any discussion nor was it included in the "Code of Conduct for Religious Organizations," found on page 84 of the edited version of the proceedings of the conference.

However, code 4 of the Code of Conduct captures the undercurrent of the conference and much of the spirit of the larger initiative.

4. **Witness:** We commit ourselves to a gentle and winsome public witness and to a creation of an environment in which staff, volunteers, and program participants are free to speak autobiographically about their own lives of faith. Our staff and volunteers are instructed to welcome and lovingly

respond to spiritual inquiry and discussion initiated by program participants, while avoiding aggressive evangelism.[8]

There has always been something unsettling to me knowing that the FBCI was staffed from the beginning with a government commitment to Christian witness.

At lunch on that second day of the conference, Christopher Beem, the Johnson Foundation's program officer, said something to the effect that he thought it was safe to bless the noonday meal, so he asked a pastor from Philadelphia to say a prayer. Now, let me say that I have been in and out of Christian churches as much as any Jewish academic in the United States. At the time of the conference, I was in my third week of teaching an adult class at a local downtown Methodist church, and we ended each class with a blessing. I held my graduate classes at Mt. Zion Baptist Church in Greensboro for three years and spent considerable time at that church helping develop the Welfare Reform Liaison Project, attending numerous services, celebrations, several baptisms, and a funeral there. So, I am accustomed to devotions and prayer in the name of Jesus.

Nevertheless, I was taken aback when the lunch on this occasion was blessed in the name of Jesus, because all morning there had been an undercurrent in the discussion about how faith-based social services, if they are to be honest participants in Charitable Choice and be respectful of people *of all faiths*, or people with no faith at all, must be bilingual. In other words, they had to be cautious to deliver social services without forcing their brand of faith on anyone, but instead do it in a "winsome" way.[9] When people were back in their own circles, they could fill the air with the spirit in the way they were accustomed.

At my lunch table, I told Mr. Beem that I thought the organizers had forgotten that there was someone of the Jewish faith present and were being insensitive by blessing the lunch in Jesus' name. Beem went into a quick flap, saying that he had been at Jewish events where "he had to wear a yarmulke." He could not have made the point I was making more precisely. The fact is that this event wasn't supposed to be an evangelical Christian event. It was called "Religion in the Public Square in the Twenty-First Century." But when attendees and leaders moved from the conference room to the lunchroom, all of the talk about being bilingual and sensitive—and there had been a good bit of it—went by the wayside. Thankfully, Elliot Wright, a mainline Methodist minister, came to my rescue and tried to point out to Beem that, especially in light of the morning's discussion, not only did insensitivity prevail but legitimate critics of Charitable Choice also feared that a broad faith-based policy would be led by Christians for whom *winsomeness* was a veiled policy agenda.

THE AFTERMATH OF THE CONFERENCE

This discussion of the Wingspread conference gives some insight into why I believe that the evangelicals' larger sense of mission could not allow for a counteranalysis where ideas would get exchanged and a redevelopment of those ideas might take place based on some combination of workability and legislation. Nothing of the sort happened at the conference, nor did it have much of a chance of happening. To me, their ideas had no chance of succeeding in creating real results-oriented partnerships.

I had until this time held back my judgment about Charitable Choice, because I thought it was too early to have the discussion—I knew it would get bogged down in church-and-state debates and nobody would ever talk about whether the proposal would actually work. In my 2001 book, *A Limited Partnership: The Politics of Religion, Welfare, and Social Service*, which I was writing between 1998 and 2000, I pleaded for a sober discussion, because I found little sobriety in the backroom discussions by the leaders of this initiative, nor in their writings leading up to it. If the gatekeepers of this initiative could not be sensitive to a Jew in the room, how could they, in their newfound glee of having their own office in the White House, really be honest about the difficulties faced in implementing a complex initiative so it could work? I argued then, and still do, that success hinges on overcoming the difficulties of developing workable, measurable, and effective social services in a complex local arena. Such an agenda was not on the table and never has been.

Stanley Carlson Thies, as he does on occasion whether I am in the room or not, acknowledges that I have not strayed from that point. At the Wingspread meeting in 2000, I was surprised when he told his brethren what I had told him in e-mails, in person, and in my critiques of his 1995 book. I am going to quote him at length because his words both capture what this book is about, and he said them before he and the other conference leaders, including Dilulio, Eberly, Willett, Streeter, and Bobby Polito (who later landed in a key government position after Bush was elected), ended up in the FCBI or one of its outposts in a cabinet department. The leaders knew the problems they had to face on the ground but they were caught in political and religious follies. Thies told the conferees:

> Bob Wineburg, among others, has reminded me several times about a haunting problem which is in fact one of my criticisms of the welfare law as well. The law assumed that we could go from essentially a government-run system of fiscal benefits to a system in which people receive community supports. But we all know that it takes a long time to build community supports. Yet the law just said to start the time clock ticking and start cutting people off welfare even though we haven't built that community support system. In fact, we can see on the ground in many places that it is a slow process to build such a system. If you want faith-based groups involved and say it's okay because of Charitable Choice, and four years later we are still debating what Charitable Choice means, then it's hard to get faith-based groups involved in the way that is supposed to be available.
>
> So, there is this problem of constructing or reconstructing the social safety net, something different than what we had before. I think that one tendency is for government officials to say, since it's not going to just develop by itself, that we have to make it happen. So we should figure out what role the faith community will play and then give it its slot, so to speak. A number of states have said, "We know what the churches ought to do. They ought to do mentoring or they ought to provide community service

positions, or they ought to do this or that," and the officials start to plan and design accordingly. The positive result is that there will be a network, but the negative thing is that the churches say, "Wait a second, you never talked to us first. You just told us what we were going to do. It's as if we are a different set of policy instruments that you're now going to pick up and use as you wish." It just doesn't work that way. It's a problem, both because the churches say, maybe that's not our role, that's not what we want to do, that's not what were best at. That's a problem. And there is the problem that not all faith-based organizations are churches, and for the government to say the way the faith communities can get engaged in a new way is by working through congregations ignores a wide range of other kinds of faith-based organizations out there. I don't think this kind of government initiative works, and the reaction out there is very negative in the faith community.[10]

Thies is also one of the few faith-based advocates who spent enough time with local leaders to recognize that the Faith-Based Initiative cannot change from a government-run system one day to one that relies on community support the next without developing comprehensive, thoughtful, and respectful ways to work with local leaders. The extremists in the movement believe that funneling federal money to Christ-centered churches is the key to an effective initiative; they simply are mistaken.

Appointed the associate director of law and policy in the FBCI, Dr. Thies understands that it takes more than blind faith to make a faith-based initiative effective. Unfortunately, the religious extremists pushed him out of the White House within a year. Even though he has advised numerous civic and religious leaders on the faith-based circuit for years, including George W. Bush as governor of Texas, Thies was considered a threat to the extremists' goals of Christianizing America because he is fair-minded, pragmatic, and respectful of the Establishment Clause in the First Amendment.

I interviewed Thies in Washington, D.C., on October 30, 2004, by which time he was no longer a White House insider. I was on my way to Greensboro from an interview in Philadelphia with John Dilulio, who had also been forced out of the FBCI. Due to scheduling problems, the only place we could meet was at Union Station before my train home left. He had just returned from a three-day, White House–sponsored, faith-based conference in Ohio. Ever the good soldier, it was no accident that Thies was in Ohio. According to Kenneth Blackwell, Ohio's secretary of state and a leading black strategist in the GOP, as well as a 2006 Republican candidate for governor there, the White House and the Republican National Committee were making "a tightly choreographed effort to become a stable majority party by targeting African-Americans and getting 30 percent of their vote in future presidential elections."[11] A tireless promoter of government support for faith-based social services, Thies was in a swing state one week before the presidential election to help black clergy earn government money and thereby to assist Blackwell toward that coveted 30 percent (Bush received 16 percent of the black vote in Ohio in 2004, up from the 9 percent he garnered in 2000).[12]

Over the din of arrival, departure, and delay announcements, I asked Dr. Thies whether those vibes I sensed regarding Jews were real or imagined: "As a Jewish man, I am nervous about the church-state stuff here. Is that a legitimate fear, or is that a 2,000-year-old fear?" He responded, "No, I think it is a legitimate fear, structurally and historically. I think it is justified."[13] He continued by informing me that he did not know many of the new people who had joined the FBCI since he left, hinting that they might have something to do with the increased radicalization.

Thies clearly stated that the extremists had prevailed over more moderate voices, but that they were not the only ones who ruled. Marvin Olasky, the right-wing ideologue, was not a Faith-Based Initiative staff member, but he held enough influence with the religious Right and President Bush to oust the moderates. Sounding somewhat slighted and apologetic, Thies explained to me that when he and other moderates started in the FBCI, there was no one there whom Jews needed to fear at all—but that that was not so today. "They weren't Marvin Olasky types," he added. Olasky may have done some good by bringing certain dimensions of human services to the public's attention, "but there is a side of that which all of us found very troubling," Thies said. While Thies noted the moderates had a Constitutional commitment to equal treatment, he emphasized that Olasky wanted the "right religious groups involved. Then everything would be okay. That is the way they have tried to do it."[14]

As I have said before, this book is not a critique of the religious Right. It is a critique about what happens when a policy relies on the construction of partnerships between different levels of government and the religious community and is guided by the supernatural. Dilulio was wrong. These were not "Mayberry Machiavellians," they were Machiavellians pure and simple, and Thies wasn't one of them. Unlike Dorothy who spun in a dream from Kansas to Oz, the Faith-Based Initiative is a modern-day Machiavellian reality. Had I only been smart enough to reread *The Prince*, I may not have been standing on my head trying to make sense of the rhetoric and actions of this initiative.

Everyone admits how praiseworthy it is in a prince to keep faith, and to live with integrity and not with craft. Nevertheless our experience has been that those princes who have done great things have held good faith of little account, and have known how to circumvent the intellect of men by craft, and in the end have overcome those who have relied on their word.[15]

CHAPTER 8

The Reverend
and the Professor

I have been both confident and irritated throughout this book. My irritation stems from compassionate conservatives forcing an unsuspecting public to discuss poverty and its solutions in simple religious terms. The case study that follows in the next three chapters explores a different reality, one shielded from the public by a skilled message machine and one in which I am most confident: service and program development. Nine years in the making, the story that follows grew from sober discussions, clear goals, and comprehensive planning.

In 1997, the Rev. Odell Cleveland and I met. At that time, the Republicans controlled both chambers of Congress, Bill Clinton's welfare reform had passed, Charitable Choice was a reality but had not yet taken hold, the economy was thriving, and the country sensed that religious efforts could mend any holes in the social safety net.

Even before then, I was trying to raise another issue into the discourse. In June 1995, I wrote an editorial for the *Greensboro News and Record* (see appendix D) that remains as relevant today as it was then. The tone of the piece was sober and straightforward, with the essence immediately identified through the first line, "Politicians want the religious community to expand its role as social service provider," followed by the caveat, "That may not be realistic." To reinforce the quintessential meaning, I concluded: "Some sober discussion, coupled with comprehensive community planning, keeping in sight a clear goal for developing strong and fair partnerships among public, private, and religious organizations, is a first step in reducing the complexity and preventing simple-mindedness."

Not too long after that editorial appeared, Reverend Cleveland and I became acquainted while playing basketball at Guilford College in mid-1996. It was an open game with people of all ages playing. On some days, we athletes pumped more energy into the political discussion in the men's locker room before and after the game than we exerted on the basketball court. Some of the most profound and often heated policy and social service issues guided the conversations in the locker room.

That locker room is where I held my first conversation with Odell, a businessman who was studying to become a minister at the time. When we met on the basketball court that day more than nine years ago, he was a young man of 37 and a former college basketball player. When he grew tired of the constant arguing in the young man's game, he started playing with us older folks. He associated well with players in either game, acting as the elder statesman and arbitrator in the young men's game and as cheerleader in the older folks' game. One of Odell's qualities I admire most is his ability to work with everyone—within the mainline white social service establishment, with welfare recipients and their families, and with churches in the African American community. This talent has earned him and his program much recognition in Greensboro and throughout the state and the nation. His ability to link different worlds—be it in basketball or faith-based social service in a diverse community—is a gift hard to come by; he has taught me a great deal.

Odell made a transition both on the basketball court and in life. Statistically speaking, he should not even have made it to college, let alone earned a degree in management in 1984 and a master's degree in theology in 1997. He was one of four children who lived with his divorced mother. In 1968, when his mother was 25, she had a stroke; after that, the family barely survived off her monthly $240 disability check. According to Odell, in those days, the court system did not insist upon child support from fathers.

In college, Odell's coaches wanted him to major in leisure studies to ensure that his grades would be adequate to maintain his sports eligibility. In other words, he was a "notch" in the career belt of some college coach and entertainer. As he remarked at a recent speech, he did not know he was providing entertainment to youngsters "who painted their faces" school colors and rooted loudly for their squad. However, Odell is a true scholar-athlete who understands that winning—be it in life, sports, or program development—requires preparation, implementation, and evaluation. Instead of leisure studies, he chose a business major. Reality arrived four years later:

> I realized I had no more basketball eligibility, no NBA contract, and a year and a half of academic requirements left to graduate. I quickly became a man. I returned to school by way of guaranteed student loans, a work-study job, an academic scholarship, a 1:30 A.M. to 6:30 A.M. job at UPS unloading trucks, and a summer job at a basketball camp. My grades suffered because sometimes I was so tired from working and studying that I dozed off in class.[1]

Eighteen months later, Odell earned his business degree and embarked on a very successful career as the top sales representative for a large trucking firm. But Odell envisioned himself living his life devoted to helping the less fortunate, and so he decided to move into a community ministry that helps women and families and much more. As it turned out, he chose the most important social policy issue in sixty years on which to hang his new hat, yet he would be the first to admit that he knew very little about welfare, welfare reform, social service delivery, or the people who receive services. His lack of knowledge was only temporary, though, for he quickly became very well informed.

While Odell and I had first become acquaintances at the basketball games, we did not develop a lasting relationship until the day I inquired about the subject of his master's thesis. He told me its title: "Some Black Churches' Response to the 1996 Welfare Reform Bill." This struck a chord, because since the early 1980s, I had increasingly focused my attention and work on community groups and the role the religious community plays in service development. My interest intensified because the government budget cuts caused more voluntary service provision and a corresponding reconfiguration of relationships in the service delivery systems locally among public, private, and sectarian service providers.

Back in 1976, while Odell was focusing his energies on becoming a high school basketball star in Charleston, South Carolina, I was organizing a town meeting on welfare reform in Utica, New York, as part of President Jimmy Carter's attempts to repair the welfare system. The Carter team visited Albany, and our community practice class from Syracuse University attended the meeting. We were so disgruntled with the way it was handled that we organized a "real" town meeting, and with some old-fashioned persuasion, the Carter entourage returned to upstate New York. Ever since that town meeting, I have been studying social welfare policy and working with local organizations and churches regarding this issue.

Our locker room chats evolved into a long-term relationship, and Odell asked me if I would work with his church in developing a nonprofit organization. Program development being one of my specialties, I told him I would be honored, thinking to myself how fortunate I was to be invited inside a church's efforts to be a community servant. I also agreed because I believed Odell was ready to entertain a more systemic way of looking at the complexities of welfare and developing an organization to address those complexities in changing times. One of the intricacies was how to balance Odell's religious fervor against community social service realities.

We spent part of almost every day in 1997 planning this new organization, the Welfare Reform Liaison Project (WRLP), which developed in response to the Personal Responsibility and Work Opportunity Omnibus Reconciliation Act of 1996, the welfare reform legislation that not only ended welfare as we knew it but also allowed direct funding of churches through Section 104, a provision called Charitable Choice. The nonprofit corporation was established both to help welfare recipients find and maintain employment and to work with small African American churches as they increase their capacity to assist people in need. Odell became the WRLP's first director.

Discussions between us over time have been intertwined with Odell's vision about how his church might implement a program to help poor women make a genuine leap into successful and sustained employment, as well as a large and changing set of local economic factors that broadened the agency's focus from welfare-to-work to workforce development. To this day, there remains the underlying concern of how a community-oriented black church could spawn and sustain a community ministry by building a strong, nonprofit organization that was both separate from and tied to the church.

We both have been very concerned how this evolving organization could not only become a magnet that attracted public and private stakeholders from the mainline white social service and philanthropic community but also sustain their high regard while joining forces with Greensboro's small and large African American churches and the white religious community, too. The WRLP became the nation's first and, at this writing, only faith-based Community Service Block Grant designee, otherwise known as the Community Action Program (CAP), a federal program that originated from the Johnson administration's War on Poverty initiatives in the 1960s. Today 1,100 CAP agencies exist nationwide, all but one secular.

While national discussion and the ideas of the political and religious Right were shaping the public discourse locally,[2] even to the point of shaping some of Odell's viewpoints, something else very important was taking place. The increasing service demands on churches beginning in earnest in the Reagan era[3] affected Mt. Zion Baptist Church of Greensboro to the point that Minister Cleveland and his senior pastor recognized the "new welfare reform" of 1996 would turn their congregation, especially its Emergency Assistance Program (EAP), into a multiservice but isolated social service agency if they did not somehow respond.

The growth of poverty and the problems facing the elderly and working poor from the Reagan and Bush Sr. years, straight through the prosperous economy of the Clinton years, had already affected local services and was causing stress for Mt. Zion. I strongly encouraged Odell and Bishop George W. Brooks, the leader of Mt. Zion, to arrange a professional evaluation of their EAP so they could decide their course of action based upon facts.

In November 1998, the Carolina Evaluation Center issued its report.[4] Among its key findings, the Center's director noted that, due to cutbacks in state and federal programs from 1988 to 1997, the nine years when the church kept statistics, Minister Cleveland's church had distributed $379,000 to help people with food, rent, transportation, prescription drugs, child care, and the like. This figure merely shows the cash outlay and did not take into account the numerous onsite programs the church offered nor the countless hours volunteers spent to administer such programs. Surprisingly, 75 percent of the people who received help were *not* members of Mt. Zion Church. Even more surprising was the large expenditures of cash during 1996, 1997, and five months into 1998.

The comments of the evaluator, Dr. Fasih Ahmed, illustrate what was happening with Mt. Zion's Emergency Assistance Program:

It is noteworthy that a comprehensive and detailed accounting system is maintained for the EAP, not typical of most programs managed by volunteers. This evaluator was pleasantly surprised when resource input data for the last three years was quickly retrieved in the format required by him. As Figure 2 shows direct emergency assistance of $80,050 and $84,150 was provided in 1996 and 1997 respectively, an annual increase of about 5%. Data for the first five months of 1998 indicates that if monthly average is maintained, the projected amount of assistance for the current year would be around $97,000, which may reflect an increase of about 15% over last year. This trend of steady increase in the need for emergency assistance portends increasing strain on the church's resources to sustain the program. On the average EAP assists around 270 persons every year, and about 70% of recipients are not members of the church, which reflects relatively high level of accessibility to the program.[5]

Data confirmed what the leadership of Mt. Zion knew from practical experience; therefore, church leaders chose to develop a nonprofit corporation to handle systematically and with community resources what might have become an exponential demand on its church. After all, even without any persuasion from the religious community, the first report of the Work First Planning Committee (the new title for welfare reform) of Guilford County (where Mt. Zion is located) included recruitment of the "faith community" to help with clothing for job searches and employment. By 1998, "Achieve Work First Goals," the county plan developed in 1997 for submission to the state in 1998, called for closer ties with the religious community and took interest in the national discussion for church-based mentoring in job searching:

> Guilford County's plan's second priority, recommendation in category #3 on page 16—Staying Off Welfare After Going To Work—seeks to "Recruit civic organizations, *faith communities*, and service organizations to serve as mentors to Work First [North Carolina's welfare program] participants.[6]

Public officials simply bought into the political discourse of the time and planned to rely increasingly upon the faith community, even though only one minister was on the eighteen-member community planning committee. In reality, not until the late spring of 2001 did the Guilford County Department of Social Services solicit a proposal for a needs assessment to determine how it could work effectively with the faith community. Since there was little effort to integrate the faith community systematically into a wider service initiative, the time was right for Odell's agency to carve out a niche that would make it a limited but essential partner in the wider community efforts to help address issues of poverty.

As a social work professor with a community education orientation involved in one of the most profound service changes in years, I had a simple mission: to help a community institution address an important social problem in a well-planned and honest way. My training in community organization twenty-five years ago was grounded in the idea that the organizer helped communities, and organizations build the capacity to help themselves. My challenge with Odell was taming his exuberance, commitment, and concern so I could restrain him long enough to develop strategies.

His challenge with me was to endure my intransigence on the require-ment that everything be planned before being implemented. He knew this trait of mine intuitively from business and basketball, but his understand-ing of what needed to occur to develop a spin-off nonprofit organization and claim a position in the local service system did not match his zeal to take action. How I differ from many proponents of the Faith-Based Initia-tive is that I insisted that Odell's organization be legally independent of his church. The Charitable Choice provision of the 1996 welfare legisla-tion made it easier for efforts like Odell's to receive federal money yet still to remain part of the legal church body, but I recommended that he legally split from the church for practical reasons, not ideological ones.

Like many U.S. communities, resources in Greensboro come from many streams. The 1998 evaluation of Mt. Zion's EAP captured the essence of the national legal debate that is still raging in the faith-based circles and that I insisted *had to cease* for practical reasons if this agency were ever to become a "bigger than life" leader in the community:

> An important aspect of the program process is the spiritual ministry. It should be noted that emergency assistance is provided irrespective of denom-inational or religious affiliation, though most of the applicants observed by this evaluator were protestant Christians. After the initial assessment of need and determination of assistance, the interviewing committee typically explores the applicant's spiritual feelings and religious inclinations. It was observed that the interviewing committee brought up spiritual matters always after informing the applicant about decision regarding assistance. As such, there is no link between spiritual counseling and decision about assis-tance. However, since the interview often involves discussion about the cli-ent's overall life situation, talking about their spirituality and religious beliefs is appropriate and warranted by the occasion. This evaluator noted that most clients were open to exploring their spirituality and found comfort in rein-forcement of their faith in the Providence.[7]

Since the rules of the local social service funding game—at least in Greensboro—start and end with accountability, I wanted to make sure no avenues that led to funding or other resources were closed. Some major community foundations and several local philanthropists do not typically contribute to churches, but do not hesitate to donate to a spin-off non-profit emerging from a church. Odell Cleveland is one of the most reli-gious people I have ever met. Yet, once he understood that he either had to spread the Good News of Jesus Christ and freeze out funders who could help the population he served or make his faith demonstrable through its good works by including the whole community of funders, he recognized the practicality of my theory and chose faith-works. He has not and does not now conduct the spiritual counseling in which Mt. Zion's EAP engaged.

However, Odell's new organization, the Welfare Reform Liaison Proj-ect, had to be permanently related to Mt. Zion for legitimacy in the white community's mind and for spirituality in the black community's mind, so it would be perceived as an African American organization, which it was and still is. Such stipulations proved important in Greensboro's community politics. The WRLP also required a connection to Mt. Zion's expansive set of congregational ministries. So the church provided it with resources, a rent-free building, and Odell's salary even though it would become a separate nonprofit. It needed nonprofit venture capital from the inception. The church's contribution of space and money for salaries initially nurtured this startup organization. Having a genuine partner from the beginning strengthened the perception and "real position" in its race for funds in this community. Thus, in chapter 2 and other pages where I pointed out that the president's Faith-Based Initiative's community intervention strategy was actually in quest of unincorporated organizations and churches, I simply became exasperated, knowing that implementation without a plan could not work in this community nor anywhere else.

I spent an entire year planning with an incredibly bright, energetic, and talented visionary who benefited from the backing of a powerful community church. Almost a year passed by as he assembled a board of directors, incorporated the WRLP, and generated enough enthusiasm to gain acceptance from the rest of the community. How would the smaller upstarts, the targets of the Bush Faith-Based Initiative, succeed with none of the resources Odell had and merely a smidgeon of outside help? Would the administration abandon them if budgets tightened or they did not succeed?

Not only did Odell accept a crash course in building a nonprofit organization, but he also solicited ones in welfare politics, social services in the community, and a home-study, brush-up course in program planning, budgeting, and development as it applied to human services. With these requirements satisfied, he progressed while learning the skills of legitimizing his efforts by building community relations in the least obtrusive manner. Such a task is not really as difficult as it may sound. We worked together regularly, with me learning as much as I could about what his church hoped to accomplish; both of us studied the new welfare reform, and together, like two well-schooled basketball players, we prepared a defined, organizational game plan.

Minister Cleveland brought none of the battle scars from years in the social service trenches to the planning process. He was a businessman and a trucking expert. If the conservative Right is correct about anything, it is that the system is in disarray; nonetheless, much of the disorder has been its own doing. Carpe diem; a wonderful opportunity exists to plan appropriately and to rid the uncertainty. The public system of services was and still is confused, and poor women, children, the mentally ill, the elderly, displaced workers, and others are unnecessarily being hurt. Consequently, good planning and community education to set the record straight about the plight of the poor is the root of the WRLP's vision.

The faith community is expected to help, but in this perplexity, it must understand that organizations with resources can now sit at the table and shape the moral environment of the community because in the real world of social service politics, those with resources make the rules. Odell's zeal, business acumen, and basketball prowess were the assets he needed for me to collaborate with him, and together, in very different ways, we began to advance his organization and community to the next stage of development in understanding where it ought to position itself in a new millennium. In basketball, business, program development, and life, the requirements for success rest solidly on the principle of preparation. As a former college basketball star, Odell knew that the big games were won after hours of preparation. *No real* community strategy exists in President Bush's Faith-Based Initiative. If it were not such a serious matter, his lack of vision would be considered humorous.

In the nine-plus years since that day we engaged in the locker room, many changes have occurred both in the national policy arena—particularly with President Bush's establishment of the White House Office of Faith-Based and Community Initiatives—and at the programmatic level with the WRLP. One fixation has remained constant; Reverend Cleveland and I still play ball together and commiserate daily about basketball, family, social policy, and the practical matters facing both the thriving and survival of his organization. We are friends; yet, I frequently feel like a yo-yo as I communicate with him by cell phone, work with his agency, return to the university for other classes, leave again to work with his staff and my student interns there, and then attend a faculty meeting. All of these activities are combined with reciprocating calls. This routine is ever present, and I cannot imagine experiencing a better situation.

CHAPTER 9

From Church to Community Nonprofit

It seems like only yesterday that I stood in the locker room at Guilford College and made the commitment to work with Odell Cleveland. I knew he was a good basketball player, and I also was aware he was a businessman studying to become a minister. Living in the South, where religion is so influential, his career change did not surprise me. Many of my students, regardless of race, are quite religious and undisturbed about lacing their analysis with religious metaphors. I view such communication as part of this culture, and communication with God layers my soul as well. My grandmother lived upstairs over my father's store, where I worked throughout grade school and high school, and she spoke to and about God regularly, shamelessly, and with such ease.

When Odell requested my help to achieve his deep and soul-felt vision, developing a program that joined the resources of the religious community with a broad-based training effort to support women progressing from welfare to work, I did not consider the religious language this "black Baptist born-again Christian" used to be threatening. In a strange way, it reminded me of my grandmother's utterances and therefore intrigued me. In fact, I learned to understand such words better than I did before working with him.

In those early days, we spoke about program development and God's purpose for both him and me. Of course, the discussions were frequently tied to Christ references. We were not really talking about theoretical issues of fire and brimstone in some religion course, although we leveled with each other where we stood regarding God, time, and space. For us, the issues *always* returned to my unyielding guideline: *What would work best in the community?*

It was then my eighteenth year in the South. Such compromise was refreshing and not completely out of the ordinary. Section 104 of the welfare reform legislation of 1996, called Charitable Choice, allowed churches to solicit government money, which they still do too slowly. On the ground, where services are delivered, the atmosphere was one of urgency, so much so that many churches felt a pervasive pressure to take some form of action.

I was on research leave in 1997 and had much going on. I was beginning to investigate and write my book *A Limited Partnership* and was also increasingly involved with individuals from Yale University's Program on Non-Profit Organizations (PONPO). PONPO subcontracted with me to study how the shift toward using more religious organizations in welfare provision was unfolding in North Carolina. I found it invigorating to work on a book about a community's response to welfare reform and the religious community's role, especially since it involved me nationally. If I were not already a believer, I would have become one, because there was such continuity between my earlier life and my present activities.

There I was, one of a handful of academics who was involved at the community level with President Carter's welfare reform. I also had continuing research experience about the meaning of the expanded involvement of the religious community regarding social service provision as far back as the Reagan years. Charitable Choice made it easier for government to fund local religious congregations. Strategists assumed that governmental assistance to churches would strengthen the safety net for women who could no longer receive welfare because of a new time limit for receiving aid. This speculation, however, was not a good one because they did not understand local practicalities.

By 1997, I had won my second grant from the Lilly Endowment, allowing me time to synthesize my years of community research and write my book, in which I supplemented what I had determined from the 1992–1995 study of how agencies in Greensboro's system of services planned for, implemented, and evaluated the use of religious resources. Then Yale extended a financial hand to broaden my study statewide and to keep me associated with scholars nationwide who were analyzing the complex dimensions of the religious community's involvement in community life. Just when I thought I could not take on any more relevant and meaningful academic undertakings, I received an invitation to visit the depths of a man's personal journey—one that went straight through a local black church's effort to develop a program responding directly to Bill Clinton's change of welfare as we knew it.

Odell came to my residence almost every day, because that is where I always was, writing. In some of our spiritual drifting, I would comment that even though I believe in free will and that I followed my nose with most of the matters that led to our working together, it surely felt like it was more than luck for us to be collaborating—as odd a couple as we were.

Those early years can be characterized as two men abuzz with documents and plans, strategizing about program development, grant proposals, and more. I became the archivist for the Welfare Reform Liaison Project (WRLP), keeping every document Odell entrusted to me. Yet, underneath the surface, we were engaged in a partnership based on a four-point credo of trust. The first four points were:

1. We do not know why we are together, but it must be for a reason.
2. Whatever our differences, we both have this large and shared concern for the plight of poor women and children.
3. I am not sure I like you, but I will listen and learn as much as I can from you while we are together.
4. Even though we may not understand each other, we will demonstrate mutual respect until something happens to steer us away.

These points formed the basis of trust needed for us to accomplish our goals on a daily basis in the community.

That second point was the "tester" between us. He was the top salesperson in a large trucking firm and liked to close deals swiftly, surpassing his quota rapidly. Similarly, he wanted this program in full operation before he laid the foundation for its success. Despite our shared interest in helping women and children, however, I was not going to progress impulsively without careful consideration of the various possibilities.

Odell seemed to keep waiting for me to do "something wrong" so he could call me on it and confirm what he never said directly: that he did not trust me, either. I told him repeatedly, showing him writings that dated back to the early 1980s, that I am not part of this effort simply because of him. He was just giving me the chance to work on behalf of the voiceless who have been bullied for the political ends of conservatives, many of whom never shook the hand of any poor people but seemed to know everything about their royal character and assumed as conservatives that they were spiritual advisors. Let me be clear: Reverend Cleveland is no liberal. But neither is he a conservative in the traditional sense; he is one of the most independent, creative, and stubborn thinkers I have ever met. However, his tenacity often comes from his assumption that we mortals do not envision as far ahead as he does. We earthbound humans are like drivers on a dark road who use low beams. I have learned never to judge him for a seemingly off-the-wall idea nor for his inflexibility in holding on to or defending it. He usually has his high beams on and can see much farther than me.

In 1997, he was frenzied about starting this program, but I lacked his eagerness. I told him again and again: "I am the turtle in the race, not the rabbit. This race is about helping women and children, and the legitimacy of an important black church in Greensboro is on the line. Let's not blow it. The stakes are too high." We did the "one, two, three, four" timidly with each other, and he did the "one, two three, four" eagerly but cautiously in the community. He did not know if he trusted me, and I was not sure if I trusted him. The community certainly did not know him well enough to trust him, although as a representative of Mt. Zion Baptist Church, he did have clout.

Unquestionably, he did not know whom to trust in the community. He had to perform double duty, gaining my trust and earning the same from the community. As noted in chapter 8, given the emergency assistance offered by Mt. Zion, any leap in requests because of the new-fangled welfare reform warranted a new response from the church. Therefore, the WRLP would have to become a separate legal corporation and would be different from being a simple ministry of the church.

A significant number of the approximately two thousand community development corporations were given birth by or are intimately tied to African American churches. The new WRLP was, and still is, closely associated with Mt. Zion Baptist Church, but not in the same financial and legal manner it was before it became a separate organization. Odell Cleveland initially received his salary from church funds as part of his ministerial duties. Mt. Zion Baptist Church also provided space and office equipment as part of a startup package, a luxury that smaller church-based ministries do not enjoy.

The architects of the faith-based initiative used intermediaries through the Compassion Capital Fund to disburse small amounts of money to "under the radar" groups. I noted in chapter 2 that a Raleigh, North Carolina–based for-profit organization then named Mission Tree received a $1.5 million Compassion Capital grant on its way to becoming an intermediary. Figure 9.1 is the text of an advertisement that appeared in the *Greensboro News and Record* on January 18, 2005. It represents the national efforts to gain buy-in locally by using a statewide disbursement process. The advertisement, from CJH Educational Grant Services, solicits for "unincorporated groups," which actually means churches.

What I want to clarify is that four years after the Bush administration's White House Office of Faith-Based and Community Initiatives was launched, its buy-in strategy consisted of placing an advertisement in a

---

Grants to Faith- and Community-Based Groups

CJH Educational Grant Services, Inc. (CJH) will soon be requesting applications from faith- and community-based nonprofit and unincorporated groups seeking funds to improve their organizational capacity and infrastructure. Funds are available to eligible groups in North Carolina and Pittsylvania County, Virginia, that have not previously received federal funds and are serving high need populations, such as the elderly, at-risk children, or prisoners. The Compassion Capital Fund Demonstration Program is annually awarded to CJH by the U.S. Department of Health and Human Services. Thirty sub-grants will be awarded with funding levels up to $20,000 per agency.

A public bidder's conference (Technical Assistance workshops) is scheduled at the Sheraton Four Seasons, January 25, 10 AM–1 PM, to provide more detail on the application process.

Figure 9.1. Advertisement from a Compassion Capital Grant Intermediary Seeking Awardees

local newspaper and conducting a three-hour workshop on how to raise a few dollars. The intervention strategy in the advertisement included no community-building aspects, and "unincorporated groups seeking funds" was merely a code for churches.

In order to understand the connection between this strategy of simply trying to disperse money to some small churches and the faith-based policy itself, it is important to revisit chapter 6, where Figure 6.1 had five bullets from "Unlevel Playing Field," the government's manifesto that outlined the civil rights violations perpetrated against small churches. Two of the most relevant bullets are listed below because this advertisement indirectly fixes the perceived injustices of:

- Burdening small organizations with cumbersome regulations and requirements
- Imposing anti-competitive mandates on some programs, such as requiring applicants to demonstrate support from government agencies or others that might also be competing for the same funds

I must restate a point I have made throughout this book: a set of standards at the community level exist, but the president's architects are still attempting to rewrite them instead of work with them because they have a poor understanding of how operations run locally. This sad revision of the civil rights concept is a stratagem for disseminating money to Christ-centered churches without being exposed. Framing these architects' self-defined problems in civil rights language casts opponents unjustly into the roles of secular extremists, antireligious fanatics, and dissenters against small black churches, where a good portion of the money is directed. Thus, one is a racist by default if he disagrees—and I do. And as Odell once said to me when I was explaining this strategy, "Wine [as he calls me], if you are racist, I am white."

When one enters the surreal world of the Washington language war, it is easy to spend so much time fending off bizarre claims that one loses sight of reality. While opponents are busy screaming, "No, you don't have it correct," the proponents are reshaping the reality. In the case of the Faith-Based Initiative, the civil rights language just does not bear credence, nor does it accomplish anything whatsoever to illuminate the *local reality* in service development. Again, if this case were not so real, so sinful, and so characteristic of the lack of a cogent intervention design, it would be a circus extravaganza. I become agitated whenever I reflect upon what has happened. Since the WRLP did not become incorporated until 1998, during all of 1997, it was one of those "unincorporated groups" that intermediaries like the ones CJH Educational Grant Services of Raleigh was targeting.

However, unlike those small organizations besieged by the Faith-Based Initiative, Odell had a mentor who supported him at no cost. If the entities the president's initiative was targeting were to succeed in a way that their results could be measured, they would have had to be burdened, the way I burdened him, with the first of many cumbersome but fundamental requirements of basic organizational development—obtaining nonprofit status so that the organization could legally and *culturally* solicit and collect charitable gifts from everywhere. As I already mentioned, some foundations, businesses, and local governments will not donate money to churches, not necessarily because they are forbidden to do so by law but because part of their donation history has shown no generosity to churches. It is unlikely that the administration will change this matter significantly through the bully pulpit or by nudging the private sector to provide more funds to these unincorporated groups.

I recognized that the survival and eventual thriving of the WRLP in the real world depended upon its obtaining nonprofit status. A requirement for even applying for its first grant from the local United Way was that an applicant have 501(c)(3) nonprofit organizational status. Ironically, this stipulation was not a government rule, a government mandate, a requirement, or burden; rather, it was the rule of the United Way, itself a nonprofit organization, which is a steward of people's voluntary gifts to solve a range of problems. Before Reverend Cleveland sought donations from the community, he clearly needed to plan for the formation of a board of directors and incorporation. He could then proceed to apply for 501(c)(3) nonprofit status for the WRLP. However, selecting a board of people who know what they are doing is not an easy task. Consequently, we spent much of the early planning time developing a board, acquiring commitments from people to serve, setting up different committees, forecasting a budget, and, most of all, becoming increasingly visible in the community. Odell was tireless.

Figure 9.2 illustrates the minutes from the first board meeting and represents hours of meetings to gain commitments and sell the program idea to people who had the expertise and energy to serve. I have conducted board retreats for many organizations over the years, but as the bottom line of the minutes shows, I supervised a retreat for this board before the agency ever saw its first clients—at its second meeting. Usually, I find myself working with an organization after it has fired off its first series of program rounds and is helping its constituents learn how to aim. This organization initiated action appropriately, contrary to the way the Bush administration has pushed others. On April 28, 1998, the WRLP was informed that it had received nonprofit status.

I informed Odell that his success depended upon the support and trust of the broader community in the local culture of services. Figure 9.3 shows selected portions of a May 4, 1998, memo from Minister Cleveland (he was yet to be ordained), chronicling completed and upcoming appointments in the community from April 15 through May 3, 1998.

Figure 9.4 reintroduces the model of the community system I used in chapter 2. The dots on the illustration represent the parts of the system with which Odell had met or intended to meet. In three weeks, he had conducted thirty meetings and started on the long and successful road of accomplishing what neither the North Carolina intermediary nor the Faith Based Initiative's entire intervention strategy has yet to accomplish: *buy-in*.

February 24, 1998

The meeting opened with Prayer by Reverend George W. Brooks.

Minister Odell Cleveland welcomed everyone to the 1st meeting of the Welfare Liaison Project and asked everyone to introduce himself to the group and tell why they were interested in serving on the Board.

Mr. Cleveland charged us to remember that this program is about women and children.

Vision of the Program: Pastor Brooks
Most programs currently in assistance are stopgap programs. It is important for us to come together collectively to see what we can do because we have been remiss in our duties to deal with the issues surrounding welfare. He compared it to the story of Cain and Abel, "Am I My Brother's Keeper?"

Committee Assignments
There are three basic committees at this time: Policy, Budget, and Program. All three committees interact with each other.

Policy: This committee will be responsible for shaping and developing an overall plan that embraces the general goals and acceptable procedures of the Welfare Reform Liaison Project.

Budget: This committee will be responsible for developing accounting procedures, gathering information from the program committee, determining program cost, and planning short-term grants and long-term endowment for the Welfare Reform Liaison Project.

Program: This committee will be responsible for overseeing the development, implementation, and evaluation of an effective service delivery system.

Everyone was asked to sign up for a committee.

Program Director
Pastor Brooks offered up the recommendation that as opposed to spending time and effort on searching for a Program Director that we select Odell Cleveland as the Director. There was consensus among the group. Mr. Cleveland will discuss the issue with his family and inform us of his decision.

Next Meeting
Dr. Bob Wineburg, Professor in the Department of Social Work at UNC-Greensboro, will be the speaker at the April 6, 1998 meeting.

Figure 9.2. Highlights of the First Board Meeting of the Welfare Reform Liaison Project

---

WELFARE REFORM LIAISON PROJECT
MEMORANDUM

TO: Welfare Reform Liaison Project Members
FROM: Odell Cleveland

DATE: May 4, 1998
SUBJECT: WELFARE REFORM LIAISON

PROJECT PROGRAM UPDATES
Below is a list of organizations and leaders that I've already met with as well as scheduled appointments for the week of May 3rd.

Completed Tasks and Appointments; 4/15 Work First-Barbara Israel, 4/20 DSS-Joyce Lewis & Phyllis Hayes, 4/22 Chavis Lifelong Learning Library-Lou Sua, 4/24 Carolina Evaluation Research Center-Dr. Ahmed, 4/24 Dr. Bob Wineburg, 4/25 operated the Welfare Reform Liaison Project's booth (along with my wife) and handed out information to fifty prospective volunteers during Mount Zion's ministry day, 4/26 Social Worker-Rufus Stanley, 4/27 Pastor Brooks, 4/29 Black Child Development-June Valdes, 4/30 Greensboro Housing Authority-Tina Akers, and 4/30 First Presbyterian-Mo Sellers.

Scheduled Appointments; 5/1 Pathways-Mark Sumerford & Cathy Osborn, 5/1 North Carolina A&T (Vice-chancellor For Research)-Dr. Earnestine Psalmonds, 5/1 Faith Action- Mark Sills, 5/1 Trinity A.M.E. Zion-Pastor Frencher, 5/1 Dr. Bob Wineburg, 5/1 U.S. Dept. of Housing and Urban Development (N.C. Sr. Community Builder)-James Blackman, 5/1 Mother Murphy Labs-Marty Golds, 5/4 Women's Resource Center-Marilyn Franklin, 5/5 Urban Ministry-Mike Aiken, 5/5 Project Independence-Ann Morelli, 5/5 Evangle Fellowship-Joy Thompson, 5/6 Dr. Ahmed & Miheal Mackey, 5/6 Community Network-Marilyn Franklin, 5/7 United Way-Antonia Monk Reaves, 5/8 Catholic Social Services-(Parish Area Coordinator) Bridget Brown Johnson.

Unscheduled Appointments; Goodwill Industries-Clinton Thomas, New Zion Missionary Baptist Church-Rev. William Wright, and HOUSING AUTHORITY RESIDENTS.

Figure 9.3. Memorandum of WRLP Activities, April–May 1998

Later, in May 1998, the WRLP applied for its first grant, with the United Way. Figure 9.5 lists the criteria the United Way used to weigh the merits of the many applications it receives. The seventh criterion notes that *coordination* with other agencies is a factor to be considered in making final decisions. The local United Way standard would seem to burden both small churches and the strategists in Washington who want to remove the imagined shackles from these church programs and agencies and to end

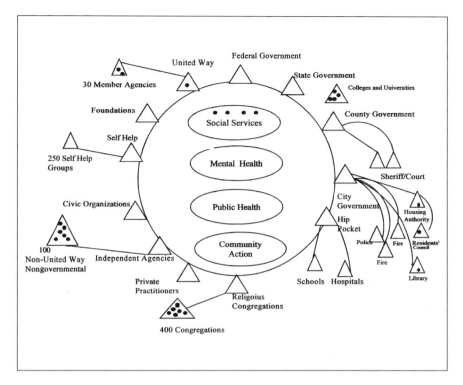

Figure 9.4. Linkages between WRLP and the Community System, April–May 1998

anticompetitive mandates through coordination. Parties who coordinate do not compete. For what possible reason would the new civil rights protectors be against coordination with other agencies and organizations, serving similar needs and populations, when it is a major factor in considering how local *nongovernmental funds* are disbursed at least in one community?

First, these so-called defenders are simply naïve in regard to understanding the community dynamics. Their strategy actually becomes anticonservative, considering the hundreds of millions of dollars that have been redirected to these small organizations; they have neglected to teach members of these groups how to play the sophisticated game locally. Second, anything that hints of "collectivism" (working together) is an anticompetitive poison in the conservatives' approach. As a result, when they assigned their strategists to find data that may look like devilishly imposed barriers on the civil rights of small churches—who realistically do not have the capacity to offer services at the same level of others in the system at the local level—the notion of coordination became a civil rights barrier and a target of elimination. As a consequence, strategists have changed the government from the "enemy" to the champion of civil rights. The same

The following factors, among others, will be considered in making
funding decisions:
1. Specific plans for measuring the impact
2. Efficient use of funding and other resources
3. Clear goals and objectives
4. Clear plans for delivery of services
5. Service to under-served or needy populations
6. Innovation
7. Coordination with other agencies and organizations serving similar
   needs and populations
8. Use of volunteer services
9. Planning for self-sufficiency
10. Lack of alternative funding

Figure 9.5. United Way Grant Criteria, 1998

situation existed when the administration played games with the Jews.
Make something out of nothing long enough, and it becomes something. Thankfully, a different interpretation of reality took place in my
community, or even I may have started praising compassionate conservatives as liberators of the small churches.

Why would coordination be a criterion for United Way funding, especially since the United Way is the charitable arm of the community's
1,600 businesses? Because the nature of the system does not lend itself to
"one-stop shopping" to solve or manage problems. The next-best option
is to know the people in the agencies and organizations in advance, so
organizations do not waste time and money, ending up with headaches
and heartaches trying to find help in the middle of emergencies.

Imagine that a consumer has a shopping basket filled with food from
each of the four major food groups and goes to pay. In one line, the cash-
ier pulls items from only one food group out of the cart. In order to pur-
chase the other items, the purchaser must move to other checkout lines
that ring up products from each of the other food groups. This system is
obviously ridiculous, time-consuming, and inefficient and would never be
tolerated by supermarket customers, but that procedure demonstrates how
social services operate in the local system. For example, if a child is a vic-
tim of incest, at minimum, five services become involved—and they are
not even housed under one roof. Representatives from child protection
and mental health services, the hospital, the police, and the courts each
have a stake in this matter.

I sent Odell on a mission to meet the people who comprise sectors with
which his efforts would eventually interface: the Department of Social
Services, Greensboro Urban Ministry, church congregants, the United
Way, United Way agencies, universities, foundations, businesspeople, the
Housing Authority, and so forth. Not only would he eventually be working with the individuals in all of these sectors, but he would also need
their support to guarantee legitimacy and to acquire funding.

In June 1998, the United Way awarded the Welfare Reform Liaison Project its first grant, $25,000. Though it was not a government grant, the organization that made the grant considered its funding decision based on solid program plans, which testifies to the reality of the burdens *small and large agencies alike* in the community must endure. Such a reality did not develop from some desire to *deny any agency anything*; it grew from simple principles of *accountability and stewardship.* In no way did the current intervention strategy of the Bush Faith-Based Initiative have the basis or savvy to create successful methods for assisting small churches in playing the game of local, organizational development, nor did it use the rules most of the community systems exercise in the thousands of cities, counties, and townships in our country. They could have allotted that money differently by both preparing the little organizations they tout so highly to play the sophisticated game of program development and helping local systems of services reconceptualize new methods of delivery appropriate for this millennium. Such methods would need to be underscored with a thoughtful integration plan for churches in ways that do no harm to themselves, those individuals in need, and other agencies in the system. From my viewpoint, whining about civil rights violations is a weak but nevertheless dangerous whimper.

Appendix E shows the award letter from the United Way to the WRLP. It is important to show what this community's standards are for spending money raised from private sources. This example takes place in the South, but there are 1,200 United Ways in the United States, and each one raises money from the private sector and uses standard practices of business to ensure the highest level of stewardship over the public's money.

CHAPTER 10

The Rest of the Story

The Welfare Reform Liaison Project's first grant request was made to the United Way's Faith Intervention and Connections Program in 1998. It proposed to conduct a needs assessment to determine if small black churches would refer people to a welfare-to-work training program that supplemented work experience with its classroom efforts. The idea behind the needs assessment was for him to survey the community's church leaders face-to-face, particularly in the African American community, in order to become familiar with the pastors of small churches, to inform them about his intentions to develop a user-friendly, welfare-to-work program, and then to develop a referral base of people who knew him and what he was trying to accomplish. In doing so, he would be earning buy-in from the community.

The grant was approved, and Odell (by now Reverend) Cleveland knocked on many church doors and became acquainted with quite a few local pastors. Odell collected data on the needs of eighty-two churches, but more importantly met the leaders who could help legitimize his efforts at the grass roots. Dr. Fasih Ahmed, who conducted the first assessment of the WRLP's Emergency Assistance Program, analyzed the data, and I suggested strategies.

That year, Reverend Cleveland met Nathan Cook, a vice president of the United Way of Greater Greensboro. Part of Cook's job involved overseeing Gifts in Kind, a program that distributes new but discarded corporate goods to the nonprofits through the United Way. Both Cleveland and Cook saw a significant potential for expanding Gifts in Kind to deliver more goods to people in need and to train some of the participants in Odell's small welfare-to-work program. The initial goal for this enlarged Gifts in Kind program was to expand the distribution so that churches and other faith-based organizations could distribute the donated corporate goods to the needy people in their communities. Because of his previous experience as the top salesperson for a regional trucking firm, Cleveland knew how to transport goods from one place to another quickly and inexpensively, a key ingredient to any successful distribution enterprise.

The Gifts In Kind aspect of the WRLP grew soon after it received that first United Way grant. Rapidly, the WRLP became a partner with both the United Way and the Weaver Foundation, and the latter in 2001 gave the WRLP a $100,000 grant to lease a 16,000-square-foot building to expand the distribution and training efforts. Over the next three and a half years, the success of the distribution/training concept compelled the agency to rent two other warehouses to expand its space for storing goods. Demand soared.

In just the last two years, the agency has distributed corporate goods valued at more than $36 million at retail prices. With the program's growth, an opportunity arose to use the warehouse as a halfway point between the classroom and the workforce to train participants in the welfare-to-work program in various skills such as bar-coding, stocking shelves, customer service, and, of course, the development of good work habits. With grants and the ability to recoup administrative fees, enough funds were generated to provide a stipend for some of the welfare-to-work participants until they learned the skills necessary for successful participation in the workforce. Today the WRLP is the largest Gifts in Kind distribution operation in the world.

Late in 2001, former Greensboro city councilman Earl Jones lost the local Community Services Block Grant due to claims of financial irregularity, so the North Carolina State Office for Community Service Block Grants requested proposals for taking over the funding and operations of Jones's $600,000 program as the county's new Community Action Program (CAP). The CAP concept started in the 1960s as part of President Lyndon Johnson's War on Poverty. The 1,100 CAP programs now in the United States receive federal money to develop self-sufficiency programs for people who live in low-income neighborhoods.

Guilford County, North Carolina, is a racially charged community, and thus the circumstances regarding Councilman Jones losing the agency had created a racially hostile tone. Surprisingly, Reverend Cleveland had not considered that the WRLP was the perfect candidate to take over Jones's program. CAPs boasted self-sufficiency, as did the WRLP, but the major difference and the new twist between them was that by 2002, the WRLP had a three-pronged approach to self-sufficiency: It had a built-in job training program tailored for both welfare recipients and others who wanted to upgrade their employability skills; its distribution center served as a place where students received real-world job training; and its hosts dispersed new goods, ranging from diapers to household items, but did so mainly through churches in low-income neighborhoods where, in a way similar to co-ops or Sam's Clubs, recipients bought memberships—except in this case, it was nonprofits and churches that bought the memberships. The WRLP was also connected to a church at a time when it was possible politically to be both a *faith-related* agency and a government entity. The WRLP provided a fine model for addressing self-sufficiency through the small churches, a major neighborhood institution, and it could do so with the credibility that usually takes considerable time to earn.

It was a natural fit for the WRLP to assume responsibility for the CAP because it could foster self-sufficiency in a combination of ways: individualized academic training, practical work experience, and the ability to help neighborhood churches expand their ministries. A small church with extra money in its ministry budget could buy diapers in bulk from the distribution center at a fraction of their retail cost and then assist families with infants and toddlers to stretch their budgets by providing diapers for little or no cost.

It is essential to understand that people on food stamps cannot buy diapers, toilet paper, dish detergent, or other household necessities with food stamps. Because they often do not have a car and live too far off the bus lines, they frequently must take taxis to larger grocery stores or huge discount stores like Wal-Mart to buy bulk items; consequently, either taxi costs consume their savings or they must shop at the local quick-marts and overpay for necessities. Toilet paper that costs fifteen cents at the distribution center costs a dollar at the quick-mart. Therefore, training the WRLP offers to church members focuses on helping them determine which items would be best for their specific congregations and neighborhoods. Objectively, these provisions are baby steps progressing toward self-sufficiency, yet finding ways for neighborhood churches to stretch the meager incomes of struggling families continually is most impressive.

The WRLP was already organizing neighborhood self-sufficiency projects by helping churches expand their ministries in the way I just described. While I had emphasized to Odell that government funding was never the answer to an organization's financial stability, the CAP funding was a grant that could be renewed if the national politics allowed it and if the agency maintained accurate books and outcome data, both of which the WRLP did from its inception.

I prompted Odell to compete with several other more established agencies, including Goodwill Industries and the Salvation Army, to make the WRLP the county's Community Action Agency. After much prayer and consultation with his board and with Bishop George W. Brooks, the leader of Mt. Zion Baptist Church, the WRLP entered the competition. The team crafted an outstanding proposal.

On the afternoon of February 13, 2002, I called Reverend Cleveland to ask him if he had heard whether or not the WRLP had become the county's new Community Services Block Grant designee. He casually informed me that the WRLP had won unanimously over five other candidates and that I needed to attend a 3:00 P.M. meeting to discuss further action.

Besides having a good proposal, the agency succeeded in the competition for other reasons as well. The WRLP had received the 1999 Best Practice Award from the U.S. Department of Housing and Urban Development. In 2000, the agency won the Best Practice Award from the state of North Carolina, and in 2001, it won the Nonprofit Sector Steward Award from the North Carolina Center for Nonprofits. During the height of the economic recovery of 1999–2000, the WRLP produced a job placement rate of 80 percent for the graduates of its program. While this list of awards and other accolades is impressive, the reason the WRLP earned such recognition is because it developed a capacity to grow through solid program planning—a strategy President Bush's Faith-Based Initiative has neglected to execute. His initiative allotted money first and then later spent millions on helping organizations develop the capacity to spend it appropriately.

The day of the CAP award, Reverend Cleveland spent nearly two hours with Nancy McLaughlin, a staff writer for the *Greensboro News and Record*, and John Robinson, the paper's editor-in-chief. The purpose of this meeting was to explain that the Welfare Reform Liaison Project was its own corporation and not a legal part of the Mt. Zion Church. Unfortunately, the session made no difference. The newspaper wanted to acknowledge publicly to the community that a highly regarded church had been named the steward of federal funds and that the two-year controversy plaguing the former program had reached its end. The headline in the local section of the February 14, 2002, *Greensboro News and Record* read: "CHURCH GETS GRANT LOST BY JONES; THE WELFARE REFORM LIAISON PROJECT IS AN OUTREACH OF MOUNT ZION BAPTIST CHURCH ON ALAMANCE CHURCH ROAD."[1]

Even so, what makes this agency unique and leaves an undeniable imprint of its connection to the church is what both organizations have provided for the community, not what they received in return. In structure, the WRLP resembles many of the nearly two thousand community development corporations nationally, many of which emerged from black churches. It *was* an outreach of Mt. Zion Baptist Church, but the finer distinctions of having its own board, its own budget, and its own mission are merely paper distinctions in the public's mind; the media made no effort to characterize the WRLP as the new Community Action Program. Three years earlier, the May 7, 1999, *Greensboro News and Record* had carried the story of the WRLP's first Guilford County Community Faith Summit, which took place at Mt. Zion Baptist Church with more than two hundred people in attendance.[2] In Reverend Cleveland's needs assessment, he had found that leaders of the faith community preferred a broader discussion of welfare reform, social services, and the role their ministries were expected to play as a result of this policy change. Undaunted that this type of event had never been staged previously in Greensboro, he called together ministers and other social service and nonprofit leaders for the first of what has become a biennial forum held at Mt. Zion. Two years later, the June 6, 2001, Guilford County Faith Summit featured the Rev. Jim Wallis of the Washington-based *Sojourners Magazine*. According to the news account, Wallis "invigorated the 275 people" attending the event at Mt. Zion.[3] We who attended the summit all learned a valuable lesson concerning working with the press: Perception is reality.

The Welfare Reform Liaison Project remains labeled as an extension of Mt. Zion Baptist Church—because it is.

More than four hundred people attended the 2003 Faith Summit, and even more attended the 2005 conference. After holding four summits in eight years, it is clear to Reverend Cleveland and I that communities need to talk. People throughout the region now attend this meeting because their own communities are not talking. Communities are not conversing because President Bush's Faith-Based Initiative remains a folly, partly because it has included no community intervention strategy whatsoever. More than a thousand Community Action Agencies across the nation serve the country's poorest people. Had the social engineers and ideologues who run this operation not seen government programs as enemies but rather as partners, and small churches as an ingredient in a recipe to improve local services instead of the recipe itself, the Faith-Based Initiative could have earned some merit.

The Welfare Reform Liaison Project has been offering this community an opportunity to converse, and Mt. Zion has provided a safe place for such discourse. The agency has united the key players to speak instead of merely to listen to Washington bureaucrats as they pretend that grants for abstinence, marriage, or prison reentry programs are the answers to the complex issues involving the huge loss of textile jobs and the disaster economic changes within a manufacturing base brings to individuals, families, and communities. Throughout the United States, manufacturing jobs have dried up, particularly in the South. Whether I am standing in the crowd of attendees at the Faith Summit or taking questions in a workshop about how to be an effective ministry in the community, the buzz is the same for me. People are hungry to help in any way they can. However, the wayward Bush political agenda, and its far-fetched idea about this church or another one being discriminated against, seems to be coming from another reality. The administration's effort to throw government money at organizations and churches without having the utmost important community discussions first is essentially bad policy.

Conclusion

I conclude this book by clarifying that a faith-based initiative is not innately threatening. The Faith-Based Initiative of President George W. Bush, however, has not only been sinister but also ideologically driven and poorly executed. Its planners' confidence, accompanied by their cheerleading, has drowned out any chance for a sober, alternative discussion. Hopefully, this book will open a new avenue for conferring about social services and the faith community. If we will ever have a genuine faith-based initiative—one in which community service systems effectively begin to serve those individuals in need and the available resources are used most efficiently—we must think in different terms. We need a national community policy that plays out locally, designed by local leaders. Sadly, the Bush administration's Faith-Based Initiative cannot improve local services.

President Bush and his cohorts have no commitment from local leaders and never will. While their stated agenda claims to fight society's ills by "rallying the armies of compassion" inside America's churches, the scheme is merely a disguise. Underneath the camouflage has been a war plan to demolish government programs, to mobilize and increase the size of the evangelical Christian voting bloc, to shift government money to churches and other faith-based organizations in the conservative-led culture war, and to develop a smoke screen of persuasive media images and baffling words to confuse detractors. Acquiring local buy-in would mean that those homegrown leaders would have a say in what societal issues deserve monetary attention and what groups receive the money to deliver the services. If local groups across the nation were to determine that their issues are not the ones Washington wants publicized (namely, substance abuse, abstinence, marriage, and prison reentry) but rather worker displacement services, illiteracy, housing, health care, child abuse, and condom use to curtail the explosion of sexually transmitted diseases, Washington could no longer control the message it sends to its base. Neither would there be the stage nor the bankroll to promote and fund the social issues that bind the Christian Right to the White House.

With their top-down planning model, compassionate conservatives have defined which issues to fund, maintained control of the purse strings, and directed local operations from Washington. Decentralizing power and yielding to the authority of locals—a requirement for effective social service development and delivery—would have exposed the faith-based camouflage. If local leaders controlled the purse strings, they would probably choose not to fund the programs the Bush Faith-Based Initiative sponsors, nor would they direct the money to small churches and pervasively Christian agencies, as the Washington Beltway architects have been doing.

Churches may be small, but they remain essential players in local social service delivery. They have a role to play, as does every provider on the local scene. We simply cannot continue to redirect scarce resources, which the White House has earmarked to suit its own political agenda, and do so in thoughtless ways with regard to bona fide service needs. Communities do not need Washington redirecting the people's money to small churches just yet. Communities must first *talk*. Second, they need accurate data about issues such as:

- How many children are homeless?
- How many cannot read?
- How many need mental health services?
- How many foster children need adoptive homes?

Communities cannot get answers to these questions if organizations do not collect data, and it is certain that small churches do not presently have the capacity for such a task. Communities must begin discussing the problems they face, one by one if need be, and do so with the same vigor and urgency that pro-life and pro-choice opponents square off. I believe it is high time we put a moratorium on the "God talk" uttered by the president and his followers and close the gates to heaven at the community level to those who love only their unborn neighbors and show no affection for their living neighbors who need help.

As we prepare to handle the unemployed victims of displaced furniture and textile factories moving overseas or to address the increasing number of hardworking Americans without adequate medical coverage, we will certainly gain a new appreciation for the interconnectedness of the individual and the community. President Bush's top-down Faith-Based Initiative has not only been anticommunity but has also provided too bold a voice to the Puritan wing of the Republican Party. The greed has been shrouded in an individualistic message that "general welfare" really means one brand of Christian charity—theirs. Helping one's neighbor has become finger-pointing moralizing instead of a means of unification. We will know we have a truly faith-based initiative when communities brand themselves with scarlet letters for each child who sleeps in a shelter because his or her family cannot afford housing or for each family whose breadwinner works forty or more hours a week but does not earn enough to afford both food and medical coverage.

We will never find clarity while addressing these complex issues if Washington politicians define them and surrogates tell us what to believe. At the community level, we can reach consensus on important matters central to community policy. We need accurate data and coherent definitions of what problems exist in our community. After discussing matters as a community and collecting data, another step in developing a community's human service policy is forming a consensus about the nature, scope, and meaning of the various troubles in the community. As the focus becomes clearer on the positive care and concern for the plight of the people to whom the policy is directed, the policy will become more effective for everyone. Many of the matters to be addressed at the community level are complicated, so we need data that are set forth impartially. For example, if the community were to offer a church-run tutoring program and it knew that a certain number of the children who attend are learning disabled, then it could budget to train tutors to teach those children. Otherwise, tutoring becomes merely a baby-sitting service, yet no one would question it because the community seemingly used data to build a consensus about the nature of and solution to the particular problem. When communities do not understand the nature and scope of the problems they face, they pay less attention to the intricacies of implementing policies to address those problems.

When planners make policies without consideration of the *interconnection* of social concerns, their efforts result in programs working at cross-purposes with each other, making it difficult to harness the energy, spirit, and commitment necessary to operate cooperatively. The federal government could play an important role in this aspect of developing community policy. Furthermore, we also must be aware of the nature, scope, and capacity of the agencies and organizations that, in our system of service delivery, must share responsibilities; they should encompass structures for cross-training, interagency communication, and joint planning efforts. Rarely are funds directed to maintaining the infrastructure to hold the necessary partnerships together. We need to see the system as one, yet respect the organizational differences and plan for more seamless interconnections. The Bush Faith-Based Initiative has encouraged more churches to enter an already tight competition for scarce funding, without ever conceptualizing how *all* the players—the bit players as well as the main actors—can fulfill their roles effectively.

As these players move increasingly to the state and local levels, the design, management, financing, and evaluation of programs will reach success more rapidly if there is local consensus about causes, effects, and solutions to problems. The best route to such ends is based on *clear-headed judgment and moral vision*, not on vague and intractable ideological positions. If we can avoid situations that attach personal and moral decay to every problem, and instead look at the local system of services the way communities look at specific concerns that hold the broader infrastructure together (e.g., charting ways to fix old sewers, bridges, and roads when they need repair), then we have a basis for some common ground.

Our local delivery systems deal with problems that range from teen pregnancy to hospice care—"womb-to-tomb" issues. Each issue bears its own gut-wrenching concerns with matters of morals, finances, and service delivery. If communities could arrange systems already in place locally to categorize each problem in terms of to what degree the efforts are preventing, managing, or eliminating it, the systems could cogently assist the public in making informed decisions. Continual community education could make great strides in shaping an environment where leaders develop delivery systems that are more effective than allowing Washington to define the problems and determine the solutions.

Communities must communicate before making plans. The Welfare Reform Liaison Project held its fourth Community Faith Summit in 2005 with approximately six hundred people in attendance. This daylong conference, entitled "Exercising Our Faith: Living Our Faith to Build a Better Community," explored subjects for discussion referred to as "building blocks." The flyer for the event explained that "each building block rests atop another, all contributing to the reconstruction of a stronger community."

The agenda for this summit is shown in appendix F because I believe it is important to document a slice of one faith community's reality in trying to address its problems in terms of broader community concerns, not the moralistic ones Washington defines. I also want readers to visualize the reality of one social service community collaborating, not (as the Bush administration portrays it) with the bureaucrats in opposition to the real faith healers. This fourth summit is only the first step in collecting community-wide data—so communities across the country that have not yet even attempted such a strategy once have a long way to go.

This community knows its reality is far different from the world of the compassionate conservatives. While my critics will say this community is only a single example, I am inclined to point out that North Carolina is a "red state" within the Bible Belt and, most importantly, that my community is achieving success in ways that President Bush's Faith-Based Initiative's community intervention strategy has not yet been able to experience. I challenge the president and his administration to find a community in the United States whose faith community has led more community-wide social service discussions with the same or higher level of participation in the last eight years than mine. The effort displayed in appendix F represents a community really pulling together. What makes the summit so exciting is that it is the fourth one in eight years and that, without any guidance from experts in Washington, its popularity continues to increase because of its necessity. What is most challenging is all the work that remains ahead. It is quite unfortunate how much money the Bush administration has wasted on redirecting grants to Christ-centered drug programs and marketing for its weakest of efforts when, instead, it could have stimulated the types of discussions engendered by these summits.

As one can clearly see from the workshop sessions and the cross-section of presenters in appendix F, the community shows much interest in partnerships exploring economic and health concerns, as well as other issues faced by the impoverished population, the social service agencies, and other organizations. The array of presenters comprises a blend of religious leaders, public agency representatives, nonprofit leaders, and entrepreneurs. This community effort, intelligently designed, obviously contrasts President Bush's Faith-Based Initiative, a deficiently designed, faith-based folly.

Welfare Reform Liaison Project Quarterly Progress Report, June 2000 Class

I have included a sample of the evaluation reports that WRLP had to submit to the State of North Carolina during 2000 and 2001 as it received funds from the state to provide welfare-to-work training classes. The purpose for its placement here is to demonstrate the complex problems the clients faced, and to show that if the agency were to be successful in placing such people in jobs, which it has been, it had to plan ways to address the range of problems they faced. This meant that WRLP had to coordinate with other agencies in the system of services to be effective. Since the early days WRLP has done just that by developing a well-thought-out case management system that employs the services of many agencies. That planning is based on developing relationships with other providers of services. Reverend Cleveland's visits outlined in Figure 9.3 represent only one important example of what needs to be done to work effectively at the community level on a continual basis. "Buy-in" for an idea or a program locally means that an organizational leader has to become acquainted with members in the system of care locally and they have to become acquainted with that organizational leader. Such a nationwide strategy to teach newcomers how to earn "buy-in" locally was sorely lacking in the Bush faith-based initiative.

Submitted by Robert J. Wineburg

2. HOW MANY INDIVIDUALS HAS YOUR PILOT PROJECT SERVED DURING THE LAST THREE MONTHS?

The June class of the Welfare Reform Liaison Project, which was the organization's fourth training class since its inception, held its second nine-week welfare-to-work training session for the reporting period of this grant. This class started out with fifteen participants, two of whom were active TANF recipients. The specific outcomes in this report will point to: (1) The progress of those two recipients on a range of variables. (2) The report will also provide information about the other eight participants as well. (3) There is a brief mention of the five people who dropped out of the June class, as three of them are trying to enter the third training class of this grant period.

It is becoming increasingly difficult to merely outline whether a student succeeds in WRLP education and training without understanding seven profoundly interrelated concerns, each of which has a bearing on the success of the program. These concerns include: (1) The complex and multiple problems of the clients such as the lack of transportation or adequate housing, which is often laced with their personal inabilities to manage time effectively or plan appropriately that in turn affects their attitude and comportment; (2) The intense and complicated interactions the students have with the staff which includes intense case management to address the above concerns, coupled with a no-nonsense educational program; (3) The unifying and supportive relationships the students have with each other; (4) The respect the staff has gained among the leaders and line staff of the other social service organizations with which it has had to form partnerships to deliver these complex services; (5) How this program and the students have become known and gained legitimacy in the low income community in Greensboro; (6) The increasingly intricate relationships the agency has developed with the institutional stakeholders in its sphere: (a) foundations, (b) businesses, (c) media, (d) United Way, (e) higher educational institutions, (f) Department of Social Services, (g) other nonprofit organizations, (h) religious congregations, and the intricacies involved in securing and maintaining all of these partnerships; and (7) The blending of the Faith Factor and Professional Factor which takes much of its form in the deeds and professional approach to service delivery of the highly trained professional staff. *These people often work well beyond the forty hours for which they get paid and rarely do they quit on people who sometimes have given up on themselves.*

It is no accident that it is difficult to just list outcomes, particularly when an organization like WRLP understands that it is building a foundation for a new type of welfare-to-work program that blends the *establishment of intense personal relationships with the students* alongside the creation of *lasting partnerships with its stakeholders in the community.* The remainder of this report might best be viewed in the context of the energy this organization is expending in building partnerships and providing education, case management, pre on-the-job-training by way of the sheltered workshop, job development services, and client follow-up.

3. BRIEFLY DESCRIBE THE OUTCOMES OBSERVED FOR THESE INDIVIDUALS

Of the two TANF recipients in the June Class, each successfully completed the Guilford Technical Community College certificate program. Each of the TANF recipients was placed in the Sheltered Workshop setting for further training. This training is subsidized by the grant for this program. Please note that the workshop is an option for up to eighteen months. Each of the TANF recipients experienced several moderate to severe structural barriers during the course of the training, most of which were overcome through intensive case management. These barriers were noted above in item #2. They included: A slight problem with *transportation* early in the training but it was solved by the end of the nine-week classroom component of the program; a moderate *housing* problem which was reduced slightly by the end of the training; a moderate *health* problem that was managed effectively by the end of the training; a student's *child was severely ill* but got treatment and was much better by graduation; one TANF recipient's *educational level* was an extremely severe limitation at the beginning of the program but was reduced to a moderate limitation in the nine-week program. These problems seem comparable to those of the TANF recipients in the last class. We noted the following in the report on that class:

Of the eight TANF participants, five had experienced problems with transportation, and through program efforts or good problem-solving skills, each person was able to do somewhat better with her transportation concerns. Two participants had health problems that were barriers to completing the program successfully, while one of those participants also had a child with health problems as well (Report for March Class).

It is worth noting the statistics on the non-TANF recipients for this fourth class. It is becoming increasingly apparent, as measured through interviews with the students, by the number of extended networks of people who came to the fourth class's graduation, and the fact that thirty people showed up for the orientation to the fifth session, that WRLP in the minds and actions of the people in the low income community has become a viable welfare-to-work training program, but more interestingly a *welfare prevention program*. So it is essential to understand the following data in the context of both the outcomes, but the constellation of factors that is making this a legitimate option for those working poor and those who want to better themselves through legitimate job training educational training, spiritual attentiveness by staff, and genuine skill development that leads to a better life as they perceive it. Of the five that dropped out three returned for the next class.

3A. OBSERVED OUTCOMES FOR NON-TANF RECIPIENTS

One recipient experienced child care problems early in the nine-week session, but it was solved by the end. Two class members had severe housing problems at the beginning of the program and one had a slight problem. By the end one person had a moderate housing problem while the other two had their problems solved. Sometimes a housing problem will mean that someone cannot meet the utilities payment, for others it might mean an eviction. Staff intervene to solve these difficulties and work on preventing them in the future. Two people had health problems at the beginning of the program; one's problem was moderate, the other's was slight. At the end of the session the person with the slight problem had no problem and the one with the moderate problem had only a slight problem. One of the non-TANF students had a problem with a parent's health that was an extreme limitation to her success. With a referral to an adult daycare program in the community this concern was no longer a barrier to successful training.

Three of the eight non-TANF recipients had educational barriers, one slight, one moderate, and one severe. Quite often, such students never had success in the classroom, and the classroom in this setting sets an extremely high level of expectation for student performance. As a consequence, students are fearful and become their own worst enemy. Case management and close monitoring helps students succeed in the classroom when one might assume such success would be but a fleeting hope. At the beginning, three of the eight had barriers to educational success, one severe, one moderate, one slight. At the end of classroom instruction, two students had slight barriers and one had a moderate barrier. At the end of the nine-week classroom training, three students were working in full-time jobs, two were interviewing for full-time work, and three were placed in the workshop, one as an administrative assistant to the executive director.

4. DESCRIBE HOW THESE OUTCOMES ARE IN LINE WITH THE GOALS AND OBJECTIVES OF YOUR PILOT PROJECT

Welfare Reform Liaison Project's major goals center on assisting families with special problems that prevent them from obtaining immediate employment or long-term employment. It is becoming increasingly apparent that meeting these goals depends on solving, managing, or preventing the complex and multiple problems of the clients such as the lack of transportation or inadequate housing, which is often laced with their personal inabilities to manage time effectively or plan appropriately that in turn effects their attitude and comportment. Whether the student is a TANF recipient or not, there is an intense and complicated set of interactions the students have with the staff.

The students trust the staff profoundly as they witness them going the extra mile in intense case management that addresses concerns that have possibly been neglected for a lifetime. The casework, coupled with a no-nonsense educational program is a formula for success on its own. A by-product of these intense relationships among staff and students is the unifying and supportive relationships that emerge among the students. They become part of a learning community and the community spirit that students have increases the program's legitimacy in the low-income community in Greensboro. This legitimacy has rolled over to the professional service community as the staff has gained increasing respect among the leaders and line staff of the other social service organizations with which it has had to form partnerships to deliver these complex services.

The primary case manager of the program has been invited to staff retreats and planning sessions for the Guilford County Department of Social Services. The partnerships between Welfare Reform Liaison Project and other stakeholders grows daily. The program is helping people find work, get further training if need be, educate themselves about other agencies, and educate the stakeholders about the complex concerns that surround placing and keeping people in viable work.

5. LIST ANY CHANGES OR MODIFICATIONS TO THE SERVICES YOU PROVIDE OR THE MANNER IN WHICH SERVICES ARE DELIVERED AS A RESULT OF THESE OUTCOMES

A social work intern has been placed in the social service division of the program to help with the intensive case management required. A local foundation has supported keeping the summer business intern that it helped support so he could implement the administrative plan introducing prospective employers to the program and the Welfare Reform Liaison participants, as well as introducing the participants to the prospective employers. All of last year, the distribution center, where the clients get placed in a sheltered environment for further training, distributed 3.5 million dollars in corporate "Gifts in Kind" to local agencies. As of this report, with four months left in the year the program has distributed over seven million dollars in corporate Gifts in Kind.

The two other changes are the co-op aspect of the program, and the job-coaching component. The co-op aspect of the program is for students of the program who are able to move out of the workshop but who are not yet ready for independent employment. They are placed with an employer but are paid the $8.00 an hour they receive in the Workshop, with funds paid with the grant. This is a win-win situation for both employer and prospective employee. What makes the program so important is that a staff member from the WRLP is acting as job coach—a broker of sorts between the employer, the student, and the project to help make a smooth transition to the workplace. The job coach has been a successful programmatic change to address the difficult transition from welfare to work.

An Envelope from Texas

by William E. Rapfogel
The Jewish Press, January 7, 2004

President George W. Bush puts his money where his mouth is. He has me convinced. Erev Shabbos Chanukah I received an envelope from a Texas accountant. Having no business in Texas, I was immediately curious. Inside was a generous contribution to the Metropolitan Council on Jewish Poverty, the organization I have run for the last decade, from George and Laura Bush.

Shocked would be a mild description of how I felt holding that check. Don't get me wrong—Met Council receives generous contributions from scores of New Yorkers. And we're grateful for each and every dollar we receive on behalf of needy Jews in New York. But this was a personal check from the president of the United States. I almost didn't believe it.

To put this into some perspective, I have met President Bush several times since his election three years ago. During the last two years the president, Attorney General John Ashcroft and other Bush administration officials have singled out Met Council in their speeches as an example for community-based organizations to follow.

This began a year and a half ago. In a speech about welfare reform at a Milwaukee church, the president said, "The Metropolitan Council on Jewish Poverty out of New York ... [is] a group of people who want to help; they feed the hungry for their community. They feed the hungry regardless of somebody's religion. They don't ask, what is your religion; they ask, are you hungry."

I met with the president several days later and we chatted about his remarks, his strong support for Israel and our mutual interest in baseball and running. When I told him that I aspired to run better than a seven-minute-mile like he did, he put his hand on my shoulder and told me, "Don't worry, just keep running."

A year ago, the White House asked me to speak at a conference in Philadelphia. I was glad to learn that the president would be there, but I was surprised to hear him again mention Met Council's work in his remarks. After his speech, he was shaking hands and came over to ask me how he did in describing Met Council. I was touched that the president's private moments matched his public words. I remember thinking, "This president is a real mentsch."

Jim Towey, the president's assistant and director of his Office of Faith and Community Based Initiatives, has been a consistent friend, advocate and supporter of our work and has spoken of Met Council in news interviews. Other White House staffers have been equally supportive of our mission to combat Jewish poverty. Merryl Tisch, the chair of my board, and her husband James, the chair of the Presidents' Conference, are friends of the First Family and have been important advocates for the Jewish community, and particularly the poor. In a few weeks, Met Council and UJA-Federation of New York will release a joint report showing a dramatic increase in Jewish poverty in New York. Indeed, while there is poverty in Jewish communities throughout America, most poor Jews live in our midst. The president's contribution serves as a recognition of that need and his appreciation of our motto, Tzedakah U'gemilos Chasodim: Acts of Charity, Deeds of Kindness.

In our conversations, the president was moved by the sheer number of people served by our crisis intervention staff, the housing we created for the elderly, the home health care we provide to the frail, the job training and counseling, the kosher food programs and our extensive network of Jewish Community Councils around New York.

It is intriguing to imagine that the president of the United States places the issue of Jewish poverty on his radar screen, and backs his words up with his personal financial support. Certainly, few would have imagined that the president would donate to a Jewish charity from New York.

President Bush's commitment to helping the needy qualifies him for the mantle of Joseph the Righteous, about whom we read in Parshas Vayigash. Joseph reunites with his brothers who sold him into slavery. He tells them not to fear his new role as viceroy of Egypt because he is rescuing the region from famine. Likewise, our president found himself in a unique role post-9/11 to lead the free world against terrorism. But he has not strayed from his domestic agenda of helping the less fortunate.

By noting the needs of poor Jews—with all that is on his plate—President Bush has endeared himself to our community and truly follows the lead of Joseph.

White House E-mail to Jewish Leaders

From: Office of Public Liaison
Sent: Wednesday, August 25, 2004 2:23 P.M.
To: Jewish Leaders
Subject: President Bush's Initiative Helps Jewish Faith-Based Institutions

One of the central accomplishments of the Bush administration has been the Faith-Based Initiative. Through executive orders, the president has greatly reduced the discrimination once faced by faith-based institutions in the federal grant applications process. Before President Bush instituted these executive orders, faith-based organizations were frequently locked out of receiving federal grants to provide much-needed social services, even if they did not proselytize. One charity was told not to apply for a grant because it had the word "Jewish" in its name, even though it served both gentiles and Jews.

President Bush's efforts have had a profound impact on the ability of faith-based organizations to be recognized for their good work, and to be welcomed into the charitable community as an equal partner. More than 20 state governors have offices to reach out to faith-based organizations—and throughout America, and especially in America's inner cities, the high-quality work of many faith-based organizations has been strengthened. At the same time, America's long tradition of separating church and state has never been altered; the standards by which all faith-based organizations are judged is no different than those used to evaluate the work of other charitable organizations.

Many Jewish organizations have received federal grants, thanks to the president's Faith-Based Initiative. Jewish social work agencies in Arizona, California, Illinois, Massachusetts, Minnesota, New Jersey, and elsewhere have received federal grants. Faith-based offices in federal agencies have provided assistance for other programs sponsored by Jewish groups, including those aimed at refugee resettlement, seniors, small businesses, torture survivors, and victims of family violence. Touro Synagogue in Newport, Rhode Island—the oldest continually used synagogue in the United States, received a "Save America's Treasures" grant, thanks to a policy change made by President Bush.

Below, I've included details on a few notable examples of faith-based organizations that are answering the call of service, thanks to grant money from the federal government:

Metropolitan Council on Jewish Poverty
New York, NY
Metropolitan Council on Jewish Poverty won a $525,645 grant in FY04 from HHS to serve as a Compassion Capital Fund intermediary.

Jewish Family Service
Albuquerque, NM
Jewish Family Service is a lead partner with Catholic Charities of Central New Mexico on the CCF-funded Stone Soup Collaborative. Jewish Family Service is receiving more than $150,000 over three years to work with synagogues across the state to help them recruit, encourage, train, and organize a strong volunteer base and also develop and expand services and programs for their surrounding communities. The Stone Soup Collaborative does this through intensive technical assistance as well as sub-awards made to regional collaborative projects.

Jewish Family & Children Services (JFCS)
Long Beach, CA
Through funding from Father Joe's Villages, a Compassion Capital Fund intermediary, JFCS provides an innovative school-based at-risk student-counseling program that promotes self-awareness and resiliency in girls.

JFCS received a $26,974 sub-grant from the Compassion Capital Fund to expand a program, called "Girls Circle," to a new site during the spring, summer and fall of 2004. Through the CCF grant, JFCS is able to serve approximately 100 additional elementary, middle school and high school girls in the Long Beach Unified School District who are considered at-risk.

Jewish Renaissance Medical Center
Perth Amboy, NJ
One of the first faith-based Community Health Centers (CHCs) to receive funding since the President launched the Initiative was the Jewish Renaissance Medical Center in Perth Amboy. As its first Federal grant, the Center was awarded a two-year award in 2002 of $1,700,000 by HHS, to expand its center and increase its care for the uninsured and underserved. Indirectly, this grant is helping expand the 5,000 patients seen a year to 20,000 patients a year.

The Weinberg Campus
Geltzville, NY
The Weinberg Campus is the newest addition to a long-standing Jewish or-
ganization that has provided housing for the Buffalo area's elderly since
1915. They now manage a nursing home, a home care agency, assisted liv-
ing apartments, and special services for the memory impaired. In 2003, the
Weinberg Campus received direct federal funding for the first time.
Through the Supportive Housing for the Elderly Program (Section 202),
HUD awarded the organization with a $4.5 million grant. The Weinberg
Campus will use the funding for the land acquisition and construction of a
new 50-unit apartment building, which will allow the organization to pro-
vide housing and care for even more elderly individuals.

Noam Neusner
Special Assistant to the President
Office of Public Liaison

Religious Community Already Is Doing Its Share to Provide Social Services

Editorial by Bob Wineburg
Greensboro News and Record, June 25, 1995

Politicians want the religious community to expand its role as social service provider. That may not be realistic.

In the rush toward welfare and social service reform, politicians, especially Republicans, are calling for more involvement from the religious community. U.S. House Speaker Newt Gingrich, R-Ga., impressed by the volunteer spirit he found in the home-building efforts of Habitat for Humanity, supports a $50 million federal grant for that organization and others that build homes for the poor. Republican Gov. Kirk Fordice of Mississippi has proposed a program—Faith in Families—where each of his state's 5,000 religious congregations would adopt a welfare family and provide them with spiritual and practical support. Republican Sen. John Ashcroft of Missouri has proposed that states, through a block grant from the federal government, contract directly with religiously based charities for delivery of social services to the poor.

Three assumptions beneath these proposals need closer scrutiny: (1) The religious community has the capacity to shift from a minor to major social service provider. (2) The religious community wants to expand its service role. (3) The religious community will provide better services than the public sector.

For 12 years I have been studying how the religious community has been supporting public and private social service agencies, trying to understand a major but little understood change brought on because of Reagan-era social policies. I have found that the religious community has increased its involvement tremendously nationally and locally. Yet the talk from Washington and some of the nation's state houses seems oblivious to the changes. Let's look at why I feel this way. Do religious congregations and charities have the capability to charge into service? During the Reagan and Bush eras, Catholic Charities alone saw a 700 percent increase in volunteers.

According to a 1992 study by the Independent Sector, an umbrella research and information organization for U.S. nonprofits, members of the nation's religious congregations provided 125 million hours a month in volunteer services to local health, welfare and educational organizations. A third of our nation's child care is housed in religious facilities, making the religious community the nation's single largest provider of such services. If you want to give blood, attend an AA meeting or start a Scout troop, chances are good that you will wind up at a local congregation's facility, not just in the Triad but anywhere in the country. When one stops to think that religious congregations first provide a gathering spot for communal worship, it is amazing how such organizations muster the energy and spirit to help their own members, offer their facilities to the community, support community agencies and reach out with money and service nationally and internationally.

My research of Greensboro's public and private agencies found a huge increase in the use of congregational resources during the Reagan and Bush years. I found that 42 percent of the agencies using congregational volunteers and 42 percent using congregational facilities started doing so during the 1982–92 period. Unbelievably, 69 percent of the agencies receiving money from the religious community started doing so in the Reagan era. There is no doubt the religious community can expand its service efforts. It is simply wrong to assume, however, that it has an unlimited capacity to expand.

Does the religious community want to increase its service efforts? I have read of no major religiously based service provider pleading to take over more of the nation's social services, with the possible exception of refugee resettlement. The calls for increased service from the religious community, and the romanticizing of its capabilities, are coming from the political arena and think tanks. Politicians who, in a subtle and patronizing way, try to co-opt the religious community into providing more services seem phony. If politicians dump their programs on the religious community without discussion and planning, they run the risk of being seen as co-opting those institutions, hurting people who need services and being blamed for weakening the relationships they seemingly want to strengthen.

Will the religious community offer better services than the public sector? If the politicians reduce the fiscal outlay for public sector services and try to meet the same demands with just religious resources, religious social services will have to expand exponentially. Extreme pressure will be on them to contribute more volunteers, space and money. These organizations are attractive in that they are small and less bureaucratic than government agencies and can solve problems and meet needs immediately. The spirit underscoring their effectiveness comes in part because their efforts are voluntary. Co-opting them, laying guilt trips on them or bludgeoning them from the political bully pulpit will not create a more humane, caring and responsive social service system.

The late social welfare historian Roy Lubove used to remind his students that social welfare policy is complex despite the simple-mindedness of its formulators. Some sober discussion, coupled with comprehensive community planning, keeping in sight a clear goal for developing strong and fair partnerships among public, private and religious organizations, is a first step in reducing the complexity and preventing simple-mindedness.

United Way Grant Approval to the Welfare Reform Liaison Project

United Way of Greater Greensboro
P.O. Box 14998
1500 Yanceyville Street
Greensboro, NC 27415-4998

Rev. Odell Cleveland
Welfare Reform Liaison Project
1301 Alamance Church Road
Greensboro, NC 27406

Dear Rev. Cleveland:

Congratulations. The Joseph M. Bryan Foundation Grant Program for Health and Human Services has approved funding of your grant proposal. The funding cycle is August 1998–July 1999. *The grant committee is awarding your agency a one-year grant of $25,000 specifically for the Welfare Reform Liaison Project.* We are pleased to be able to assist you in assessing the community's outreach programs that benefit the needy. Prior to receiving funds we need a comprehensive report detailing how you plan to measure your outcomes. Please submit this plan to us no later than August 15, 1998.

All grantees are required to attend a one-day outcome measurement training workshop. The workshop is scheduled for July 21 or August 5, 9:00 A.M.–4:00 P.M. in Rooms 2–3 at United Way, 1500 Yanceyville Street. Lunch is on your own. The workshop is designed to enable you to determine the benefits for participants in your program during or after their involvement with the program. In addition, the workshop will assist agencies in tracking a program's success on outcomes. Outcomes are benefits or changes for individuals or populations during or after participating in program activities. They are what participants know, think or can do; or how they behave, or what their condition is, that is different following the program.

In addition, we need to have monthly financial reports and monthly program reports. These reports should be submitted within ten days of the end of the reported month. Funds will be dispersed on a quarterly basis, if all required documents are submitted and approved by United Way staff. Additional information regarding reporting guidelines will be mailed to you under separate cover.

Please feel free to call Antonia Monk Reaves (378-6600) if you have any questions regarding the grant process or the reporting requirements. *Registration forms are due by July 16, 1998.*

We appreciate your interest in the grant program and look forward to hearing great things about this initiative and the impact it will have on the Greater Greensboro community.

Sincerely,

(signed)
Ron Bruner
Committee Chairperson

Agenda for the 2005 Guilford County Community Faith Summit

2005 Biennial Guilford County Community Faith Summit
Sponsored by Welfare Reform Liaison Project, Inc., O.I.C.-C.A.A.
Hosted by: Mt. Zion Baptist Church of Greensboro, Inc.

**Exercising Our Faith: "Living Our Faith to Build a
Better Community"**
*Each Building Block Rests Atop Another, All Contributing To
The Reconstruction Of A Stronger Community*

Thursday, June 30, 2005

Time	Event
8:00 A.M.–9:00 A.M.	Pre-Registration, On-Site Registration, Continental Breakfast
9:00 A.M.–9:30 A.M.	**Opening Session**
Welcome Remarks	Bishop George W. Brooks, Senior Pastor, Mt. Zion Baptist Church of Greensboro, Inc., Co-Founder, Welfare Reform Liaison Project, Inc., O.I.C.-C.A.A.
	Welfare Reform Liaison Project, Inc., O.I.C.-C.A.A, Board Chairman Ron Surgeon
	City of Greensboro City Council Representative
	City of High Point City Council Representative
Invocation	Father Phillip Kollithanath, Christ the King Catholic Community

Introduction of
    Keynote Speaker   Bishop George W. Brooks

9:30 A.M.–10:30 A.M.   **Keynote Speaker**

                             Clarence H. Carter, Former Director of the Federal
                             Office of Community Services (OCS)

10:30 A.M.–10:45 A.M.   Special Announcements/Break

                             Nancy McLean, Welfare Reform Liaison Project, Inc.,
                             O.I.C.-C.A.A.

10:45 A.M.–12:15 P.M.   **First Building Block:** *From the Pulpit to the*
                             Community: Building Capacity in the Faith
                             Community

2:15 P.M.–3:45 P.M.   *Facilitator:* Deborah Moore, Assistant Director, Guilford
                             County Department of Social Services

This session is designed to provide information on building capacity within
the Faith Community. Attendees will learn tips on how to tap into community resources; how to strengthen faith-based ministry through collaboration with other faith-based organizations, federal and state agencies,
corporations, and other agencies from both the public and private sector;
and how to expand community ministry beyond the four walls of the
church. Highlighted are two local "Best Practice" models: Macedonia
Family Resource Center of High Point, presented by Rev. Ronald Wilkins
(Board Member) and Welfare Reform Liaison Project's "Gift In Kind
Program," presented by Rev. Odell Cleveland, Founder. Other workshop
highlights will be presented by Dr. Robert Wineburg, a Professor at the
University of North Carolina at Greensboro, and national expert on build-
ing capacity for faith-based organizations; and Deborah Moore, Guilford
County Department of Social Services.

10:45 A.M.–12:15 P.M.   **Second Building Block:** *Through African American*
                             Philanthropy

2:15 P.M.–3:45 P.M.   *Facilitators:* Earnest Miller (morning session), Owner,
                             Chem Care Co., Inc., and Tony Roper (afternoon
                             session), Executive Director, Macedonia Family
                             Resource Center

This session will focus on educating the community about African American philanthropy. Come and learn how faith-based giving in the African
American community can be used to address social problems in the community. This workshop will give you a new appreciation for the word
"philanthropy" and a greater understanding of how philanthropy among
African Americans can impact the whole community. McArthur Davis from
Black United Fund; Renee Smith from the United Way of High Point
(African American Initiative); and Nicole Beatty from the United Way
of Greater Greensboro (African American Leadership) will present this
workshop.

10:45 A.M.–12:15 P.M. **Third Building Block:** *Providing Safe Affordable Housing in Our Community*

2:15 P.M.–3:45 P.M. *Facilitator:* Angelia Ijames, United Way of Greater Greensboro

This session is designed to address housing issues facing low-income citizens in our community. Topics will include the lack of safe and affordable housing, lead found in some low-income housing, and strategies for transitioning families from tenants to homeowners. Karen Young from the Housing Authority will present the Section 8 Home Ownership Program; Beth McKee Huger from the Housing Coalition will present the Housing Hotline and Social Service.com; Bob Kelly from Habitat for Humanity will present on Home Ownership; and Linda Golden from the City of Greensboro will present on Inspection Ordinances and Lead-Based Paint.

10:45 A.M.–12:15 P.M. **Fourth Building Block:** *Healthcare Options in Guilford County*

2:15 P.M.–3:45 P.M. *Facilitator:* Antonia Monk-Reaves, Vice President and Chief Program Officer, Moses Cone–Wesley Long Community Health Foundation

This session will empower service providers by covering information on promoting better health among the families that they serve. It will focus on ways to assist low-income people to access affordable, quality healthcare services. More than 40 million people in America have no health insurance. Rev. Katherine McWilliams, Certified HIPPA Specialist, will present on patient awareness and rights; Brian Ellerby will discuss services offered at HealthServe Community Health Clinic; and Lelia Moore will discuss the Congregational Nurse Program.

10:45 A.M.–12:15 P.M. **Fifth Building Block:** *Through Volunteerism*

2:15 P.M.–3:45 P.M. *Facilitator:* Lynn Wells, Volunteer Coordinator, Moses Cone Health System

This workshop will focus on the theme "Volunteers the Hands and Feet of Your Organization." Topics covered will include: how to engage members of your congregation; volunteers and risk management; how to set up a volunteer ministry; and, the importance of volunteer appreciation. Robin Lindsey from the Volunteer Center; Wes Ward from Agents of Grace; Evelyn Parks from Greensboro Urban Ministry; and Lynn Wells from Moses Cone Health System will present this workshop.

10:45 A.M.–12:15 P.M. **Sixth Building Block:** *Be Your Own Boss! Dare to Believe Your Dreams Through Entrepreneurship*

2:15 P.M.–3:45 P.M. *Facilitator:* Ed Kelley, SCORE—Counselors to America's Small Business

Participants in this workshop will be motivated to dare to dream! Entrepreneurship is an essential driver of the American economy, contributing jobs and innovation. As the ethnic makeup of our nation continues to change, entrepreneurship will fuel the next generation of growth in business development and job creation. If you are an educator this session will introduce the concept of starting entrepreneurship classes in your church or community center. It will equip you with what it takes to start, maintain, and be successful in implementation of an entrepreneurship program. Silvia Collins from Triad Economic Development Corporation; and Kathy Elliot from the Greensboro Chamber of Commerce will present this session.

10:45 A.M.–12:15 P.M.	**Seventh Building Block:** *Building Wealth in the Faith Community*
(Morning only)	*Facilitator:* Nancy McLean, Welfare Reform Liaison Project, Inc., O.I.C.-C.A.A.

This workshop is filled with insightful information about building wealth in the faith community. Also covered in the workshop is information on increasing access to faith-based social services. Presenters will be Bishop George W. Brooks, Senior Pastor of Mt. Zion Baptist Church of Greensboro, Inc. sharing practical tips on the creation of wealth from a corporate standpoint; William V. Thompson, a Financial Strategist sharing why "Money Is Just An Idea;" and Rev. Kenneth D. Price, Team Coordinator for Project Gilead will discuss plans to launch Project Gilead in the Greensboro region and what this means for faith-based organizations and community agencies. Project Gilead was the first, faith-based organization to receive a grant from the U.S. Department of Commerce National Telecommunications and Information Administration. Faith-based leaders and members alike will learn innovative strategies to create wealth and expand their service capacity from these three dynamic presenters.

10:45 A.M.–12:15 P.M.	**Eighth Building Block:** *Digital Media/Entrepreneurial Initiative (CopyCents)*
2:15 P.M.–3:45 P.M.	*Facilitator:* Merna Pettit, Welfare Reform Liaison Project, Inc., O.I.C.-C.A.A., Program Trainee

Individual and organizational self-sufficiency requires a combination of factors: clear direction, organizational strength to skillfully take advantage of market opportunities without jeopardizing institutional integrity, staff and students that understand entrepreneurial principles and who are interested in success, and quality products and services that meet the marketplace needs. This workshop will introduce an entrepreneurial model that has the potential to develop self-sufficiency for participants as well as provide organizational financial stability. Also, learn how your agency or church can get your message out to a broader audience by utilizing the services offered by this unique program model. This workshop will be presented by Jeffrey Black, Welfare Reform Liaison Project, Inc., O.I.C.-C.A.A. (CopyCents) Program Manager; Tonya Scales, Program Trainee; and Pastor Duke, Senior Pastor of Outreach Missionary Baptist Church.

12:15 P.M.–12:30 P.M.   Break

12:30 P.M.–2:00 P.M.   Working Lunch
Topics: Session I—Schools and Children
          Session II—Homelessness in Guilford County
          Session III—Substance Abuse

2:00 P.M.–2:15 P.M.   Break

2:15 P.M.–3:45 P.M.   **Ninth Building Block:** *40 Years into the War on Poverty*

(Afternoon only)   *Facilitator:* Mary Reaves, Welfare Reform Liaison Project, Inc., O.I.C.-C.A.A.

This workshop will take a closer look at 40 years into the war on poverty with a review of the Moynihan Report (1965). In 1964, President Lyndon B. Johnson declared war on poverty. In 1965, Daniel Patrick Moynihan wrote a controversial report entitled "When Politics and Sociology Collide." In this report, Moynihan warned that if more children grew up without the presence of fathers, the result would be social chaos, including crime. The presenter, Dennis Parker, has observed a weakness in this report that omits a fundamental strength of the African American family. He will update the report with an asset-based perspective focusing on Faith and the "Black family." Dennis Parker is the Founder of Carieton & Associates in Richmond, Va. He has more than 15 years of experience in community development and grassroots efforts. He is a consultant for the Department of Social Services, State and Federal Government.

Notes

INTRODUCTION

1. For example, see Amy E. Black, Douglas L. Koopman, and David K. Ryden, *Of Little Faith: The Politics of George Bush's Faith-Based Initiatives* (Washington, D.C.: Georgetown University Press, 2004).

2. Mark Chaves, *Congregations in America* (Cambridge, Mass.: Harvard University Press, 2004, 50.

3. Bob Wineburg, *A Limited Partnership: The Politics of Religion, Welfare, and Social Service* (New York: Columbia University Press, 2001).

4. George W. Bush, "Rallying the Armies of Compassion," January 2001, ii, 6, http://www.whitehouse.gov/news/reports/faithbased.pdf; emphasis added.

5. See Marcus Borg, "Paul's Unconventional Wisdom," 2005, http://www.beliefnet.com/story/142/story_14275_1.html.

6. Heidi Rolland Unruh and Ronald J. Sider, *Saving Souls, Serving Society: Understanding the Faith Factor in Church-Based Social Ministry* (New York: Oxford University Press, 2005), 98.

7. Unruh and Sider, *Saving Souls*, 98.

8. Kevin Nunley, "Soft Sell Marketing," *Insider Reports*, 2005, http://www.insiderreports.com/storypage.asp_Q_ChanID_E_MR_A_StoryID_E_20000087.

9. Jim Towey, "Next Steps for Faith-Based Social Services 2005 and Beyond," *Plenary Session Transcripts*, Roundtable on Religion and Social Welfare Policy, Rockefeller Institute of Government annual conference, Washington, D.C., December 2004, 1–45.

10. Towey, "Next Steps," 9.

11. Towey, "Next Steps," 13.

12. Tom Cochran, U.S. Conference of Mayors executive director's column, May 7, 2004, http://www.usmayors.org/uscm/us_mayor_newspaper/documents/05_10_04/cochran.asp.

13. George W. Bush, "Remarks by the President in Announcement of the Faith-Based Initiative," January 29, 2001, http://www.whitehouse.gov/news/releases/20010129-5.html.

14. Don Eberly and Ryan Streeter, *The Soul of Civil Society: Voluntary Associations and the Public Value of Moral Habits* (Lanham, Md.: Lexington Books, 2002).

15. Mark Silk, "Old Alliance, New Rules," *Washington Post*, February 18, 2001.

16. Ram A. Cnaan, with Stephanie C. Boddie, *The Invisible Caring Hand: American Congregations and the Provision of Welfare* (New York: New York University Press, 1999).

17. John Dilulio, personal interview, Philadelphia, October 26, 2004.

CHAPTER 1

1. Dominionists believe the federal government should recede into the background. This would be achieved through massive tax cuts. Then churches would assume responsibility for welfare and education. Tax cuts, faith-based initiatives, and school vouchers are the cornerstones of Bush administration domestic policies. These policies are putting the United States on the path toward becoming what the Texas Republican Party platform calls a "Christian" nation; see Theocracy Watch, "Texas Republican Party Platform," http://www.theocracywatch.org/texas_gop.htm.

2. Marvin Olasky, *The Tragedy of American Compassion* (Washington, D.C.: Regnery Gateway, 1992).

3. Silk, "Old Alliance, New Rules."

4. Alexander Hamilton, *The Federalist Papers: Alexander Hamilton, James Madison, John Jay*, ed, Clinton Rossiter (New York: New American Library, 1961), 422.

5. Anne Farris, "New Bush Budget Slashes Domestic Spending, but Retains Money for Some Faith-Based Programs," Roundtable on Religion and Social Welfare Policy, February 7, 2006, http://www.religionandsocialpolicy.org/news/article.cfm?id=3836.

6. See "Attendees at Faith Based Event," http://www.whitehouse.gov/news/releases/20010129.html.

7. Texas Freedom Network, "Faith-Based Initiative Reaps Bitter Fruit in Texas," press release, October 10, 2002, http://www.tfn.org/pressroom/display.php?item_id=50.

8. Olasky, *Tragedy of American Compassion*, viii.

9. "An Interview with Marvin Olasky," Roundtable on Religion and Social Welfare Policy, December 20, 2004, http://www.religionandsocialpolicy.org/interviews/interview.cfm?id=77&pagemode=featured.

10. John Shore, "Displaced Worker Committee Meeting Reminder," e-mail, September 4, 2003.

11. American Atheists, "Faith-Based Treatment Director Boasts Evangelical Conversion of 'Completed Jews,'" May 28, 2001, http://www.atheists.org/flash.line/faith20.htm.

12. George W. Bush, State of the Union Address, January 28, 2003, http://www.whitehouse.gov/news/releases/2003/01/20030128-19.html.

13. HopeNetworks, "Louisiana Using Faith-Based Approach to Drug and Alcohol Treatment," 2004, http://www.hopenetworks.org/OAD_Press_Faith.html.

14. U.S. Department of Health and Human Services, Substance Abuse and Mental Health Services Administration, "New Program Promotes Choice, Accountability In Substance Abuse Treatment," press release, March 3, 2004, http://www.samhsa.gov/news/newsreleases/040303nr_atr.htm.

15. Matt Chancey, "'Faith-Based' ... in Big Government: The Religious Right Feeds at the Federal Trough," *Augusta Free Press*, February 7, 2005, http://www.augustafreepress.com/stories/storyReader$31379.

16. Tim Stafford, "The Criminologist Who Discovered Churches," *Christianity Today*, June 14, 1999, 35–39.

17. Paul D. Robbins, "Celebrating Fifty Years of God's Faithfulness," *ChristianityToday.com*, 2006, http://www.christianitytoday.com/anniversary/features/welcome.html.

18. Stafford, "Criminologist Who Discovered Churches," 37.

19. Rebecca Sager, personal correspondence, February 12, 2005. This quote was recorded in her notes taken at the White House Conference on Faith-Based Initiatives, June 1, 2004, in Washington, D.C. At that time, she was a doctoral student at the University of Arizona writing her dissertation on the Faith-Based Initiative. I have been unable to locate a transcript of Towey's remarks that day, but I trust Sager's citation, as she has been a meticulous scholar.

20. "Interview with Marvin Olasky."

21. Joseph Loconte, "Faith Healing: Teen Challenge and Prison Fellowship," *Public Interest* (Spring 2004): 89.

22. Aaron Todd Bicknese, "The Teen Challenge Drug Treatment Program in Comparative Perspective" (Ph.D. diss., Northwestern University, 1999).

23. Brian C. Anderson, "How Catholic Charities Lost Its Soul," *City Journal* 10, no. 1 (Winter 2000).

24. Pioneer Institute for Public Policy Research, review of Joseph Loconte, *Seducing the Samaritan: How Government Contracts Are Reshaping Social Services* (Boston: Pioneer Institute for Public Policy Research, 1997), http://www.pioneerinstitute.org/research/piopaper/summ13.cfm.

25. Eberly and Streeter, *Soul of Civil Society*, 5.

26. Child Welfare League of America, "Child Protection: Facts and Figures," n.d., http://www.cwla.org/programs/childprotection/childprotectionfaq.htm#seriouslyinjure.

CHAPTER 2

1. U.S. Department of Health and Human Services, "Foster Care: Numbers and Trends," 2006, http://www.childwelfare.gov/pubs/factsheets/foster.cfm.

2. To understand the complexity of this issue and grasp the point I am making, it is useful to examine the legislative history of federal child abuse legislation, available at http://www.childwelfare.gov/pubs/factsheets/about.cfm. If one goes through it, the point I am making about the passing of money and authority from federal to state levels is clear. Since there are so many dimensions to this problem—from abuse that occurs when a child is born addicted, sexual abuse, and adoption, for example—the money goes in numerous directions. However, take sexual abuse. Money is in the legislation for assessment. Is it feasible to shift money away from or hold the line on these services and put it into the faith community with the hope that it can help? States have statutes and guidelines for how to make these sensitive assessments and who is qualified to do so. I seriously doubt that a shift can be made without disruption to services unless comprehensive and detailed planning have taken place.

3. Child Welfare League of America, "Child Protection: Facts and Figures."

4. U.S. Department of Health and Human Services, Administration on Children, Youth, and Families, "Victims: Child Maltreatment, 2003," in *Child Maltreatment, 2003* (Washington, D.C.: GPO, 2005), available at http://www.acf.hhs.gov/programs/cb/pubs/cm03/chapterthree.htm.

5. American Academy of Child and Adolescent Psychiatry, "Child Sexual Abuse," July 2004, http://www.aacap.org/publications/factsfam/sexabuse.htm.

6. One Church, One Child of Illinois, "The Adoption Advocacy Program," 2004, http://www.state.il.us/dcfs/adoption/index.shtml.

7. Charles Murray, preface to the 1995 edition of Olasky, *Tragedy of American Compassion* (Washington, D.C.: Regnery Gateway, 1995).

8. Anderson, "How Catholic Charities Lost Its Soul."

9. This estimate was provided to me by Robert Tuttle, professor of law at George Washington University and an expert in faith-based law, in e-mail correspondence on May 3, 2006.

10. A list of presidential speeches on the Faith-Based Initiative is given at http://www.whitehouse.gov/government/fbci/archive.html.

11. Chaves, *Congregations in America*, 50.

12. White House Office of Faith-Based and Community Initiatives, "Guidance to Faith-Based and Community Organizations on Partnering with the Federal Government," 2003, http://www.whitehouse.gov/government/fbci/guidance/index.html.

13. Chaves, *Congregations in America*, 47.

14. Chaves, *Congregations in America*, 46.

15. Robert Wineburg, "An Investigation of Religious Support of Public and Private Agencies in One Community in an Era of Retrenchment," *Journal of Community Practice* 3, no. 2 (1996): 50.

16. MADD, "Stats and Resources," http://www.madd.org/stats.

CHAPTER 3

1. Chaves, *Congregations in America*, 222; emphasis added.

2. Sheila Suess Kennedy and Wolfgang Bielefeld, *Charitable Choice at Work: Evaluating Faith-Based Job Programs in the States* (Washington, D.C.: Georgetown University Press, 2006).

3. I want to thank Professor Mark Chaves, chair of the University of Arizona's Sociology Department and one of the most renowned survey research methodologists in the world, for guiding me through this analogy. Needless to say, I was intimidated asking him to review this survey section. I did not want to trivialize survey research and felt if the analogy passed his standards it would pass anywhere. I was trained in experimental and quasi-experimental work by a student of Donald Campbell who "wrote the book" on this type of inquiry and felt comfortable translating its essence into shorthand. I would like to thank Professor Chaves again for looking that part over as well.

4. Jean-Philippe Laurenceau et al., "Community-Based Prevention of Marital Dysfunction: Multilevel Modeling of a Randomized Effectiveness Study," *Journal of Consulting and Clinical Psychology* 72, no. 6 (2004): 933–43.

5. U.S. Department of Health, Education, and Welfare, Public Health Service, Alcohol, Drug Abuse, and Mental Health Administration, National Institute on Drug Abuse (NIDA), "An Evaluation of the Teen Challenge Treatment Program," Services Research Report (Washington, D.C.: GPO, 1977). After NIDA's report but before Bicknese's, another quantitative study of Teen Challenge was

undertaken. The investigator was Dr. Roger Thompson, criminologist at the University of Tennessee at Chattanooga. This 1994 project, a mail survey, ran into response-rate problems, as Dr. Thompson confirmed on the phone; 44 subjects out of 213 responded, yielding a response rate of only 21 percent. I am very grateful to Dr. Thompson for his advice to me and for the ideas I gleaned from his survey instrument. Bicknese does an excellent job of clarifying the misinformation around the NIDA and Thompson studies.

6. Bicknese, "Teen Challenge Drug Treatment Program," 10–11, 124, 126.

7. Malachi House serves only adult males; the Bicknese study compared only men as well.

8. Bicknese, "Teen Challenge Drug Treatment Program," 125–26.

9. Bicknese, "Teen Challenge Drug Treatment Program," 126.

10. Stephen V. Monsma, *Putting Faith in Partnerships: Welfare-to-Work in Four Cities* (Ann Arbor: University of Michigan Press, 2004).

11. Stephen Monsma and Carolyn Mounts, "Working Faith: How Religious Organizations Provide Welfare-to-Work Services," report, Center of Research on Religion and Urban Civil Society, University of Pennsylvania, 2002.

12. Monsma, *Putting Faith in Partnerships*, 36.

13. Stephen V. Monsma, "Myths, Lies, and Soundbites: Reactions to President Bush's Initiative," Sixth Annual Henry Lecture, April 29, 2002, http://www.calvin.edu/henry/archives/lectures/monsma.pdf, 5.

14. Chaves, *Congregations in America*, 63–64.

15. Chaves, *Congregations in America*, 53–54.

16. Kennedy and Bielefeld, *Charitable Choice at Work*, 141.

17. Kennedy and Bielefeld, *Charitable Choice at Work*, 144.

18. Steven Rathgeb Smith and Michael R. Sosin, "The Varieties of Faith-Related Agencies," *Public Administration Review* 61, no. 6 (2001): 351ff, available at http://www.questia.com/PM.qst?a=o&d=5000926074.

19. Smith and Sosin, "Varieties of Faith-Related Agencies."

20. Mark Chaves, "Secularization as Declining Religious Authority," *Social Forces* 72, no. 3 (1994): 749–74.

21. Nancy Ammerman, *Pillars of Faith: American Congregations and Their Partners* (Berkeley: University of California Press, 2005).

22. See, for example, Cnaan, *Invisible Caring Hand*; Chaves, *Congregations in America*.

23. Chaves, *Congregations in America*, 50.

24. Chaves, *Congregations in America*.

25. Wineburg, "Investigation of Religious Support."

CHAPTER 4

1. John Dilulio, personal interview, Philadelphia, October 26, 2004.

2. Dilulio, quoted in Ron Suskind, "Why Are These Men Laughing?" *Esquire*, January 2003, available at http://www.ronsuskind.com/newsite/articles/archives/000032.html. The letter from Dilulio to Suskind is posted at http://www.esquire.com/features/articles/2002/021202_mfe_diiulio_1.html.

3. Bill Berkowitz, "Pat Robertson Counts His Federal Blessings: Reverend's Controversial Charity Awarded Faith-Based Grant from HHS," *TomPaine.com*, October 15, 2002, http://www.liberalslikechrist.org/about/robertsonblessings.html; Laura Meckler, "Robertson's Group Gets Faith-Based Funding," Associated Press, October 3, 2002, available at http://www.beliefnet.com/story/114/story_11457_1.html.

4. Dilulio, personal interview.

5. U.S. Department of Health and Human Services, Administration for Children and Families, "Summary," in *Child Maltreatment, 2004* (Washington, D.C.: GPO, 2005), available at http://www.acf.dhhs.gov/programs/cb/pubs/cm04/summary.htm.

6. Children's Defense Fund, "Analysis: Number of Black Children in Extreme Poverty Hits Record High," May 28, 2003, http://www.childrensdefense.org/pdf/extreme_poverty.pdf.

7. Child Welfare Information Gateway, "Foster Care: Numbers and Trends," 2005, http://nccanch.acf.hhs.gov/pubs/factsheets/foster.cfm.

8. Kimberly Jane Wilson, "What About Adoption?" National Center for Public Policy Research, February 2003, http://www.nationalcenter.org/P21NVWilson Adoption203.html.

9. Human Rights Watch, "United States—Punishment and Prejudice: Racial Disparities in the War on Drugs," vol. 12, no. 2, May 2000, III, available at http://www.hrw.org/reports/2000/usa/Rcedrg00-01.htm.

10. Becky Pettit and Bruce Western, "Mass Imprisonment and the Life Course: Race and Class Inequality in U.S. Incarceration," *American Sociological Review* 69 (April 2004): 151–69; U.S. Department of Justice, "Prison and Jail Inmates Report High Rates of Physical and Sexual Abuse before Their Confinement," press release, April 11, 1999, http://www.ojp.usdoj.gov/bjs/pub/press/parip.pr; Terry Maxwell, "A Closer Look: Illiteracy—The Crisis Nobody Talks About," *Arizona Range News*, May 3, 2006, http://www.willcoxrangenews.com/articles/2004/04/28/news/editorial_opinions/edit2.txt.

11. William J. Bennett, John J. Dilulio Jr., and John P. Walters, *Body Count: Moral Poverty—and How to Win America's War against Crime and Drugs* (New York: Simon & Schuster, 1996).

12. John Dilulio, "Two Million Prisoners Are Enough," *Wall Street Journal*, March 12, 1999.

13. Dilulio, personal interview.

14. Amy Sherman, "Seven Habits of Highly Effective Charities," *Philanthropy* (September–October 1999), available at http://www.hudson.org/index.cfm?fuseaction=publication_details&id=57.

15. Sherman, "Seven Habits."

16. Roundtable on Religion and Social Welfare Policy, "Legal Updates," http://www.religionandsocialpolicy.org/legal.

17. Robert Tuttle, e-mail message to author, May 3, 2006.

18. Chancey, "Faith-Based."

19. Museum of Broadcast Communications, "Pat Robertson," http://www.museum.tv/archives/etv/R/htmlR/robertsonpa/robersonpa.htm.

20. John Dilulio Jr., "Know Us by Our Works," *Wall Street Journal*, February 14, 2001.

CHAPTER 5

1. See Robert Wineburg, P. Spakes, and J. Finn, "Budget Cuts and Human Services: One Community's Experience," *Social Casework* 64, no. 8 (1983): 489–96.

2. Ram A. Cnaan, with Robert J. Wineburg and Stephanie C. Boddie, *The Newer Deal: Social Work and Religion in Partnership* (New York: Columbia University Press, 1999).

3. Leon Wynter, "Reagan Is Host to Black Ministers; Reagan Defends His Policies to Black Ministers," *Washington Post*, March 27, 1982.

4. Wynter, "Reagan Is Host to Black Ministers."

5. Herbert H. Denton, "Reagan Urges More Church Aid For Needy," *Washington Post*, April 14, 1982.

6. Denton, "Reagan Urges More Church Aid"; For complete text of this speech, see Ronald Reagan, "Remarks at the Annual National Prayer Breakfast, February 4, 1982," http://www.reagan.utexas.edu/archives/speeches/1982/20482a.htm.

7. Randy Frame, "The Religious Nonprofits Fight for Government Funds," *Christian Century* 39, no. 14 (1995): 65.

8. Eberly and Streeter, *Soul of Civil Society*, 5.

9. See Robert Wineburg, "Assessment of Potential Partnerships between Guilford County Department of Social Services and the Faith Community," report to Guilford County, NC DSS, May 6, 2002.

10. Amy L. Sherman, "Implementing 'Charitable Choice': Transcending the Separation between Church and State," *Philanthropy* (January–February 1999), available at http://www.philanthropyroundtable.org/article.asp?article=1231&paper=0&cat=147.

11. Sherman, "Implementing 'Charitable Choice.' "

12. Sherman, "Implementing 'Charitable Choice.' "

13. John J. Dilulio Jr., "The Three Faith Factors," *Public Interest* (Fall 2002), available at http://www.brook.edu/views/articles/diiulio/pi_fall2002.htm.

14. Amy L. Sherman, "Faith in Communities: A Solid Investment," *Society* 40, no. 2 (January–February 2003): 19–27.

15. NIDA, "Evaluation of Teen Challenge."

16. Roger Thompson, "Teen Challenge of Chattanooga Survey of Alumni: Final Report," 1994; Bicknese, "Teen Challenge Drug Treatment Program." Bicknese actually wrote in his dissertation that the reason he conducted his study was because the two earlier studies (NIDA and Thompson) cited by Sherman were not statistically valid.

17. Sherman, "Faith in Communities," 22.

18. "Interview with Marvin Olasky"; emphasis added.

19. Loconte, "Faith Healing," 89.

CHAPTER 6

1. For example, see International Fellowship of Christian and Jews, "Endorsements," http://www.ifcj.org/site/pageserver?pagename=endorsements.

2. Centers for Faith-Based and Community Initiatives, "Unlevel Playing Field: Barriers to Participation by Faith-Based and Community Organizations in Federal Social Service Programs," August 2001, available at http://www.whitehouse.gov/news/releases/2001/08/unlevelfield.html.

3. See Ed Cone, "Scholar vs. Dollar," 2003, http://radio.weblogs.com/0107946/stories/2003/09/30/scholarVsDollar.html.

4. Centers for Faith-Based and Community Initiatives, "Unlevel Playing Field."

5. Centers for Faith-Based and Community Initiatives, "Unlevel Playing Field," 2.

6. Lou Cannon, *Ronald Reagan: The Presidential Portfolio; A History Illustrated from the Collection of the Ronald Reagan Library and Museum* (New York: PublicAffairs, 2001), 81.

7. Douglas Kneeland, *New York Times*, August 6, 1980.

8. Mary Leonard. "Bush Targets Support of Blacks: Faith-Based Efforts Focus on Churches," *Boston Globe*, March 11, 2001.

9. Peter Wallsten, Tom Hamburger, and Nicholas Riccardi, "Bush Rewarded by Black Pastors' Faith: His Stands, Backed by Funding of Ministries, Redefined the GOP's Image with Some Clergy," *Los Angeles Times*, January 18, 2005.

10. "President Visits Bradley Grantee," *Lion Letter* (Bradley Foundation), Summer 2002, http://www.bradleyfdn.org/lionletter/LL02summer.pdf.

11. House Committee on Financial Services, Housing and Community Opportunity Subcommittee, *Strengthening America's Communities: Examining the Impact of Faith-Based Housing Partnerships*, 108th Cong., 1st sess., 2003, 68–69.

12. House Committee on Financial Services, Housing and Community Opportunity Subcommittee, *Strengthening America's Communities* as reported in memo to members 8.13 3/28/03 National Low Income Housing Coalition. "Faith-Based Regulatory Changes Come under Scrutiny" found at http://www.nlihc.org/.

13. Thomas B. Edsall, "Grants Flow to Bush Allies on Social Issues: Federal Programs Direct at Least \$157 Million, *Washington Post*, March 22, 2006.

14. Edsall, "Grants Flow to Bush Allies."

15. American Jewish Congress, "AJ Congress Asks Court to Stop Americorps from Sponsoring Religious Teaching in Sectarian Schools," press release, December 22, 2003.

16. Bill Berkowitz, "Christian Zionists, Jews and Bush's Reelection Strategy," *Working for Change*, May 28, 2004, http://www.workingforchange.com/article.cfm?itemid=17021; Jane Lampman, "Mixing Prophecy and Politics," *Christian Science Monitor*, July 7, 2004.

17. George W. Bush, "Remarks on the Faith-Based Welfare Initiative in Milwaukee," July 2, 2002, available at http://www.presidency.ucsb.edu/ws/print.php?pid=64207.

18. Bush, "Remarks on the Faith-Based Welfare Initiative."

19. Jim Towey, speaking at the Roundtable on Religion and Social Welfare Policy annual conference, Washington, D.C., October 23, 2002, panel 1: "The View from Washington—Administrative Efforts to Involve Faith-Based Groups in Social Service Delivery," http://www.religionandsocialpolicy.org/docs/transcripts/10-23-2002_annual_conf_welcome_view_from_washington.pdf, 8.

20. Steven Windmueller, "Are American Jews Becoming Republican? Insights into Jewish Political Behavior," *Jerusalem Viewpoints* (Jerusalem Center for Public Affairs) 509, December 15, 2003, http://www.jcpa.org/jl/vp509.htm.

21. George W. Bush, "President Bush Implements Key Elements of His Faith-Based Initiative," press release, December 12, 2002, http://www.whitehouse.gov/news/releases/2002/12/20021212-3.html.

22. Jim Towey, interview by Gwen Ifill, "Faith Based Initiatives," *News Hour with Jim Lehrer*, December 25, 2002, http://www.pbs.org/newshour/bb/religion/july-dec02/faith-based_12-25.html.

23. Towey, "Faith Based Initiatives."

24. John Ashcroft, "Prepared Remarks of Attorney General John Ashcroft," White House Faith-Based Conference, Tampa, Florida, December 5, 2003, http://www.usdoj.gov/archive/ag/speeches/2003/agfull120503.htm.

25. E. J. Kessler, "Candidate Contribution," *Forward*, January 2, 2004.

26. William E. Rapfogel, "An Envelope from Texas," *Jewish Press*, January 7, 2004, available at http://www.ourjerusalem.com/opinion/story/opinion20040203.html.

27. Judith Weiss, "Jewish Philanthropy: Benefiting from the Faith-Based Initiative," *Kesher Talk*, August 25, 2004, http://www.hfienberg.com/kesher/2004/08/jewish-philanthropy-benefiting-from.html.

28. E. J. Kessler, "Bush-Cheney Stumps to Get Out the Orthodox Vote," *Forward*, September 3, 2004.

29. Kessler, "Bush-Cheney Stumps."

30. Adena Kaplan, personal conversations, December 18 and 30, 2004. On December 30, I reconfirmed the facts, and Kaplan claimed that all the information was correct, but she asked me to note that she was acting merely as a conduit for the CEO of the agency, Rapfogel, who verified that the information Kaplan gave me was correct.

31. Jonathan Weisman, "2006 Cuts in Domestic Spending on Table," *Washington Post*, May 27, 2005.

32. E-mail from Noam Neusner, special assistant to the president, to Jewish leaders, August 24, 2004; copy provided by Tom Hamburger, *Los Angeles Times* Washington Bureau.

33. Weiss, "Jewish Philanthropy."

34. "Jewish Vote in Presidential Elections," *Jewish Virtual Library*, http://www.jewishvirtuallibrary.org/jsource/US-Israel/jewvote.html; Pew Research Center,"Religion and the Presidential Vote: Bush's Gains Broad-Based," December 6, 2004, http://people-press.org/commentary/display.php3?AnalysisID=103.

CHAPTER 7

1. Stafford, "Criminologist Who Discovered Churches," 39.

2. Stafford, "Criminologist Who Discovered Churches," 39.

3. John Dilulio, preface to *Religion and the Public Square in the 21st Century: Proceedings from the Conference, the Future of Government Partnerships with the Faith Community, April 25–26, 2000, at Wingspread, Racine, Wisconsin*, ed. Ryan Streeter (Indianapolis, Ind.: Hudson Institute, 2001).

4. See the Center for Public Justice website, http://www.cpjustice.org/.

5. Amy Sherman, "How Do Congregations Serve the Larger Society? How Should They?" address to the Alban Institute First Annual National Conference, Alexandria, Virginia, October 19, 1999, http://www.hudson.org/index.cfm?fuseaction=publication_details&id=1912.

6. Elena Curti, "Special Report: God and Government," *Tablet*, July 1, 2000, 909–10.

7. Bush, "Rallying the Armies of Compassion," 1, 6.

8. Streeter, *Religion and the Public Square*, 84.

9. Dictionary.com (2006), thesaurus for winsome found at http://thesaurus.com/search?8=winsome.

10. Stanley Carlson Thies, in Streeter, *Religion and the Public Square*, 47.

11. Leonard, "Bush Targets Support of Blacks."

12. Peter Wallsten, Tom Hamburger, and Nicholas Riccardi, "Bush Rewarded by Black Pastors' Faith," *Los Angeles Times*, January 18, 2005; http://news.orb6.com/stories/latimests/20050118/bushrewardedbyblackpastorsfaith.php.

13. Stanley Carlson Thies, personal interview, Washington, D.C., October 30, 2004.

14. Thies, personal interview.

15. Niccolò Machiavelli, "Concerning the Way in Which Princes Should Keep Faith," chapter 18 of *The Prince* (1513), trans. W. K. Marriott (Medieval Sourcebook, http://www.fordham.edu/halsall/basis/machiavelli-prince.html).

CHAPTER 8

1. Odell Cleveland, personal conversation, Greensboro, N.C., 1997.

2. Ruth DeHoog and Jonathan Mattiello, "North Carolina County Reports: Policy Choices and Welfare Reform, 1997–2000, Guilford County," 2000, http://www.unc.edu/depts/welfare/Guilford%20Co.pdf, 17–18.

3. See Robert J. Wineburg and Catherine R Wineburg, "Localization of Human Services: Using Church Volunteers to Fight the Feminization of Poverty," *Journal of Volunteer Administration* 4, no. 3 (1986): 1–6.; Catherine R. Wineburg and Robert J. Wineburg, "Local Human Service Development: Institutional Utilization of Volunteers to Solve Community Problems," *Journal of Volunteer Administration* 5, no. 4 (1987): 9–14; Robert J. Wineburg, "An Investigation of Religious Support of Public and Private Agencies in One Community in an Era of Retrenchment," *Journal of Community Practice* 3, no. 2 (1996): 35–56.

4. Fasih U. Ahmed, "Evaluation Report: Emergency Assistance Program, Mount Zion Baptist Church of Greensboro, Welfare Reform Liaison Project" (Carolina Evaluation Research Center, 1998).

5. Ahmed, "Evaluation Report," 2–3.

6. Work First Planning Committee, *Guilford County Work First Plan for 1998–2000* (Greensboro, N.C.: Guilford County Work First Welfare Reform Planning Committee, 1998); emphasis added.

7. Ahmed, "Evaluation Report," 5.

CHAPTER 10

1. Nancy McLaughlin, "Church Gets Grant Lost by Jones; The Welfare Reform Liaison Project Is an Outreach of Mount Zion Baptist Church on Alamance Church Road," *Greensboro News and Record*, February 14, 2002.

2. Margaret Moffett Banks, "Church Help Is Key in Welfare Reform; Churches Can Go a Long Way Toward Easing the Transition for Welfare Recipients about to Lose Their Benefits," *Greensboro News and Record*, May 7, 1999.

3. Margaret Moffett Banks, "Summit Rallies to End Poverty; Religious People Have to Make Poverty Morally Unacceptable, the Keynote Speaker Says," *Greensboro News and Record*, June 8, 2001.

Index

About the Author

BOB WINEBURG is the Jefferson Pilot Excellence Professor of Social Work at the University of North Carolina, Greensboro. He is the author of many book chapters, published articles, and the books *A Limited Partnership: The Politics of Religion, Welfare, and Social Service* and *The Newer Deal: Social Work and Religion in Partnership*. He was an advisor to Catholic Charities USA on its Vision 2000 Project, and served as a panelist on the President's Faith-Based Initiative at the United Jewish Communities bi-annual conference, along with Senator Joseph Lieberman, Congressman Jerrold Nadler, and USA Freedom Corps Director John Bridgeland.